OXFORD LEGAL PHILOSOPHY

Series Editors

TIMOTHY ENDICOTT
JOHN GARDNER (1965–2019)
LESLIE GREEN

The Right of Redress

Andrew S. Gold is a Professor at Brooklyn Law School. His primary research interests address private law theory, fiduciary law, and the law of corporations. He is a co-editor of multiple books on fiduciary theory, including Contract, Status, and Fiduciary Law (Oxford University Press, 2017); and Philosophical Foundations of Fiduciary Law (Oxford University Press, 2014). He is also co-editor of The Oxford Handbook of the New Private Law (Oxford University Press, 2020). Professor Gold has been the Bruce W. Nichols Visiting Professor at Harvard Law School; an HLA Hart Visiting Fellow at the University of Oxford; and a Fulbright Visiting Research Chair at McGill University. He is a co-founder of the North American Workshop on Private Law Theory and a member of the American Law Institute.

OXFORD LEGAL PHILOSOPHY

Series editors: Timothy Endicott, John Gardner (1965–2019), and Leslie Green

Oxford Legal Philosophy publishes the best new work in philosophically oriented legal theory. It commissions and solicits monographs in all branches of the subject, including works on philosophical issues in all areas of public and private law, and in the national, transnational, and international realms; studies of the nature of law, legal institutions, and legal reasoning; treatments of problems in political morality as they bear on law; and explorations in the nature and development of legal philosophy itself. The series represents diverse traditions of thought but always with an emphasis on rigour and originality. It sets the standard in contemporary jurisprudence.

In memory of John Gardner
1965–2019

ALSO AVAILABLE IN THE SERIES

Property Rights: A Re-Examination
JE Penner

A Theory of Legal Personhood
Visa AJ Kurki

Law and Morality at War
Adil Ahmad Haque

Ignorance of Law
A Philosophical Inquiry
Douglas Husak

Reason and Restitution
A Theory of Unjust Enrichment
Charlie Webb

Allowing for Exceptions
A Theory of Defences
and Defeasibility in Law
Luís Duarte d'Almeida

The Ends of Harm
The Moral Foundations
of Criminal Law
Victor Tadros

Corrective Justice
Ernest J. Weinrib

Conscience and Conviction
The Case for Civil Disobedience
Kimberley Brownlee

The Nature of Legislative Intent
Richard Ekins

Why Law Matters
Alon Harel

Imposing Risk
A Normative Framework
John Oberdiek

The Right of Redress

ANDREW S. GOLD

OXFORD
UNIVERSITY PRESS

OXFORD
UNIVERSITY PRESS

Great Clarendon Street, Oxford, OX2 6DP,
United Kingdom

Oxford University Press is a department of the University of Oxford.
It furthers the University's objective of excellence in research, scholarship,
and education by publishing worldwide. Oxford is a registered trade mark of
Oxford University Press in the UK and in certain other countries

First published in 2020
First published in paperback 2022

Published in the United States of America by Oxford University Press
198 Madison Avenue, New York, NY 10016, United States of America

British Library Cataloguing in Publication Data
Data available

Library of Congress Cataloging in Publication Data
Data available

ISBN 978–0–19–881440–5 (Hbk.)
ISBN 978–0–19–286612–7 (Pbk.)

In loving memory of my parents, Arthur and Estella Gold

Without injustices, the name of justice would mean what?[1]

– Heraclitus

[1] As translated (somewhat loosely) in Heraclitus, *Fragments* (Brooks Haxton, transl.) (Penguin Books 2003) (Fragment 60) 39.

Preface

Rights of redress have been a preoccupation of mine since law school. This book has thus had a long path to completion, and it represents several stages of my thinking about private law. A much wider swath of the field is covered than I first anticipated when this project began, and this book examines redress from angles that would not have occurred to me even a few years ago. Indeed, some of these angles only became visible in the final weeks of writing.

The late John Gardner's influence should be evident throughout, both in the express discussion of his ideas and in more implicit ways, like the selection of puzzles to be solved. I am not certain I would have written this book without John's early encouragement, and I am grateful for several especially fruitful conversations we had on the book's theory. Needless to say, he would likely have disagreed with a number of my claims, but I am hopeful that he would also have enjoyed seeing them worked out in print. I am truly thankful for John's generosity in helping me to think more deeply about the kinds of justice in private law.

The arguments were further developed during the course of years of conferences, workshops, articles, and discussions over coffee—especially discussions over coffee—and I can't hope to thank everyone who contributed in some way. With that noted, I am grateful for helpful comments from Lisa Austin, Miriam Baer, Aditi Bagchi, Shyam Balganesh, Kenworthey Bilz, Brian Bix, Sam Bray, Curtis Bridgeman, Rick Brooks, Nico Cornell, Hanoch Dagan, Seth Davis, Simone Degeling, Robin Effron, Scott Hershovitz, Kim Ferzan, Stephen Galoob, Mark Geistfeld, Matthew Harding, Tonja Jacobi, Greg Klass, Adam Kolber, Ethan Leib, Daniel Markovits, Nate Oman, Diego Papayannis, James Penner, Arthur Ripstein, Arden Rowell, Matt Sag, Irit Samet, Prince Saprai, Anthony Sebok, Matthew Shapiro, Emily Sherwin, Seana Shiffrin, Ken Simons, Zoe Sinel, Jason Solomon, Rob Stevens, Victor Tadros, and Laura Valentini.

I also owe a debt of gratitude to my colleagues at Brooklyn Law School and to my dean, Mike Cahill, for their support. I am especially thankful for suggestions that Julian Arato, Ted Janger, Christina Mulligan, and Alice Ristroph made at a book workshop held at Brooklyn Law School. I am similarly thankful for a symposium on the manuscript held at King's College London, and co-sponsored by the Notre Dame Law School Program on Private Law. I am grateful to the participants at that conference, including Sinead Agnew, Noam

Gur, Yael Lifshitz, Catherine MacMillan, Nick McBride, Colm McGrath, Paul McMahon, Nick Sage, Prince Saprai, Victor Tadros, Emmanuel Voyakis, Charlie Webb, Fred Wilmot-Smith, and Ekow Yankah. Profound thanks are owed to Paul Miller and Irit Samet for organizing the symposium. I thank my former colleagues at DePaul for suggestions—including David Franklin, Mark Moller, Song Richardson, Josh Sarnoff, and Stephen Siegel. And I am likewise grateful to the professors who helped me develop my thinking on private law when I was still a student at Duke Law School: these include Paul Haagen, Martin Stone, Laura Underkuffler, and William Van Alstyne. While there are major differences in approach, Ernest Weinrib's writing was also an early influence, and this book owes much to his work.

Several scholars made continuing contributions to the development of the manuscript—often discussing multiple chapters—and I wish to offer them my particular thanks. These include Evan Fox-Decent, John Goldberg, Paul Miller, Henry Smith, Stephen Smith, Deb Tuerkheimer, and Ben Zipursky. Their comments—frequently from quite different perspectives—contributed substantially to this book's development. Assistance from Jamie Berezin, Alex Flach, and the other editors at Oxford University Press was also invaluable.

I benefited greatly from my time as an H.L.A. Hart Visiting Fellow at University College, Oxford; as a Fulbright Visiting Research Chair at McGill University; and as a Visiting Professor at Harvard Law School. A sabbatical visit at the University of New South Wales was very helpful as well. I also thank Trinh Nguyen for suggesting that Positano would be a good place to complete the final stages of the manuscript. In different ways, each of these settings was a perfect writing environment. Several bookstores likewise made a difference, but I have to single out the Seminary Co-op Bookstore in Chicago and the Raven Bookstore in Cambridge, Massachusetts for attention. An incalculable number of cafes contributed caffeine and a comfortable writing space.

I am very grateful to Trinh as well for her unwavering support and patience during a lengthy writing process. My family also helped me in many ways, only some of which are academic. I thank my brother Matt for his support, and also for the example of his idealism. It is safe to say that he appreciates rights of all kinds, legal and moral. I wish my parents could have seen this book. Their influence on me, on my writing, and on so many other things is always there.

Andrew S. Gold
Le Sirenuse
Positano, Italy
3 August 2019

Acknowledgements

As noted in the Preface, this book has had a long gestation period and it consequently reflects substantial earlier research. Material drawn from several of my prior works (often significantly revised) appears in the following chapters.

Chapter 2 includes material from 'A Theory of Redressive Justice' (2014) 64 U Toronto LJ 159. Chapter 4 includes material from 'A Property Theory of Contract' (2009) 103 Northwestern U L Rev 1, and also draws on arguments in 'Contract, Promise, and the Right of Redress' (2018) 9 Wm & Mary Bus L Rev 389. Chapter 5 includes material from 'A Theory of Redressive Justice' (2014) 64 U Toronto LJ 159.

Chapter 6 includes material from 'The State as a Wrongful Fiduciary' in Evan Criddle, et al. (eds), *Fiduciary Government* (CUP 2018). Chapter 7 includes material from 'Private Rights and Private Wrongs' (2017) 115 Michigan L Rev 1071. Chapter 8 includes material from 'Equity and the Right to Do Wrong' in Dennis Klimchuk, Irit Samet, & Henry E Smith (eds), *Philosophical Foundations of the Law of Equity* (OUP 2020), and from 'Derecho Privado y El Problema de la Justicia por Eleccion' in Diego M Papayannis & Esteban Pereira Fredes (eds), *Filosofia del Derecho Privado* (Marcial Pons 2018).

Chapter 8 also draws on ideas developed in 'Justice and the Right to do Wrong' in Simone Degeling & Jason Varuhas (eds), *Equitable Compensation and Disgorgement of Profit* (Hart 2017). Chapter 9 includes arguments from 'On Selling Civil Recourse' (2014) 63 DePaul L Rev 485 and 'Contracts with and Without Degradation' (2012) 40 Capital L Rev 657.

Contents

Detailed Contents

1
Introduction

I. An Introduction to the Right of Redress

Imagine that you just purchased a unique and expensive gift for a family member. As you leave the store, a stranger approaches and steals your shopping bag from you, taking the gift and fleeing. You run after the thief, calling out for help. Fortunately, the thief is not as fast you are, and he stumbles so that you have a chance to grab the bag back. You also see that there are no police in sight and, if the thief gets away, your gift will never be recovered. Is it morally acceptable for you to grab the bag? If you successfully take your bag back, is that a kind of justice?

This book will offer a new theory of private law. It will suggest that there is a special kind of justice involved in cases like the one described above. This type—which I will call redressive justice—governs right holders when they undo the wrongs they have suffered, and it governs third parties like the state who act on their behalf. Redressive justice is an importantly different kind of justice from the kind we get when a wrongdoer fixes his own wrong and, as I will argue, it is a kind of justice that can help us to understand private law.

Authorship matters here, and the type of justice that governs a right holder's acts of redress is different in kind from the type of justice authored by a wrongdoer. In part, this is because the moral ledger of the wrongdoer varies depending on who fixed his wrong. We have better complied with our obligations when we fix our own wrong, rather than standing by while another person fixes it for us. As we will see, it also makes a difference whether justice is authored by the state, or by the state in combination with a right holder. Co-authorship matters for private law as much as sole authorship.

There is another reason to care about redressive justice. Thinking about redress from a right holder's perspective makes us focus on legitimacy. Not every case in which we have a moral right to something—even a remedial right—will also be a case in which we can legitimately use coercion or force in support of our right. We may be in a position to remonstrate, blame, warn, request, and also forgive. But none of these is the same as using coercion or force in the ordinary case. Indeed, even in the absence of force, we may

The Right of Redress. Andrew S. Gold, Oxford University Press (2020). © Andrew S. Gold.
DOI: 10.1093/oso/9780198814405.001.0001

not have standing to just take something from another person without permission. When we are concerned with redress, we are concerned with the standing to enforce.

Imagine I have promised to have lunch with you on Saturday and I don't keep my word. You will now have a remedial moral right to my having lunch with you on another occasion, or else you will have a right to whatever happens to be the next best thing. You may also feel that I should apologize. But you cannot make me have lunch with you. You lack an enforcement right.[1] It would be different if you had promised me something—say a prized possession—in return for my performance of an arduous task. Having performed the task, I may now have moral standing to insist on the promised object, and even to take the object for myself in some cases.

Much of private law reflects questions of justice that track this enforcement question; that is, much of private law tracks the question of when we can legitimately enforce our rights, morally speaking. Indeed, the justice that results is fundamental for understanding the law of contracts, torts, fiduciary relationships, and unjust enrichment. In different ways, each field is significantly concerned with rights of redress.

As noted above, redress raises questions of authorship. The most common form of authorship at issue in this book is the kind involved when we initiate a lawsuit and pursue that suit to fruition. A variant is also available in cases of self-help, like recaption of chattels. In each case, authorship means that one has initiated and successfully pursued the undoing of a transaction (typically, a wrongful transaction). As we will see, additional forms of authorship also make a difference. A second form of authorship potentially overlaps with this form. A right holder may not only initiate redress, but, in addition, her conduct may be attributed to her; in that case, she is not merely a stand-in for a public actor or a third party on whose behalf she undoes the wrong. Both forms of authorship are valuable, but for different reasons.

There is a third form as well. Notice that partial authorship of our lives is also at stake when we engage in redress. This is a salient concern with respect to our primary rights, when they have been violated by a wrong. Those primary rights and the projects they enable may be significant to the arc of our lives. Redress often restores our capacity to pursue the projects that a wrong

[1] I use 'right' as a shorthand here. In Hohfeldian terms, rights of redress would be a privilege, or a protected privilege held by the party seeking redress against the wrongdoer or, in unjust enrichment cases, against the party from whom redress is sought. Note that there is also frequently a claim right involved when right holders seek the state's assistance in providing a remedy.

otherwise interfered with. Such authorship is likewise significant with respect to our enforcement rights, as redress itself can be a meaningful thing. Granted, these are not the only ways that redress is valuable, but they are some of the more important ways. Redress is likewise valuable for its expressive effects, deterrence of future wrongs, efficiencies of various kinds, and a multitude of other less heralded benefits.

Even if we possess a moral enforcement right, it need not follow that the state or any other third party has an obligation to help us out when we have been wronged. Some have suggested the state owes us its assistance under a Lockean social contract theory. This is a classic civil recourse account—civil recourse theories seek to explain private rights of action in light of the principle that a wronged party should be able to act against the person who wronged her (with state assistance), and Lockean understandings of pre-legal rights are one way of supporting this approach. I will instead offer a view of the state's obligation to provide civil recourse from a different angle. This book will draw on public fiduciary theory. From this perspective, the state owes certain obligations to its citizens in light of its assertion of discretionary power over their lives. Among other things, the state often prohibits self-help, and this context bears on what the state owes. The resulting state obligations in turn include an obligation to provide rights of redress or effective equivalents.

But the state's role need not involve a private right of action, let alone a measure designed to directly bring about redressive justice. The state could also facilitate other types of redress, whether by making room for self-help, or by allowing for arbitration. Indeed, one of the themes of this book is that the justice in redress takes multiple forms. Some of these forms are paternalistic, as when a guardian brings suit on behalf of a ward. Some are substantially more private than the norm (recaption of chattels, arbitration), while others involve potentially circumscribed plaintiff control (think of class actions).

Most striking are instances in which the state acts to impede redress, or at least fails to facilitate it. This classically happens through broadly equitable doctrines, such as the unconscionability doctrine in contract law. It is also exemplified by cases of estoppel, unclean hands, and laches. For example, suppose that Jack brings suit against Jill to enforce a contract that is both procedurally and substantively suspect. Even though Jack may have a right to performance under the contract, if the unconscionability doctrine applies, the court will refuse to enforce that right. As Seana Shiffrin has suggested, the state in such cases may act from self-regarding motives; it may refuse to assist the right holder because it should not have to be complicit in the right holder's conduct.[2] Where courts adopt this view, they effectively limit the degree to which the state is caught up in morally wrongful enforcement of legal rights.

Still, the possibility that right holders will seek justice when it is morally wrongful to do so is just one of the concerns regarding rights of redress. Another concern is that redress isn't feasible because a full 'allocation back', or undoing of a transaction, isn't possible.[3] While justice is often thought of as an 'all or nothing' proposition, it need not be. One can have partial redress, and the result is a type of partial justice. In some cases, that is desirable, as when a plaintiff who possesses the virtue of equity chooses to accept less than her due. In other cases, partial redress is the best we can hope for, as commonly arises in tort settings when an injury is sufficiently severe or difficult to undo fully. Partial redress is still a kind of justice in either case, and understanding the significance of such fact patterns will help us to make sense of private law doctrine.

What of cases in which the state is not directly involved? These cases may not be common in the case law, but they are significant nonetheless. Recall our example where a thief has run off with your bag and you take it back. These are also instances of redress and they can be fully legitimate even if they involve unilateral coercion. Rights of redress can be reasonable and worthy of our support even if the party seeking redress is acting on her own behalf, and even if she is not a stand-in for a public office holder. The justice in redress is thus a feature that links self-help, arbitration, conventional private rights of action, massive class actions, and in some cases *parens patriae* suits. It not only intersects with multiple private law fields, it runs through multiple channels.

As we will see, legal rights of redress are ultimately enabling and their exercise is intrinsically valuable. This book seeks to show various ways in which this holds true. The resulting account of private law offers a new path, differing from the leading Kantian analyses, and differing from influential pictures of corrective justice. This account also offers a new direction for civil recourse theory: one that is much more closely linked to justice between individuals. As I will argue, the justice in redress is fundamental to private law.

[2] *See* Seana V Shiffrin, 'Paternalism, Unconscionability Doctrine, and Accommodation' (2000) 29 Phil & Pub Aff 205.

[3] *See* John Gardner, 'What Is Tort Law For? Part 1: The Place of Corrective Justice' (2011) 30 Law & Phil 1, 9–10.

II. Overview of the Argument

The chapters of this book are arranged to show different angles on the importance of rights of redress. Chapter 2 begins with an introduction to rights of redress and the distinctive kind of justice that governs them: redressive justice. The next step, in Chapter 3, is to consider why this kind of justice is valuable. I will suggest, among other reasons, that the justice in redress offers various types of authorship (self-authorship and otherwise) to right holders who have suffered a wrong. Chapters 4 and 5 consider how specific private law fields match the contours of redressive justice. Chapter 4 will elaborate on contract law, while Chapter 5 will elaborate on torts. In different ways, contract law and tort law are illustrative of the strengths and limits to a redress-focused account of private law.

The following three chapters draw out implications related to the courts' participation (or non-participation) in acts of redress. Chapters 6 and 7 address the state's role in enforcement, with Chapter 6 discussing the plausibility of a fiduciary conception of the state and Chapter 7 critiquing a Kantian alternative. These chapters also draw important links between redress and self-help, and more generally assess the significance of self-help for private law. Chapter 8 then addresses problems raised by the optionality of redress, including cases where people fail to sue (even if they ought to), and where people choose to sue (even if they ought not to). This chapter further indicates how equitable doctrines like estoppel or unclean hands allow courts to limit the concern that they are complicit in morally wrongful acts of redress.

Chapter 9 returns to the question of what makes rights of redress valuable, beyond their link to a kind of justice. This chapter will again indicate how redress ties in with various types of authorship (each of which are valuable in unique ways), in this case emphasizing features of contemporary law. Whether it is an arbitration or a class action, a suit between corporations or a highly personal dispute between individuals, redress offers an important category of justice in each case.

A. The idea of redressive justice

Chapter 2 will introduce the type of justice that governs rights of redress: redressive justice. It will begin, however, with a more famous candidate for the type of justice in private law. This is corrective justice. The contrast between some leading definitions of corrective justice and redressive justice will help to show why the latter type is important. While corrective justice takes many forms—varying with the theorist—the approach to corrective justice discussed here will be an approach that centres on a wrongdoer's obligations to repair the effects of her wrong. In particular, this chapter will emphasize a conception of corrective justice that calls for allocation back—that is, one that calls for the undoing of a transaction.

As John Gardner indicates, the Continuity Thesis helps to make sense of corrective justice in this sense.[4] Under this thesis, the reasons for one's primary obligations continue in existence even when those primary obligations can no longer be met. For example, someone who promises to take their kids to the beach on a given day can no longer do so once they have missed the promised time. But the reasons that supported keeping this promise continue in existence, and the promisor may be morally required to do the next best thing. The reasons for keeping the initial promise support new secondary obligations to take the kids to the beach at the next available opportunity, or whatever would be the next best thing under the circumstances. The Continuity Thesis thus underpins moral norms of corrective justice, and Gardner suggests that legal norms of corrective justice can be justified in light of these moral norms.

I agree with this understanding of the Continuity Thesis, but I doubt that it is adequate to explain and justify the legal norms that undo wrongs in private law. Note, first, that it is far from clear the courts are acting on behalf of a wrongdoer when they order damages—if the courts are acting on behalf of a litigant in such cases, it appears to be the right holder. But beyond that concern, note also that remedial rights are not equivalent to enforcement rights. While it is true that a right holder's remedial rights are correlative to a wrongdoer's remedial duties for purposes of corrective justice, a right holder's enforcement right (if it exists) need not follow. And, if we want to avoid substantial problems of over-inclusiveness—after all, many moral wrongs are quite appropriately left alone by private law—it is enforcement rights that we need to address.

Redressive justice is another type of justice that governs allocation back. It stands in clear contrast to corrective justice as Gardner defines it. On his account, corrective justice governs allocation back by a duty bearer, or someone acting on her behalf. Redressive justice governs allocation back by a right holder, or someone acting on her behalf. Importantly, the two types of justice are not mirror images of each other. As we will see, the change in authorship

[4] *See* ibid at 33.

matters, and I will argue that it is redressive justice that better fits private law doctrine and structure.

In part, the change in authorship that is a hallmark of redressive justice matters because it leads to remedial asymmetries. As Chapter 2 will indicate, there are cases in which duties to correct do not correspond to rights of redress, as well as cases in which duties to correct support different remedies from legitimate redress. Such asymmetries are one reason to think that redressive justice is an important and separate category of justice. They are not the only reason. Another reason is that the moral status of the individuals involved differs depending on which type of justice is implicated. When a wrongdoer has undone her own wrong to the extent possible, she is in a different moral position from her position if someone else undid that wrong. Likewise, the right holder who fixes a wrong she suffered experiences a form of self-reliance she would not otherwise achieve.

As significantly, this category of justice matches an understanding of legal remedies which sees damages as an outcome provided on behalf of right holders rather than wrongdoers. It also has the advantage of fitting comfortably with the special standing doctrines that civil recourse theorists emphasize in their account of tort law. Nor is the theorist faced with difficult problems of vicarious agency that can beset some corrective justice accounts. A category of justice that applies where right holders (or parties acting on their behalf) undo the wrongs committed against them solves several interpretive puzzles that are otherwise raised by private law's structure and reasoning.

B. The value of a right to redress

Chapter 3 develops the value of a right to redress. Such rights are valuable in part because they provide an important type of justice between the parties, but this is not their only benefit. They may deter future wrongdoing, or they may communicate something about the dignity of a wronged plaintiff. This chapter outlines a particular kind of value that the right to redress advances in addition to these others: redress provides a right holder with distinctive kinds of authorship (both of her life's narrative writ large, and also more narrowly at the level of her specific choices). Within that subcategory of value, rights of redress may also provide a notably *private* authorship that is hard to obtain elsewhere.

It bears emphasis that there are a variety of positive features to a right of redress. Rights of redress may serve an important expressive function, and in the private right of action context this may comprise a 'best of both' worlds: communicating both the state's support of a claim and a plaintiff's self-reliance.[5] Rights of redress may be useful for their contribution to efficient outcomes, not least because of the deterrent effect that redress often provides. Rights of redress may restore opportunities for self-authorship that are an intended feature of primary rights, such as various opportunities for private choices associated with property rights. And, where redress is linked to distinctive private law institutions—such as tort, contract, property, and fiduciary law—it may accentuate the menu-like qualities of private law institutions.[6] This latter consequence may contribute to a desirable form of autonomy.

Note, however, that several conceptions of authorship are at work in private law, and they operate at several levels. At one level, redress can restore a right holder's means, enabling her to advance various projects that she finds meaningful. Thus, by restoring an approximate status quo ante with respect to property ownership, a right of redress can give a trespass victim the ability to engage in whatever projects her property ownership originally facilitated. At another level, it allows victims of a wrong to stand up for themselves. Authoring redress itself thus often has significant meaning for a right holder who seeks to allocate back. More subtly, the way in which that redress is attributed to a right holder also matters. Private rights of action may provide a kind of authorship that is not readily obtained in other settings, and it is this topic to which I will now turn.

A right holder might be an author of redress in the sense that an allocation back is the product of that right holder's choice. That is a comparatively common type of authorship, and private law offers many such occasions for its appearance. But one might also author an act of redress in a further respect, depending on how the right holder's actions are attributed to her by the law. Significantly, a legal system can ascribe redressive acts to a private party, rather than to the state. This private attribution of redress will give a right holder a different understanding of what she has done in fixing a wrong.

There is a conceptual challenge, to the extent we don't think that private plaintiffs really act through the courts when they bring suit.[7] This challenge has been raised against civil recourse theories more generally, but it does not succeed here. As Chapter 3 will develop, private rights of action are appropriately

[5] For development of this idea, *see* Jason M Solomon, 'Equal Accountability Through Tort Law' (2009) 103 Nw U L Rev 1765, 1795.
[6] Cf. Hanoch Dagan, 'Pluralism and Perfectionism in Private Law' (2012) 112 Colum L Rev 1409.
[7] Ori Herstein, 'How Tort Law Empowers' (2015) 65 U Toronto LJ 99.

understood (albeit not inevitably) as means for private parties to act against the parties who wronged them.

Problems of attribution are not new to private law theory. Kantian private law theorists seek to attribute authorship to the state—to an omnilateral will—and other theories are concerned with attribution as well. But quite possibly what ought to be valued is an attribution to a private right holder, and that perspective has received less attention. A unilateral will, or a will shared by a small group, offers something that can be desirable in its own right. It gives a right holder a different standing with respect to the party that wronged her—and just as importantly it gives her a different standing with respect to the state. In such cases, the right holder acquires a special kind of independence, different from the kind that is often elaborated in republican political theory. In such cases, the right holder need not act by the grace of another, and she need not feel that the credit for her enforcement rights properly goes to someone else. To the extent a state allows for private authorship of redress in this sense, it is offering something valuable indeed.

C. Applications to contract law and tort law

Chapter 4 then turns to applications in specific private law fields, beginning with the law of contracts. Private law theorists very frequently begin with tort law. In itself, this is hardly cause for concern, but tort-focused accounts can draw a theorist's attention to those concepts that best fit tort law's central features, potentially at the expense of concepts that are central to contract law, fiduciary law, or other private law subfields of equal importance. This book will begin with contract law, as it best illustrates how focusing on redress can shed light on private law doctrine. If that results in a less tort-centred account it is an unintended consequence, but it may also be a desirable one.

Contract theorists often begin with the reasonable premise that promissory morality helps make sense of contract obligations. Assume then that our goal is to account for contract law in a way that draws on norms of promissory morality. If so, one of the more significant puzzles in contract theory will be the expectation damages remedy. For some theorists, it is puzzling why this remedy should be the standard remedy, as opposed to reliance damages, or specific performance, or even an apology.[8] In promissory settings, each of these remedies

[8] Cf. Nathan B Oman, *The Dignity of Commerce: Markets and the Moral Foundations of Contract Law* (Chicago 2016) 114–26 (challenging the fit between both legal remedies and standing doctrine in light of promissory morality).

might fit under the right circumstances, assuming that we seek to explain the law in light of a promisor's moral obligations. The reality that some promises are legally enforced, while others are legally inconsequential, is similarly challenged. So, too, is contract law's substantive standing doctrine, whereby in the ordinary case it is only a wronged promisee who can sue following a breach.

Shifting our attention from a wrongdoer's obligations to a right holder's moral right to demand performance can help to solve these puzzles, as promisees may have a moral right to demand performance even in cases where a promisor would otherwise only have a duty to apologize. At least some of the remedial puzzles thus fall away.[9] Indeed, when right holders have standing to demand performance, they can quite reasonably complain if they are instead offered a reliance-based remedy. In addition, turning to the right holder side of the picture may help account for a plaintiff's special standing to bring suit, which is less easily explained if our focus is on a breaching party's obligations. Third parties may lack standing to demand that a breaching party perform, at least in the absence of an appropriate link between the third party and the promised performance.

Yet a shift to the right holder's perspective does not adequately capture what is at stake in contract law, at least not if we are just thinking of the right holder's standing to demand performance. Various moral relationships implicate a special standing of some sort, and these types of standing have arguable legal counterparts. Some private law theorists emphasize a right holder's special standing to make demands, analogizing this standing to the standing a plaintiff has to bring a private right of action. Others look to a wronged party's standing to complain about a wrong. Each approach offers insights, yet neither of these types of standing will inexorably lead to the standing to enforce. And, in order to explain contract law, we need standing to enforce, and not merely standing to make a demand or to make a complaint.

Chapter 4 pursues a particular way that standing to enforce post-wrong can be explained and justified: if the right to performance is understandable as a property interest or at least property-like.[10] If contract obligations are property interests—or suitably analogous to property interests—then they fall into a category that is commonly viewed as apt for enforcement. This chapter will

[9] Though new remedial puzzles arise. If standing to demand performance is our focus, this raises the question of how we are to explain why specific performance isn't the standard remedy for breach.

[10] Prior contract theories that build on property or property-like interests in performance include Stephen A Smith, 'Towards a Theory of Contract' in Jeremy Horder, (ed.), *Oxford Essays in Jurisprudence (Fourth Series)* (OUP 2000) 107, 120–9; Andrew S Gold, 'A Property Theory of Contract' (2009) 103 Nw U L Rev 1; Peter Benson, 'The Idea of Consideration' (2011) 61 U Toronto LJ 241, 268.

suggest that various principles of just property acquisition can be adapted to contractual settings such that contract obligations are different in kind from ordinary, unenforceable promises.

If we focus on moral enforcement rights (as opposed to a promisor's moral obligations or a promisee's standing to make demands), the preference for expectation damages over specific performance makes sense as well. Even where performance is owed and can be appropriately demanded, it may not be morally acceptable to coerce that performance. And, seeing contract principles in this light also offers insights into one of the more troubling doctrinal puzzles in the common law of contracts: it can help to make sense of the doctrine of consideration. Rights of redress accordingly may not only fit contract law, they may assist in explaining core doctrinal features.

Tort law turns out to be the greater explanatory challenge. It is not, however, an insurmountable challenge, and in some respects rights of redress are an especially good match for tort law doctrine. Chapter 5 suggests that substantial parts of tort law are readily explained by a redress-focused account, most notably torts like conversion or negligence torts that involve straightforward applications of make-whole remedies. Even cases involving make-whole remedies that are plainly inadequate can still fit a redressive justice framework. At the same time, the exceptions are substantial, as punitive damages and certain other remedies simply don't fit an allocation back mode of reasoning.

As noted, those parts of tort law that emphasize make-whole remedies are a natural fit for a redressive justice perspective, as they structurally match the idea of allocation back. But some torts make for an easier case of allocation back than others. Certain strict liability torts like conversion are especially strong examples. Indeed, their features echo the contract law analysis in Chapter 4. The idea that one may have a proprietary interest in contractual performance is if anything a variation on the theory of conversion, where a taking of property is exactly what the plaintiff complains of.

On the other hand, that ease of application disappears in several common tort law settings. Thus, some argue that negligence torts involving permanent physical harms—not to mention intentional torts, such as battery, that implicate serious emotional and physical injuries—are ill-suited for an allocation back rubric. One can't fully undo the harm suffered when a victim loses a leg, and this is taken to mean that these cases must be explained in some other way.[11] That critique misses the way in which an allocation back works

[11] *See* Scott Hershovitz, 'Corrective Justice for Civil Recourse Theorists' (2011) 39 Fla St U L Rev 107, 116.

in practice. Full allocation back is an ideal, but ultimately aspirational in the ordinary case. An allocation back can be partial and, by extension, redressive justice can govern in cases where partial allocation back is the best we can get. Not every type of justice is an all or nothing proposition, and this type of justice operates by degree.

Yet other cases pose genuine fit problems. Injunctive relief, nominal damages, and punitive damages are each challenges in their own ways. As this book rejects an equation of primary rights and obligations with secondary rights and obligations, injunctive cases are best seen to involve a different type of justice from redressive justice. Preventive justice and redressive justice diverge, and tort law instantiates both types. In addition, nominal damages are not realistically cases of allocation back. They may serve expressive purposes, and even provide a kind of justice, but it is not redressive justice. Punitive damages are likewise a different phenomenon, and they occupy a central place in tort law.

An ancillary goal of this book is to turn private law theory in a more pluralist direction, and in particular to encourage accounts that allow for local coherence rather than global coherence. The above exceptions would be a fatal flaw for a unifying account. As I will endorse a pluralist picture of tort law, and private law more generally, these exceptions are not a flaw from this book's perspective. Tort law is, if anything, a good illustration of private law's pluralistic features, and a multi-faceted image of the field is congenial to my argument. I will suggest, however, that tort law's combination of private law values and doctrines need not call for an amorphous, ad hoc style of pluralism. The way in which tort law's different remedies fit together allows for more coherence than some other forms of pluralism permit.

D. Understanding the state's role

The next two chapters are concerned with the state's role in providing for redress. Chapter 6 begins with an introduction to the fiduciary account of the state's obligations. This chapter will be particularly concerned with the question of why the state owes a responsibility to provide private rights of action or their equivalent. Chapter 7 will address a Kantian alternative account. In assessing this account, this chapter will also discuss the importance of self-help remedies as a mechanism of redress. While the state may take on a responsibility to offer substitutes for self-help remedies where they are prohibited, we also need to understand those cases in which self-help is permitted.

To begin with Chapter 6, note that there are multiple ways to explain why the state owes its citizens a private right of action (or something akin to one). Civil recourse theorists have explained the state's obligation to provide for private rights of action in terms of a social contract. On this view, the state owes its citizens a means to act against a wrongdoer, given that the state has largely prohibited self-help. I will suggest an alternative to a social contract theory: the state may be a fiduciary to its citizens. A fiduciary account can help make sense of what the state owes to those it has discretionary power over, even in cases where a social contract may be doubtful.

Given the proposed origin of the state's fiduciary obligations, citizen well-being should not be understood in aggregate, but on an individual level. Individual preferences are then particularly salient, although they are not the only concern; broader conceptions of an individual's best interests will also require advancement. And, in contexts where the state has substantial discretionary power over the lives and assets of its citizens—which is to say, in most cases—it is also important that the state facilitate whatever it is that its citizens individually find meaningful in life. This latter responsibility is especially significant for the design of private law.

It is no simple task to figure out what each individual finds meaningful, and efforts at discerning the average case are likely to backfire. Meaningfulness is highly individualized, even if it shows patterns across populations. Furthermore, what we each find meaningful may depend in part on the degree to which we have advanced our projects and comprehensive goals without assistance. Pre-wrong private law institutions are a solution to this problem, at least in part: the primary rights and duties associated with property, tort, contract, and fiduciary law fit this template. But private rights of action are just as important. As I will argue, the state may owe its citizens a viable mechanism for redress as a substitute for their pre-legal enforcement rights, in light of what those enforcement rights can mean for their possessors.

Chapter 7 turns to an important concern with such accounts, based on Kantian moral premises. The Kantian objection suggests that rights of redress aren't legitimately exercisable in a state of nature. On this view, one person cannot unilaterally impose their will on another person to redress a wrong, and that is precisely what occurs in many cases of redressive justice, or it is what occurs in the absence of a neutral third party like the state. While Kantians make a crucial exception for ex ante self-defence, this exception does not hold for ex post cases of rights enforcement.

A response to this objection is to revisit the subject matter of our interpretive endeavour. In various contexts, private law seemingly allows one private party to impose their will unilaterally on another.[12] A classic example is the doctrine of recaption of chattels. Assuming we adopt a doctrinal fit criterion that emphasizes how courts actually decide cases, this is a challenge for the view that private parties don't get to unilaterally coerce in order to undo a wrong. A possible reply from the Kantian side is to suggest that in recaption cases and similar self-help settings, the private party is actually acting as a stand-in for a public office holder. Yet that reply is a debatable interpretation of existing precedents, at least in some jurisdictions. And so the legal perspective is at best an ambiguous support for the Kantian perspective.

Ambiguity still might be resolved to support the Kantian view if other interpretive criteria favour that view. Once again, it will be helpful to turn to interpretive methodology. What of the morality criterion that private law theorists often apply when comparing theories? Perhaps that tips the scales in favour of the Kantian understanding?

As others have noted, the idea that post-wrong enforcement of remedies is morally unacceptable has very counterintuitive implications.[13] It appears to preclude remedies in a range of cases where these remedies are often considered not only acceptable, but highly desirable. While there is room to debate whether the Kantian position is correct on the morality of ex post remedies, however, that debate need not be resolved here. The key question for interpretive purposes is whether courts *could* consider unilateral enforcement to be morally legitimate, not whether they have accurately ascertained that morality. Courts can reject the Kantian view on coercion while still falling well within the moral mainstream, and this in combination with doctrines like recaption of chattels and other self-help remedies leaves plenty of room for other interpretations of private law.

It might instead be argued that there is a concern under a justice criterion, and that this concern should tip the interpretive scales. Consider the contention that civil recourse theorists should interpret private law in a way that conceptually links civil recourse to justice between individuals. This book supports such a justice criterion. This same justice criterion might be thought to bar a Lockean perspective on pre-legal rights of redress, in favour of a Kantian alternative. Can it be consistent with principles of procedural justice to permit one party to impose their will unilaterally on another? What of the *nemo iudex*

[12] For discussion, *see* Andrew S Gold, 'Private Rights and Private Wrongs' (2017) 115 Mich L Rev 1071; Scott Hershovitz, 'The Search for a Grand Unified Theory of Tort Law' (2017) 130 Harv L Rev 942, 944.

[13] *See* Victor Tadros, 'Independence without Interests?' (2011) 31 Oxford J Leg Stud 193.

in sua causa principle, which holds that a person should not be a judge in his or her own cause?

Chapter 7 addresses these questions as well. Private law is a context where doing one type of justice may mean failing to do another type of justice. Without casting any doubt on the *nemo iudex* principle, it is not enough to show that a redressive justice-centred perspective requires that principle's violation. Multiple principles of justice may operate in private law contexts, and occasionally it is impossible to fully comply with each of these principles of justice in combination. In cases where it is impossible to fully comply with or advance multiple principles of justice, the law may then need to engage in justice trade-offs. And I will argue that this is what happens in several private law settings.

A good illustration appears in cases of self-defence and in other cases of ex ante, preventive justice. It is ordinarily impossible to act in self-defence while also conforming to the *nemo iudex* principle. This means that preventive justice frequently will call for sacrifice of a norm of procedural justice if it is to occur at all. Yet this is not ordinarily considered inconsistent with the possibility that preventive justice qualifies as a genuine type of justice between the parties. I will suggest that something similar occurs with respect to redressive justice and the *nemo iudex* principle. (And, in a different way, we will see examples of justice trade-offs in Chapter 8, where equity and redress are in tension.)

Self-help and private rights of action are closely connected in an important respect. They are both examples of private parties enforcing their rights on their own behalf, with the difference being that in one case the enforcement is mediated by the state while in the other case it is not. In this regard, the right of redress extends beyond cases of civil recourse, for some instances of its application do not involve recourse to the state for help. But whether or not the state helps, a more Lockean reading or a fiduciary reading are not only plausible alternatives to the Kantian one, they may be a better fit for legal doctrine.

E. Redress and equity

The optionality of redress raises a different set of concerns, and these concerns are the subject matter of Chapter 8. Initially, it might be thought that redressive justice is not properly understood as a norm of justice, given that right holders have no duty to bring it about. This challenge is effectively a definitional one and it draws on a commonly held sense of how justice works. Still, it is reasonable to conclude that not all norms of justice create duties for right holders; preventive justice is widely recognized as a type of justice, yet right holders do not have duties to defend themselves if they choose not to. Even so, if we think that norms of justice necessarily create reasons for action, we still might question whether a truly optional form of justice (like redressive justice) merits the name 'justice'.

One answer is to note that redressive justice norms may ground reasons for action, even if those reasons are commonly outweighed in the real world. Another possibility is to again analogize to the preventive justice in self-defence contexts. Regardless of our preferred answer, commonly recognized norms of justice are optional from the right holder perspective in precisely the way that redressive justice is. On the other hand, resolving this definitional point only begins the inquiry. Even if redressive justice can qualify as a type of justice while still retaining its optionality, the exercise (or non-exercise) of that option raises a complex set of normative concerns.

First, there are cases where it would be better along various dimensions if a plaintiff were to bring suit. It is a striking feature of private law that a plaintiff nonetheless has the freedom to choose not to sue even if it would be better (for her or for society) if she did sue. Perhaps our worry in such contexts is specific to the right holder: people ought to stand up for themselves when they are wronged in certain ways. Or perhaps our worry is a matter of social benefit: not enough people sue to deter certain wrongs, or to develop an adequate precedent pool. These concerns are genuine, and they are not easily solved in a way that shows adequate respect for a right holder's freedom of choice whether to exercise her rights. That difficulty, however, should not deter us from recognizing that the justice in private law may mean that wrongs go unfixed when it would be better for them to be redressed.

Second, there are cases in which people sue to undo a wrong, yet their choice to seek redress wrongs the other party in the process, or it is at least morally wrongful. Can it still be just for such claims to be brought? I will suggest that it is possible to do justice while wronging another person as a result. That, however, is not the typical private law outcome. More problematically, it is possible for a right holder to do justice when, all things considered, it would be better if the right holder chose not to stand on her rights. Rights of redress can bring about redressive justice even when it is morally wrongful to exercise those rights; even when the right holder is being a stickler in a bad way. These latter cases are a particular concern for private law, especially in light of the state's potential complicity.

This concern is not a minor one, but it is alleviated to some extent by equitable doctrines like unconscionability, estoppel, unclean hands, and laches. Indeed, recognizing the relationship between redress and the morality of its pursuit can help to account for equity in certain settings. In some instances, the state ought to assist right holders in seeking redress, irrespective of the morality of the right holder's choice. Legal right holders may have a legal and moral right to do wrong, and in appropriate contexts the state may owe it to them to lend its support in enforcing their rights. In other instances, the state should not have to help out despite the presence of a plaintiff's legitimate right of redress. Equity significantly limits the more severe cases of potential state complicity in these latter instances.

In practical terms, the availability of equitable doctrines also means that there will be fewer cases of morally wrongful redress. And, importantly, redress itself can be modified by equitable considerations. A central mechanism for limiting the more severe cases is through encouragement of settlements; right holders may thus seek redress in a more equitable fashion when they have the choice of obtaining partial redress instead of a complete allocation back. Admittedly, these cases may result in a partial allocation back rather than an allocation back to its fullest degree; recall, however, that a partial allocation back can still do justice.

F. Redress and contemporary law

Chapter 9 considers contemporary developments in private law. We live in a world that increasingly includes statutory encroachments on common law principles, and some of these revisions alter the way legal claims are pursued. A focus on rights of redress offers different perspectives on several of these developments, sometimes offering grounds for critique and sometimes providing support. In light of contemporary legal doctrine, I will suggest that private law now offers a range of pathways to redress, and that these pathways bring out different dimensions of redressive justice.

Some developments are notable for their effects on remedial outcomes. Damages caps are one of the more striking legal revisions, as they frequently force courts to give substantially less than a full allocation back. Other examples are more significant for what they say about the identity of claimants. Litigation finance can change the claimant's effective identity in one respect; claims by corporate right holders change that identity in another respect. There are also new developments that impact the degree to which redress is private rather than public. Arbitration is a leading example. And, finally, there are contexts in which right holders have limited control over their legal claims. Class actions often have this feature.

In the end, redress occupies multiple continuums. It can be more or less complete; it can be brought about by parties with more or less personal interests in a legal outcome; it can be more or less private; it can be subject to more or less right holder control; and it can be more or less unilateral. I will argue that understanding what makes each type of redress valuable (or in some cases costly) is crucial to appreciating how private law operates, and part of the inquiry requires us to look at each continuum. At the same time, while the redress in private law helps in obtaining diverse goals, we should not lose sight of what else it accomplishes. In each case, redress is a kind of justice.

III. On Interpretive Method

Before concluding, a brief note on methodology is also in order. A primary goal of this book is to offer an interpretation of private law that takes seriously its self-understanding. This does not amount to a case-by-case doctrinal account of private law, but it is also not what is usually meant by a normative or prescriptive account. If this interpretation is a descriptive project, it is description at a higher level of abstraction than the form typical of doctrinal analysis. Throughout, the analysis will draw on moral and political theory with the goal of providing an interpretation that makes various doctrinal features intelligible and, within certain limits described here, coherent.

At a more fine-grained level, this book's interpretive methodology fits broadly within a 'New Private Law' rubric. That is, it endorses moderate criteria for interpretive success—the kind of criteria that allow for judicial error.[14] Private law doctrines on this view need not be morally correct, but they should ordinarily be understood in a way that a judge could reasonably think is morally correct. Likewise, judicial opinions need not be perfectly transparent, but a theorist should at least be able to explain why judges would claim to reason in the way that the language of their opinions suggests.

As with other private law theories, this one adopts criteria of fit, coherence, morality, and transparency. Yet the basis and content of these criteria will differ

[14] For a leading development of such criteria, see Stephen A Smith, *Contract Theory* (OUP 2004) 7–32. For discussion of the relation between such approaches and New Private Law methodology, see Andrew S Gold, 'Internal and External Perspectives' in Andrew S Gold, John CP Goldberg, Daniel B Kelly, Emily L Sherwin, & Henry E Smith, (eds), *Oxford Handbook of New Private Law* (OUP forthcoming).

from some other leading accounts. The moderate morality criterion provides a good example.[15] Interpretive theorists have good reason to care about the morality of the legal principles they describe: judges are unlikely to endorse a set of legal principles that they couldn't even think are morally appropriate (whether or not the courts are correct in that assessment). This conclusion is based on sociological and psychological premises, in light of the large numbers of judges deciding cases over long periods of time.

It bears emphasis that this is not a Dworkinian approach to interpretation, and it notably does not seek an interpretation according to which the law is actually justified. Nor will this approach rely on the premise that the law claims authority. While law makes a prominent claim to authority, this appears to be a claim to moral binding-ness, not moral correctness.[16] Law's claim to authority is thus a shaky support for a morality criterion. The moderate morality criterion used here rests solely on the language and apparent thinking of judges and other legal actors. To the extent a judge could believe a legal principle is moral, that is enough. On the view adopted here, private law doctrine does not have to actually be moral, and efforts to discern law's self-understanding should allow for this.

This book will also offer some refinements to previous methodologies. I will argue that, in addition to a moderate morality criterion, private law should be interpreted pursuant to a justice criterion. Torts, contracts, fiduciary law, and related fields should be interpreted in a way that judges could plausibly think does justice between the parties. This tracks the law's self-understanding, given the way judicial opinions are commonly written. As noted, a justice criterion poses challenges for some civil recourse accounts; but it is also a fruitful approach for assessing private law theories more generally.

In addition, I will adopt a relatively lax coherence criterion. This is largely a reflection of how private law develops piecemeal in a system of authoritative precedents, with large numbers of judges authoring opinions over many years. Modularity and information costs may also play a role in the law's development in this fashion, as pockets of local coherence can cut down on complexity in a way that attracts judicial notice. Given this backdrop, it is quite plausible to think that private law is locally coherent rather than globally coherent, and in certain fields I will suggest that multiple values and types of justice are in play. For scholars who seek to unify all private law features, this openness to

[15] For a leading account that adopts a moderate morality criterion, see Smith, *Contract Theory* (n. 14) 18–20.

[16] See generally John Gardner, 'How Law Claims, What Law Claims' in *Law as a Leap of Faith* (OUP 2012).

pluralism may seem a methodological flaw. On the other hand, if a relatively weak coherence criterion is justified, such pluralism should not be a concern. The significance of these moderate interpretive criteria will become apparent as the book progresses.

***

As developed above, the rights of redress in private law can be viewed from multiple angles. My hope is that this book will offer the beginning of a more complete understanding of private law doctrine, rather than a final word on it. The present account is avowedly pluralist, and it should be evident that rights of redress lead to different things in different settings, not to mention that some parts of the law involve other phenomena. Much future work could examine the linkages between separate private law subfields, not least where rights of redress overlap with the right to hold someone accountable. However these pieces are woven together, rights of redress are a common thread running throughout the private law. They are also one of the most important threads.

2

The Idea of Redressive Justice

I. Introduction

Corrective justice theories and civil recourse theories face significant but largely independent challenges. Redressive justice can help explain private law in a way that avoids most of these challenges, while incorporating strengths from each alternative theory. As this chapter will explain, redressive justice is a distinctive type of justice that governs the undoing of transactions (or allocation back). It differs from corrective justice as commonly formulated in that it specifically governs the conduct of right holders or parties acting on their behalf when they force an allocation back to occur. The resulting account is not a mirror image of corrective justice theory from the right holder's perspective, nor is it simply a variation on civil recourse theory.[1] Redressive justice offers a distinctive way to explain core features of private law.

This chapter will begin with a review of the allocation back account of corrective justice, as this account provides an important backdrop for redressive justice. It helps to illustrate the relevance and distinctiveness of the redressive justice category. I will then introduce redressive justice, indicating its conceptual features. This discussion will show how redressive justice is applicable in contexts where corrective justice is not, and vice versa. Furthermore, it will suggest that authorship of an allocation back has moral significance: it matters whether an allocation back is brought about by a right holder or a duty bearer. Lastly, this chapter will indicate the differences between redressive justice and other prominent categories of justice, including preventive, retributive, and distributive justice. It will also conclude with a key continuity between self-defence and redress.

[1] It is possible, however, for a particular type of civil recourse account to be reconciled with a redressive justice account. Sometimes private rights of action provide civil recourse in a way that also amounts to redressive justice. While redressive justice is not co-extensive with civil recourse, this type of justice can be instantiated through civil recourse. Note, however, that civil recourse theories do not generally recognize any necessary conceptual link between civil recourse and justice between individuals.

The Right of Redress. Andrew S. Gold, Oxford University Press (2020). © Andrew S. Gold.
DOI: 10.1093/oso/9780198814405.001.0001

II. The Corrective Justice Picture of Allocation Back

Corrective justice generally concerns the repair or rectification of wrongs or wrongful losses. It thus has a characteristic mode of operation. In Aristotle's famous description, corrective justice involves an arithmetic relation.[2] For example, if A has wrongly taken four apples from B, corrective justice would call for A to provide B with four apples, or with their equivalent in value. Four apples would be subtracted from A's holdings, while four would be added to B's holdings. Note also that justice is done as between these two specific parties. The wrongful gains acquired by A correspond to the wrongful losses suffered by B, and corrective justice effectively reverses the transaction that produced A's gains and B's losses.

While the above example is simple enough, elaborating the principle of corrective justice is not a straightforward task. Defining corrective justice with precision is difficult, given the many areas in which theorists disagree on its features.[3] There is disagreement as to whether the losses required to invoke corrective justice must be wrongful.[4] There is also disagreement as to whether corrective justice is concerned with rectifying wrongful losses, or rectifying wrongs as such.[5] And there is disagreement as to what counts as a wrong.[6] Each of these disputes is substantial.[7]

It is thus challenging to prove that one account is the proper understanding of corrective justice. Yet, if we accept certain premises about corrective justice, we can clearly distinguish corrective justice from another equally important type of justice: redressive justice. With this in mind, the following subparts will describe John Gardner's recent account of corrective justice.[8] There are other influential views of corrective justice that the reader might adopt for these

[2] Aristotle, *The Nicomachean Ethics*, bk V, ch. 7 (JEC Welldon trans. 1987).

[3] *See* Jules L Coleman, 'The Practice of Corrective Justice' (1995) 37 Ariz L Rev 15, 19 (describing significant variations among corrective justice accounts of tort law).

[4] Ibid. (noting disagreement as to a wrongfulness requirement).

[5] Cf. Jules Coleman, *Risks and Wrongs* (OUP 1992) 320–4 (discussing this distinction and arguing for a view under which it is wrongful losses that are corrected), with Ernest J Weinrib, 'Correlativity, Personality, and the Emerging Consensus on Corrective Justice' (2001) 2 Theoretical Inq L 107, 132 n. 33 (contending that Coleman has misunderstood the juridical conception of corrective justice). Weinrib's account of corrective justice in tort law is set forth at Ernest J Weinrib, *The Idea of Private Law* (1995) 134–6.

[6] Coleman, 'Corrective Justice' (n. 3) 19 (noting disagreement as to what counts as a wrong).

[7] Additional areas of divergence are now appearing. In recent years, new conceptions of corrective justice have been introduced, which differ significantly from prior conceptions. *See*, e.g. Scott Hershovitz, 'Corrective Justice for Civil Recourse Theorists' (2011) 39 Fla St U L Rev 107 (describing a theory of corrective justice that focuses on 'getting even'); Stephen A Smith, 'Why Courts Make Orders (And What This Tells Us About Damages)' (2011) 64 Current Legal Problems 51, 85 (describing a communicative conception of corrective justice instantiated by court orders).

[8] John Gardner, 'What Is Tort Law For? Part 1: The Place of Corrective Justice' (2011) 30 L & Phil 1.

purposes, but Gardner's theory presents the relevant issues most directly.[9] With this background in place, we will then be ready to consider redressive justice.

A. Corrective justice and allocation back

One of the most basic concerns for corrective justice theory is to explain how corrective justice differs from distributive justice.[10] Like other recent corrective justice theorists, Gardner seeks an account of corrective justice that views it as a distinct norm of justice, separable from distributive justice. Yet, he does not argue that corrective justice is different from distributive justice based on its concern with agent-relative reasons for action.[11] Indeed, he rejects the view that the relevant duty to correct a wrong is agent-relative.[12] On this view, 'be it corrective or distributive, an injustice perpetrated by anyone is in principle everyone's business, and anyone at all has reason to help in securing its avoidance'.[13]

Something else makes corrective justice distinctive. According to Gardner, corrective justice addresses a special type of allocative question. It involves an allocation back from one party to another. As he explains:

> Something has already shifted between the two parties. The question of corrective justice is not the question of whether and to what extent and in what form and on what ground it should now be allocated among them *full stop*, but the question of whether and to what extent and in what form and on what ground it should now be allocated *back* from one party to the other, reversing a transaction that took place between them.[14]

[9] As will become apparent, a key concern is whether a corrective justice theory views corrective justice as governing the conduct of duty bearers in particular. In addition to Gardner's account, other theories that take this approach include the 'mixed conception' of corrective justice. *See* Coleman, *Risks and Wrongs* (n. 5) 303–4 (presenting this conception); Stephen R Perry, 'The Mixed Conception of Corrective Justice' (1992) 15 Harv JL & Pub Pol'y 917 (discussing this conception).

[10] For a helpful discussion of this issue and an attempt to address it, see Coleman, *Risks and Wrongs* (n. 5) 303–11. A related issue concerns our ability to justify corrective justice, in light of distributive justice norms. For works assessing the relationship between the two types of justice, see Peter Benson, 'The Basis of Corrective Justice and its Relationship to Distributive Justice' (1992) 77 Iowa L Rev 515; Stephen R Perry, 'On the Relationship between Corrective and Distributive Justice' in Jeremy Horder, (ed.), *Oxford Essays in Jurisprudence* (Fourth Series 2000).

[11] But cf. Coleman, *Risks and Wrongs* (n. 5) 314–15 (describing a view of corrective justice that involves agent-relative reasons for acting).

[12] *See* Gardner, 'What Is Tort Law For?' (n. 8) 11.

[13] Ibid.

[14] Ibid. 9–10.

This feature separates corrective justice from distributive justice. As Gardner explains: 'A norm of corrective justice is a norm that regulates (by giving a ground for) the reversal of at least some transactions.'[15]

On the other hand, Gardner adopts a 'proposition (c)', which states as follows: '[A] norm of corrective justice only regulates the actions of the person from whom the transfer back is to be made *or another person acting on behalf of that person*.'[16] This proposition takes into account the common view that corrective justice is a type of justice that concerns the conduct of the wrongdoer in particular, while opening up the possibility that individuals other than the wrongdoer can play a role in its exercise.[17]

We will return to proposition (c) later in this chapter, as it is a significant boundary line for corrective justice. Before doing so, the next section will explain how Gardner's approach ties into questions of morality. Gardner provides an illuminating account of how the legal norm of corrective justice may be justified in moral terms, and, indeed, how it may be justified in light of a moral norm of corrective justice.

B. The Continuity Thesis

One of the common goals for a corrective justice theory is to show its relationship to private law doctrine. Gardner seeks to show how corrective justice can help explain tort law. If corrective justice is aptly described in terms of allocating back, subject to proposition (c), then tort law may indeed fit a corrective justice pattern. Tort law allocates back, and, arguably, it involves the state apparatus acting on behalf of the wrongdoer. Tort law may thus instantiate a legal norm of corrective justice. Assuming these premises, however, we may still need something more. A legal norm of corrective justice could itself call for justification.[18] Can the legal norm also be supported by a moral norm

[15] *See* ibid. 10.

[16] *See* Gardner, 'What Is Tort Law For?' (n. 8) 10.

[17] That said, Gardner does not believe that proposition (c) provides us with a difference between corrective justice and distributive justice. For example, when the state redistributes wealth through a system of taxation, he argues that 'it does so on behalf of those from whom it levies taxes.' *See* ibid. 13. What distinguishes corrective justice from distributive justice is that corrective justice involves allocating back.

[18] For helpful discussion of why the legal norm of corrective justice could itself require justification, see ibid. 14–17. Among other concerns, the legal norm may amount to an empty vessel, subject to radically different interpretations. This flexibility means that both deontological and consequentialist accounts are explanatory options. *See*, e.g. Richard A Posner, 'The Concept of Corrective Justice in Recent Theories of Tort Law' (1981) 10 J Legal Stud 187 (providing an efficiency account of corrective justice). A moral norm of corrective justice can thus fill a significant explanatory gap that is not resolved by noting a legal norm of corrective justice.

of corrective justice? Gardner's response to this challenge is based on an idea he calls the 'Continuity Thesis'. This thesis suggests that, all else equal, those reasons that justify a primary obligation will also justify a secondary obligation when the primary obligation has not been met.[19]

Consider the following example, which Gardner uses to illustrate his theory:

> I promise to take the children to the beach today, but an emergency intervenes and I renege on the deal. Let's say I was amply justified in doing so. One of my students, let's say, was in some kind of serious and urgent trouble from which only I could extricate him, and only by devoting most of the day to it. In spite of this ample justification for letting the children down today I am now bound, without having to make a further promise, to take them to the beach at the next suitable opportunity (if there is one).[20]

Of course, on these facts it is no longer possible to keep the promise perfectly. The day at the beach has already passed; any future visit to the beach is at best a close substitute. A substitute performance will nevertheless be called for.

While it may no longer be possible to meet the original obligation (which was either performed or not), 'those reasons in favour of the action that contribute to its obligatoriness can be conformed to more or less perfectly.'[21] It is still possible to conform to some degree to the reasons for action that supported the original obligation to take the children to the beach. As Gardner notes, every reason for action 'is potentially a reason for multiple actions.'[22] It may no longer be possible to take the children to the beach today, but it may be quite possible, and obligatory, to take the children to the beach on the next suitable occasion.

Based on these common sense moral intuitions, Gardner suggests the following principles:

> If all else is equal, the reasons that were capable of justifying a primary obligation are also capable of justifying a secondary one. I will call this the 'obligation in, obligation-out' principle. And the explanation for it that I have just sketched out I will call the 'continuity thesis'. It is the thesis that the secondary

[19] *See* Gardner, 'What Is Tort Law For?' (n. 8) 33. A related norm is also described by Joseph Raz. *See* Joseph Raz, 'Personal Practical Conflicts' in Peter Baumann & Monika Betzler, (eds), *Practical Conflicts: New Philosophical Essays* (CUP 2004) 172, 189–93 (analysing the continuity of reasons for action).

[20] *See* Gardner, 'What Is Tort Law For?' (n. 8) 28.

[21] Ibid. 30.

[22] Ibid. 31.

> obligation is a rational echo of the primary obligation, for it exists to serve, so far as may still be done, the reasons for the primary obligation that was not performed when its performance was due.[23]

This is also a groundbreaking insight. The Continuity Thesis indicates how the rights and duties involved in corrective justice are often related to individuals' primary rights and duties, but it does so without requiring us to say that primary and secondary rights and duties are identical. Secondary rights and duties will commonly echo primary rights and duties even if these secondary rights and duties *are not* transformed versions of primary rights and duties.

If we accept these principles, we can now also see the basis for a moral norm of corrective justice. Payment for the losses that one wrongfully occasions by breaching an obligation is a way to provide the 'best still-available conformity with, or satisfaction of, the reasons why one had the obligation'.[24] Corrective justice is supported by the continuity of our reasons for action when we have wronged others.[25]

C. The enforcement challenge to the Continuity Thesis

The above account offers an elegant analysis of corrective justice, its distinctive features, and its potential moral grounding in an individual's reasons for action. It may even be accurate as an account of corrective justice as a moral norm. If this account also fit private law, little more would need to be said. Unfortunately, given an aim of explaining private law, the above account is problematic. Proposition (c) is a potential sticking point in several respects.

[23] Ibid. 33.

[24] Ibid. 34. The basis for the primary and secondary obligations will of course vary with the complexities of each fact pattern. As Gardner indicates, however, there is no reason to think that promissory cases are a unique circumstance for present purposes. *See* ibid. 38–39.

[25] For Gardner, the Continuity Thesis is, in part, a means of explaining the manner in which secondary obligations echo primary obligations. An alternative approach to this continuity concern is to suggest that an individual's obligation continues in existence after a wrong is committed. For examples of this approach, see Ernest J Weinrib, 'Two Conceptions of Remedies' *in* Charles Rickett, (ed.), *Justifying Private Law Remedies* (2008) 3, 26; Arthur Ripstein, 'As If It Had Never Happened' (2007) 48 Wm & Mary L Rev 1957. Note that Stephen Smith has recently critiqued the versions espoused by Gardner, Weinrib, and Ripstein. See Stephen A Smith, *Rights, Wrongs, and Injustices: The Structure of Remedial Law* (OUP 2019) 180–201. Gardner has responded to some of Smith's arguments at John Gardner, 'Damages without Duty' (2019) 69 U Toronto LJ 412. In my view, Smith's critiques are more compelling with regard to Weinrib's and Ripstein's versions of the Continuity Thesis than Gardner's. In addition, not all of these critiques apply with the same force to the redressive justice account developed in this chapter, given that it is not focused on the continuity of obligations.

Initially, we might conclude that Gardner's conception of corrective justice focuses in the wrong place. Even if we assume that the moral norm of corrective justice that Gardner describes is a sound moral norm, private law is very much concerned with a wronged party's rights. The Continuity Thesis is very much a duty-focused account. This raises a potential question of doctrinal fit, since rights-based and duty-based accounts of private law need not converge. They clearly can converge, and on some views of rights and duties they must converge, but this is not something that we should just assume. Does a focus on an individual wrongdoer's conformity with corrective duties match legal reasoning?

There is a ready answer for this first concern. As Gardner notes, the Continuity Thesis is consistent with a rights-based understanding of allocation back. Indeed, the reasoning that supports the 'obligation-in, obligation-out' principle allows us to recognize what he calls the 'right-in, right-out' principle: 'whoever has a primary right (e.g. a right not to be libelled) also gets a secondary right (a right to reparative damages in a libel suit) upon violation of that primary right'.[26] Rights and duties in this context at least are correlative.[27] In light of the relationship between a wrongdoer's duties and a right-holder's corresponding rights, a right-in, right-out principle follows readily from the Continuity Thesis.

The real difficulty is not with an emphasis on rights versus an emphasis on duties in legal reasoning. Instead, the difficulty is in the structure and aim of that legal reasoning. Recall that proposition (c) is the proposition that 'a norm of corrective justice only regulates the actions of the person from whom the transfer back is to be made *or another person acting on behalf of that person*'. Private law often forces a wrongdoer to correct a wrong, but it is not obvious how this coercion occurs *on behalf of* the wrongdoer. Thus, if we follow Gardner's account, we will need to develop an explanation of private law in terms of vicarious agency, such that the state effectively acts for the wrongdoer.[28] And in this case, we will need a theory of how one party can act on behalf of another where the beneficiary of that agency relation is effectively coerced.[29]

[26] *See* Gardner, 'What Is Tort Law For?' (n. 8) 46.

[27] *See* ibid. 45–6 (explaining why, on this account, primary and secondary obligations will correspond to primary and secondary rights).

[28] As Gardner puts it, we need to explain 'how there can be an agent who acts on my behalf, such that on occasions I can be regarded as having conformed to norms of corrective justice even though it was someone else that did the allocating back for me'. Ibid. 11.

[29] Cf. Richard W Wright, 'Right, Justice, and Tort Law' in David G Owen, (ed.), *Philosophical Foundations of Tort Law* (OUP 1995) 159, 178 (questioning whether coerced conduct can satisfy a corrective justice obligation).

This vicarious agency problem is not a minor difficulty for corrective justice theories of private law.[30] How is a court acting on our behalf when it orders us to pay damages to someone else? When a tort plaintiff sues, is her claim understandable as a claim that the defendant should be assisted in meeting his responsibilities? Admittedly, vicarious agency may not be an insoluble problem. If we are ready to view the government as acting on our behalf when it forces us to meet norms of distributive justice through taxation, we could conceivably do the same for corrective justice.[31] This would, nonetheless, call for an intricate explanation of our private law system. Even if a theory of vicarious agency is up to the job, it is reasonable to seek a simpler explanation of how private law is related to justice in allocating back.[32]

Furthermore, as a factual matter, courts may *not* be acting on behalf of wrongdoers when they coerce a defendant to pay up. The possibility that they could be so acting does not mean that they are—it depends. The answer to this question is contingent on the content of judicial reasoning. Whether or not vicarious agency allows us to link corrective justice to private law in the abstract, there is still a descriptive concern regarding the actual legal point of view. Thus far, we have only suggested that it is possible in the abstract for vicarious agency to do the necessary work.

Given our private law system, we have reason to question whether courts are acting on behalf of wrongdoers, or at least whether they understand themselves to be doing so. In part, the concern is structural.[33] As the civil recourse theorists suggest, the plaintiff's private right of action is a central component of private law. This structure gives plaintiffs a right of redress through the legal

[30] Gardner himself suggests that explaining how vicarious agency would work is 'a tricky task' and he does not provide a full account in his tort theory paper. *See* ibid. This task may be rendered more difficult by self-help cases, as it seems questionable whether the individual performing self-help is acting for the wrongdoer who necessitated this remedy. I thank Rick Brooks for noting this point.

[31] *See* ibid. (giving this example). *See also* Gerald A Cohen, 'If You're An Egalitarian, How Come You're So Rich?' (2000) 4 *Journal of Ethics* 1, 2 (discussing the view that individuals discharge their responsibilities collectively through taxation). Liability insurance is also a potentially helpful illustration for these purposes. *See* Gardner, 'What Is Tort Law For?' (n. 8) 11 n. 25 (discussing the insurance case).

[32] It should be noted that, even if corrective justice is considered adequate to the explanatory job, it may still be that redressive justice provides a more convincing account. The arguments to come are thus not dependent on the reader's rejecting the possibility of a corrective justice-based interpretation of private law. It may even be that private law is explained by several types of justice in combination. In such a case, a convincing corrective justice account need not rule out a redressive justice component to private law.

[33] This concern may also be grounded in the nature of court orders, if one accepts the view that damages orders do not replicate secondary obligations. *See* Smith, 'Why Courts Make Orders' (n. 7) 70 (suggesting that, in explaining court orders of damages, the starting assumption 'should be that the courts are trying to do something other than to give effect to a moral duty'). *See also* Stephen A Smith, 'Duties, Liability, and Damages' (2012) 125 Harv L Rev 1717, 1727 (describing a view which 'supposes that insofar as it makes sense to speak at all of legal duties to pay damages, such duties are created—not confirmed—by damage awards').

system. Yet, this right of redress will only occasionally be exercised by plaintiffs and this sporadic quality raises doubts whether the aim of private law adjudication is to bring about a wrongdoer's compliance with her remedial duties. In some cases, it is also debatable whether a defendant owes a pre-judgment duty of repair, at least as a matter of legal doctrine. It could well be that existing legal doctrine is consistent with a duty-based understanding of corrective justice, but it is by no means an obvious inference from corrective justice norms to private rights of action.

In addition, the Continuity Thesis does not adequately ground rights of redress: there is a potential mismatch between those cases in which a right holder can legitimately seek redress and those cases in which a wrongdoer will have a remedial duty to do 'the next best thing'. Even a right-in, right-out principle does not entail a right of redress, at least not if redress is understood as a type of enforcement.[34] A right of redress is in Hohfeldian terms a privilege or a protected privilege to undo a wrong or otherwise unjust transaction (ordinarily held by a victim vis-à-vis a wrongdoer, or held by someone acting on behalf of that victim), and it may or may not exist in conjunction with a remedial claim right that the wrongdoer undo that wrong. A right to enforce a remedy (or have someone else enforce that remedy) is thus different from a remedial right.[35] This is because the remedial right could exist without the right holder (or perhaps anyone else) being able to legitimately enforce it.

For example, if one person promises to have lunch with another, we can readily conclude that the lunch promise creates a moral duty to have lunch. If that promise is breached, then all else equal, we can readily conclude that the promisor has a remedial moral duty to have lunch at the next best opportunity, or to provide some other version of the 'next best thing'. Each of these duties would correspond to a moral right in the promisee. It in no way follows from the practice of promising that the promisee could enforce this promise by coercive means. The promisee might have a remedial moral right to have

[34] Here, there is an important ambiguity to avoid. If 'right of redress' were to refer to a right to the outcome when wrongful losses have been corrected—by whichever party—then the right-in, right-out principle would be on point. The distinctive feature of the private right of action, however, is the right holder's ability *to bring about* that outcome. It is this aspect that we cannot readily explain by a right-in, right-out principle. A 'right of redress', for present purposes, concerns such enforcement.

[35] It should be emphasized that we are concerned with moral rights at this stage rather than legal rights. Some contend that legal rights are by definition enforceable by coercion. Cf. Matthew H Kramer, 'Rights Without Trimmings' in *A Debate Over Rights* (OUP 1998) 7, 9 ('A genuine right is enforceable. (Unlike a purely moral claim—which is also enforceable in certain ways—a genuine legal claim is enforceable through the mobilizing of governmental coercion, if necessary.)'). I do not hold that view, but its merits are not at issue here.

lunch with the promisor, but many of us would still find that she has no moral *enforcement* right.[36]

We might thus conclude that the Continuity Thesis is correct, yet never think that the right holder is justified in forcing the rectification of a wrong. Nothing in the Continuity Thesis is sufficient on its own to justify a coercive right of redress. A principle of 'obligation-in, obligation-out' is not the same as a principle of 'obligation-in, right of redress-out,' and a 'right-in, right-out' principle need not lead to a 'right-in, right of redress-out' principle. This raises an interpretive difficulty, since private rights of action are plausibly premised on a plaintiff's right of redress. In other words, Gardner's analysis could be accurate as an account of a moral norm of corrective justice, but this vision of corrective justice may not be what justifies private law.

D. Summary

Corrective justice theorists have ably shown how corrective justice can be viewed as an independent norm of justice. Given certain conceptions of corrective justice, corrective justice need not collapse into distributive or retributive justice. In addition, as corrective justice accounts have grown increasingly sophisticated, the case for the soundness of corrective justice as a moral norm has been strengthened. While the contours of corrective justice are much debated, the idea of corrective justice as a desirable and distinctive norm is increasingly plausible.

The explanatory role for corrective justice, on the other hand, continues to be a challenge in legal contexts, at least for corrective justice accounts of a certain type. Several recent corrective justice theorists have focused on a type of justice that governs the conduct of the wrongdoer. Doing so has provided important insights about corrective justice as a moral norm. This perspective, however, can make it more difficult to explain the coercive role of the state in private law settings. Is a coerced party really meeting his or her obligations? Is the coercive party really acting on the wrongdoer's behalf? More generally, is the state really acting on the wrongdoer's behalf? Given these questions, it is worthwhile to consider whether there is a type of justice that governs the conduct of the right holder who wishes to undo a wrongful transaction. This chapter will suggest

[36] Even if the reader concludes that some form of remedial enforcement right is legitimately present here, the key point is that this is a contingent outcome. The mere presence of a remedial moral right does not logically entail a moral enforcement right, nor does the Continuity Thesis point to the presence of such a right.

that there is such a type and that it is distinct from corrective, distributive, retributive, and preventive justice.

III. The Place for Redressive Justice

This brings us to the idea of redressive justice. A major insight in Gardner's account is the recognition that there is a distinctive type of justice concerned with allocating back. This formulation provides a clean boundary line between corrective justice and distributive justice. It also opens up the conceptual space for the account of justice offered in this chapter.[37] For, given proposition (c)—an intuitively plausible constraint on corrective justice—there is room for another form of justice in allocating back. Significantly, not all allocations back are made by a wrongdoer, or made on a wrongdoer's behalf. This part will explore the type of justice applicable to allocations back that are made by a right holder, or made on a right holder's behalf.

A. Redressive justice defined

Let's start with two parties to a dispute. Suppose that we are concerned with 'the question of whether and to what extent and in what form and on what ground [something] should now be allocated back from one party to the other, reversing a transaction that took place between them'.[38] Suppose, however, that we address this question to the conduct of the *right holder* in seeking redress, rather than the responsibilities of the duty bearer in correcting a wrong. Our concern then is with the question of whether and how something may be allocated back by a right holder from a duty bearer, reversing a transaction that took place between them.

It is reasonable to think that this question is concerned with justice, even if it is not necessarily concerned with corrective justice. After all, this question is a distinctly allocative question.[39] In addition, much like corrective justice,

[37] That said, it should be noted that the conception of redressive justice described here might still be accepted by someone who rejects Gardner's particular account of corrective justice. The argument is not contingent on acceptance of a specific corrective justice theory (although on certain accounts redressive justice would become a subset of another category of justice).

[38] Cf. Gardner, 'What Is Tort Law For?' (n. 8) 9–10 (using this formulation—with appropriate adjustments—to describe the question of corrective justice).

[39] *See* ibid. 6 (arguing that norms of justice are 'norms for tackling *allocative* moral questions, questions about who is to get how much of what'). *See also* Herbert LA Hart, *Punishment and Responsibility* (2nd edn) (OUP 2008) 21 (describing principles of justice as principles 'concerned with the adjustment of claims between a multiplicity of persons').

the concern is with allocating back, that is, the undoing of transactions. The primary distinction from the corrective justice case is that we now have a different party who is responsible for accomplishing the allocation back, or (if the state is involved) a different party on whose behalf the allocation back is made. Where it is the right holder who is responsible for the allocation back, we have redressive justice.

The duty to correct will admittedly exist in many redressive justice cases, and it is common to analyse wrongs in terms of breached duties. Yet, there is nothing unusual in thinking that there could also be norms of justice peculiarly concerned with the permissible actions of right holders. Preventive justice—the type of justice concerned with such things as self-defence—involves the permissible actions of right holders. In that context, we may ask when it is appropriate for a right holder to use force to prevent a wrong. At least in the abstract, then, we might imagine a distinct type of justice that governs the use of force to redress a wrong.

Care is needed in defining what type of right holder conduct is at issue. Redress can mean different things to different people.[40] Here, redress covers the enforcement of primary or secondary rights. Under this definition, redress does not mean getting satisfaction against someone who committed a wrong. The concern of redressive justice, like corrective justice, is with the undoing of transactions—allocation back—rather than with responding to wrongs as such.[41] Moreover, for legal explanatory purposes, a focus on undoing transactions is vital. Many private law remedies are a closer fit with norms of allocation back than with ideas of getting satisfaction or getting even.[42]

So construed, redressive justice takes the following form. It is the type of justice that governs whether and to what extent and in what form and on what ground something should be allocated back from one party to another,

[40] This is evident from recent work in the civil recourse literature, where redress has sometimes (though not always) been associated with the redress of wrongs involving personal injury. *See* John CP Goldberg & Benjamin C Zipursky, (2011) 'Civil Recourse Revisited' 39 Fla St U L Rev 341, 352 (suggesting that 'the paradigmatic contract case' will 'take us outside the realm of redress', but not outside the realm of civil recourse). Redress, as used in this book, will cover the standard remedies in a breach of contract case.

[41] On some theories, the annulling of wrongs as such is a retributive concern. *See* Coleman, *Risks and Wrongs* (n. 5) 325 (distinguishing corrective justice from retributive justice on this basis). It should be noted, however, that Coleman's views of corrective justice have evolved. *See* Jules L Coleman, 'Epilogue to Risks and Wrongs (Marcial Pons, Spanish Translation 2010)', available at: http://ssrn.com/abstract=1679554 (describing Coleman's recent views). The annulment of wrongs is, in any event, a distinct concern from the concern of redressive justice.

[42] Cf. Andrew S Gold, 'A Moral Rights Theory of Private Law' (2011) 52 Wm & Mary L Rev 1873, 1915–19 (discussing remedies for contract breach and for unjust enrichment which do not fit well with a retribution or satisfaction-based norm).

reversing a transaction that took place between them. However, this type of justice is subject to a proposition that I will call 'proposition (d)': *redressive justice regulates the actions of a right holder in allocating back, or of someone acting on the right holder's behalf.*[43] This proposition is what divides the redressive from the corrective.

Significantly, this form of justice between individuals allows us to explain the allocations back that private law courts regularly mandate, without calling on us to adopt the view that courts are acting on behalf of the wrongdoer when they issue such orders. In other words, we can avoid the vicarious agency challenge raised by proposition (c), and we can avoid the interpretive concern that courts, from an internal point of view, may be acting on behalf of right holders rather than wrongdoers.

B. The Asymmetries between corrective justice and redressive justice

A significant reason for our interest in redressive justice is the difficulty posed by proposition (c). But why not just revise proposition (c)? We could adopt a disjunctive version of the rule. Corrective justice might be defined as the justice of allocating back, subject to a 'proposition (c′)': *corrective justice regulates the action of a duty bearer in allocating back, or someone acting on the duty bearer's behalf,* or *it regulates the action of a right holder in allocating back, or someone acting on the right holder's behalf.* This would resolve the vicarious agency challenge, and there would be no need for proliferating categories of justice.

The answer to this question is twofold. First, it turns out that redressive justice and corrective justice are not mirror images. Not all fact patterns that implicate corrective justice necessarily implicate redressive justice, and vice versa. Second, we will likely lose important insights about justice in allocation back if we fail to attend to the differences between allocation back by duty bearers, and allocation back by right holders (or parties acting on their behalf).

The possibility of collapsing categories of justice into a smaller set does not mean we will gain greater insight by doing so. For example, as Gardner notes, it is possible to re-describe the addition and subtraction that are characteristic of corrective justice in distributive justice terms.[44] Corrective justice can thus

[43] One might reject a role for vicarious agency with respect to redressive justice, but I can see no reason for doing so. Unlike the corrective justice case (in which we may doubt that courts act on behalf of wrongdoers), there is nothing counterintuitive in thinking that courts act on behalf of right holders.

[44] *See* Gardner, 'What Is Tort Law For?' (n. 8) 9.

be seen as distributive justice. Such a move, however, 'fails to bring out that the [corrective] result depended on a special kind of norm designed to tackle a special kind of allocative question.'[45] Attending to this special kind of norm leads us to important insights about interpersonal morality.

This chapter will suggest a similar conclusion if we characterize redressive justice in terms of an expansive corrective justice category: such thinking would fail to bring out that there is a special norm involved when we pursue redressive justice. Even if we could adopt a view of corrective justice that would absorb redressive justice (i.e. by adopting proposition (c′)), there are good reasons not to. The hypothetical fact patterns in the next section will show that redressive justice is a salient conception of justice in allocating back, and also that it can apply in circumstances where corrective justice is not necessarily applicable. There are cases where corrective justice applies such that a duty bearer has a duty to allocate back, yet the right holder has no right to enforce her rights. There may also be important cases where a right holder can appropriately enforce his or her right to allocate back—an act of redressive justice—yet the counter party has no corresponding duty to allocate back.

Furthermore, it is a common intuition that it makes a difference whether a particular allocation back is authored by a wrongdoer rectifying his wrong, or a right holder enforcing her rights. We often care if a wrongdoer gets the chance to fix the results of his conduct. Redressive justice may reverse wrongful transactions, but it does so with the wrongdoer in a different role and, consequently, with a different effect on the wrongdoer's status. Even if both a wrongdoer and a right holder could legitimately reverse a transaction, it matters which party is responsible for bringing about this outcome. A morally distinct type of justice results depending upon the author of the allocation back.

Each of these points will be developed below, using a series of hypothetical examples.

1. Duties to perform without corresponding enforceable rights

Suppose that Allen casually promises his coffee mug to Beth, knowing that she has long admired the mug. Two minutes later, before Beth has relied in any way, Allen changes his mind. He tells Beth he is going to keep the coffee mug. Under these circumstances, Allen would initially have a primary moral duty to perform as promised, and Beth would have a primary moral right to performance. Given his breach of promise, Allen would have a remedial moral duty to provide the coffee mug, and Beth would have a remedial moral right to the

[45] *See* ibid.

coffee mug.[46] But notice that, if Allen refused to hand it over, Beth could not, consistent with morality, force Allen to keep his word.[47]

Let's call this the 'Ordinary Promise' case. In this first case, corrective justice would govern Allen's conduct in providing the mug. Beth, however, would not be able to take the mug for herself, at least not consistent with justice in allocating back. Whatever rights Beth has with respect to the mug, they are not enforceable rights.[48] Redressive justice would not support efforts by Beth, or by a party acting on Beth's behalf, to coerce compliance with this ordinary promise.[49]

2. Duties to perform with corresponding enforceable rights

Suppose instead that Allen promises Beth his coffee mug, if Beth will spend the day fixing a problem with his computer for him. The task is both difficult and, at times, mind-numbing. The mug is an ordinary mug and probably worth much less than the hours of Beth's time. Beth agrees to the task, however, and at the end of the day she asks for the mug. Allen recognizes she performed exactly as agreed, but refuses to turn over the mug, which he says he actually rather likes. Under these circumstances, many of us would conclude that it is perfectly appropriate for Beth to walk over to Allen's cubicle, pick up the mug, and walk away with it. If we feel uncomfortable with Beth enforcing her rights unilaterally, we may conclude that this case is appropriate for enforcement by the state on Beth's behalf.

Let's call this the 'Contract for Personal Property' case. Beth initially has a primary moral right to Allen's performance of his promise. Should Allen

[46] This chapter will bracket the question whether the remedial moral duty might give the promisor an option between specific performance or payment of damages. Cf. Jody S Kraus, 'The Correspondence of Contract and Promise' (2009) 109 Colum L Rev 1603, 1629–31 (analysing the complexity of remedial moral duties in the promissory setting). Likewise, I take no position on the possibility that contractual promises create disjunctive primary duties. Cf. Daniel Markovits & Alan Schwartz, 'The Myth of Efficient Breach: New Defenses of the Expectation Interest' (2011) 97 Va L Rev 1939 (suggesting this possibility).

[47] It is possible that, as a practical matter, Beth could enforce her rights by demanding compliance and publicly shaming Allen. This sense of enforcement is not the sense used in this chapter, as it would not take the choice of compliance away from Allen.

[48] On the enforceability of ordinary promises and its relevance to contract theory, see Andrew S Gold, 'A Property Theory of Contract' (2009) 103 Nw U L Rev 1, 20–1. *See also* Peter Benson, 'The Idea of a Public Basis of Justification for Contract' (1995) 33 Osgoode Hall LJ 273, 293 (critiquing Charles Fried's promissory account of contracts because it 'does not explain how the obligation to keep a promise is construed as something other than a merely ethical duty').

[49] To the extent that Beth might be able to take the coffee mug for herself without coercing Allen—say, by removing it from Allen's desk—this would still involve an asymmetry. Corrective justice would be met by Allen providing the coffee mug, yet it would not be just for Beth to take the mug for herself where the only basis for her conduct is an ordinary promise with which Allen refuses to comply. I thank Brian Bix for emphasizing this non-coercive type of case.

refuse, she has a remedial moral right to his handing over the coffee mug after the fact. Yet, this remedial moral right may be violated, just as the primary moral right may be violated. If it is clear that Allen is not going to provide the coffee mug, she has an enforcement option. All else equal, Beth may take the mug herself or the state may legitimately take the mug on Beth's behalf.[50] In either event, this example differs from the Ordinary Promise case because it involves an enforceable right.

Corrective justice would again govern Allen's conduct. Allen would have a duty to provide the mug to Beth, in this way correcting the wrong he has committed by breaking his word. Should he do so, it would be corrective justice. In addition, redressive justice could now also have a role. Assuming that Allen is not going to correct the wrong in a timely fashion, redressive justice would govern Beth's conduct in taking the coffee mug for herself. In such a case, Beth (or the state) would not be acting on Allen's behalf; the acts of redress would be made on Beth's behalf.

3. Enforceable rights without corresponding duties to correct

There may also be cases in which corrective justice would not apply, while redressive justice would apply. Imagine, instead of the above agreement between Allen and Beth, that Beth has mistakenly left her coffee mug on Allen's desk, intending to give the mug to another individual as a gift. Allen takes the mug, thinking it is a gift to him. Beth then calls Allen up on the phone, explaining her mistake. Assume that Allen has not changed his position in any way in reliance on the mistaken delivery. Nor has Allen committed any wrong. Allen may be unjustly enriched by Beth's error, however.

As Stephen Smith suggests, there is reason to question whether, as a matter of morality, one acquires an affirmative duty to return benefits that were transferred by mistake.[51] In such cases, the enriched party has neither consented to a duty, nor committed a wrong. There is no obvious manner in which the enriched party has harmed the party who made the mistake.[52] Arguably, what

[50] This chapter will leave open the question whether legitimate enforcement always requires a neutral third party. Cf. Arthur Ripstein, 'Private Order and Public Justice: Kant and Rawls' (2006) 92 Va L Rev 1391, 1418 (discussing this concern). Whether it is Beth, or someone acting on her behalf, in either case it would be redressive justice that governs the enforcement conduct. Further discussion of the significance of a neutral third party will be provided in Chapter 7.

[51] *See* Stephen A Smith, 'Justifying the Law of Unjust Enrichment' (2001) 79 Tex L Rev 2177, 2194 (suggesting 'that we reject the idea that there is in principle a duty to return benefits transferred by mistake.').

[52] Cf. ibid. at 2182 ('The first normative problem raised by the orthodox account [of unjust enrichment law] is how to explain the existence of a duty that seems inconsistent with the harm principle.').

the enrichee owes in unjust enrichment cases is a duty not to interfere when the transferor seeks to retrieve the property at issue.[53]

Perhaps we will feel that the enrichee does have a moral duty to return the property if it is easy to do so (e.g. if Allen could just walk across the room and place the coffee mug on Beth's desk). This is particularly likely if we focus on unenforceable moral duties, rather than duties that third parties can force Allen to comply with. But suppose instead that it would be quite costly for Allen to return the coffee mug. We might assume that Allen was transferred to a different office in another country, and could only send the mug back to Beth at great expense. It will cost him substantial expenses to return the mug, and hours of effort. Let's call this the 'Unjust Enrichment' case.

In the Unjust Enrichment case, Beth can legitimately retrieve her property. Allocation back is appropriate and redressive justice applies to her enforcement actions. On the other hand, it is debatable whether Allen would have a moral duty to return the coffee mug, especially given that doing so would be quite costly.[54] Intuitions differ in this sphere, but given a common perspective on moral duties, corrective justice is a questionable fit while redressive justice is a match.[55]

4. Redressive remedies that diverge in content from duties to perform

Finally, we may recognize cases in which corrective justice and redressive justice would both apply to the same fact pattern, but the content of the remedies appropriate to each would diverge. Suppose that we modify the prior contractual fact pattern. Imagine that, instead of providing a coffee mug to Beth, Allen has agreed that he will mow Beth's lawn for a week in return for Beth's work in fixing Allen's computer. Beth performs as agreed, and then Allen refuses to mow the lawn. In this case, it would be morally legitimate for Beth or

[53] Cf. ibid. at 2194 (suggesting 'that we regard our fundamental duty in this area of the law as a duty not to interfere with another's attempt to retrieve defectively transferred property').

[54] Several commenters have suggested there is a moral duty to return the enrichment under the given fact pattern. The present argument is not intended to resolve the question whether such a duty exists. The point is that the asymmetry described here is conceptually possible, and that it is an asymmetry that arises under a mainstream account of the morality of unjust enrichment fact patterns. Moreover, an asymmetry may exist as a legal matter, even if it is not otherwise present in morality. In some legal systems, unjust enrichment law may involve legal liabilities rather than duties to return enrichments. Cf. Stephen A Smith, 'The Restatement of Liabilities in Restitution' in C Mitchell & W Swadling, (eds), *The Restatement Third, Restitution and Unjust Enrichment: Comparative and Critical Essays* (Hart 2013) 227.

[55] To use Stephen Smith's example: 'Suppose that what has been transferred by mistake is a cow, and suppose further that the owner of the cow lives a thousand miles away. Would anyone accept as self-evident that the transferee is under a duty to return the cow to its owner?' *See* Smith, 'Justifying the Law' (n. 51) 2187.

the state to force monetary compensation (depending on the means used), but it would not be appropriate for Beth to coerce Allen to mow the lawn.[56]

Let's call this the 'Contract for Services' case. Coercing performance here would interfere improperly with Allen's autonomy, or with his dignity as a fellow human being.[57] Allen does owe a corrective duty to mow the lawn, but Beth's enforcement right would only allow her to take the equivalent in value—expectation damages. The 'next best thing' for Allen to do is the act he promised to perform. Yet the available remedies that Beth can legitimately bring about have a different content. Redressive justice and corrective justice are both potentially applicable, but their remedial implications differ.

5. Summary

What we can see from these four examples is that there are plausible cases where a) Allen would have a duty governed by corrective justice, but Beth would have no enforcement right under redressive justice (the Ordinary Promise case); b) Allen would have a duty governed by corrective justice and Beth would have an enforcement right governed by redressive justice (the Contract for Personal Property case); c) Allen arguably would have no duty under corrective justice, but Beth would have an enforcement right governed by redressive justice (the Unjust Enrichment case); and d) Allen would have a duty governed by corrective justice and Beth would have an enforcement right governed by redressive justice, but the remedies under each would diverge (the Contract for Services case). As these examples indicate, there is no necessary symmetry between corrective and redressive justice.

C. The significance of authorship

Differences in outcome are not the only reason to differentiate corrective justice and redressive justice. Even if we put to one side those fact patterns where duty bearers have a duty to correct and right holders have no right to coerce (e.g. the Ordinary Promise case), and those fact patterns where duty bearers may have no duty to correct, but right holders do have a right to coerce (e.g. the Unjust

[56] For further analysis of this type of problem, see Gold, 'A Property Theory' (n. 48) 53–58.

[57] *See* ibid. 56 (discussing this concern as it relates to contract enforcement). *See also* Anthony T Kronman, 'Paternalism and the Law of Contracts' (1983) 92 Yale LJ 763, 779 (describing a legal point of view under which 'even a contract of short duration that calls for the performance of routine and unobjectionable tasks is a contract of self-enslavement and therefore legally unenforceable if it bars the employee from substituting money damages for his promised performance').

Enrichment case), there is an additional reason to be interested in redressive justice as a distinct form of justice. It matters whether allocation back occurs at the hands of a wrongdoer, or at the hands of a right holder or someone acting on her behalf. Something is lost if our account of justice does not attend to this question of authorship.

Let's return to the coffee mug examples. Assume that Allen has wrongly taken Beth's coffee mug. He simply converted it to his own use. Imagine that Allen and Beth have an office mate, Charles, who is known for his absent-mindedness. Charles removes the coffee mug from Allen's desk in order to admire the mug's pattern. In the midst of conversation, he then inadvertently sets it down on Beth's desk. At this point, it is too late for Allen to correct much of the harm caused by his breach. He is largely unable to do the 'next best thing' by returning the mug, because Beth now has her coffee mug.

Allen's duties with respect to reversing the transaction (other than perhaps an apology) have become substantially moot.[58] Assuming Allen eventually felt bad about his breach, this is unfortunate from his perspective. Perhaps he can still try to make it up to Beth in some other way, but he cannot return her coffee mug himself. In addition, even if Allen feels no remorse, the outcome differs depending on which party repairs the effects of a wrong. For, in a corrective justice case, Allen has done as much as he can to comply with his duties. Corrective justice has a meaning for Allen, and for Beth as well, and that meaning is different from a mere return of the coffee mug by any means that happen to transpire.[59] It is a distinctly just outcome if Allen returned the mug himself, of his own choice.

A similar point holds when we compare corrective justice with redressive justice. It is meaningful whether the wrongdoer has repaired the effects of the wrong, or the right holder has repaired the effects of the wrong. Indeed, this is one reason why a redressive response is often considered inappropriate when we are certain that the wrongdoer will allocate back if given the opportunity.

[58] On apologies and their relation to corrective justice, see Scott Hershovitz, 'Harry Potter and the Trouble with Tort Theory' (2010) 63 Stan L Rev 67, 97–98. *See also* Tony Honoré, 'The Morality of Tort Law—Questions and Answers' in David G Owen, (ed.), *Philosophical Foundations of Tort Law* (OUP 1995) 73, 82 ('The *form* that our responsibility for an outcome should take remains an open question. An apology or telephone call will often be enough.'). While some corrective justice theories incorporate apologies, however, it is not clear that an apology will always be an allocation back.

[59] This fact pattern also helps illustrate how redressive justice, like preventive justice, is concerned with liability rather than desert. The duty holder does not deserve to be subjected to redressive acts as such; she is appropriately subjected to them if needed to undo the transaction. Cf. Jeff McMahan, 'Self-Defense and the Innocent Attacker' (1994)104 Ethics 252, 259–60 (describing an analogous feature of preventive justice). Since it would no longer be necessary for Beth to retake the mug in order to undo the transaction—she now has it, thanks to a lucky accident—redressive justice would no longer support Beth in taking a mug from Allen.

In an important respect, it is preferable—and differently just—if the wrongdoer has fixed the harms he caused.[60] If corrective justice is not forthcoming, however, redressive justice may be entirely fitting as a second best outcome.

Corrective justice theorists have reason to emphasize the wrongdoer's duty to correct, and they are onto something important when they adopt constraints like Gardner's Proposition (c). The fact of having wronged someone may never vanish, but the extent of a wrongdoer's cause for regret can vary significantly based on that wrongdoer's subsequent conduct.[61] The outcome is normatively different, as between the wrongdoer's rectification of a wrong, and anyone else's rectification of that wrong. Corrective justice and redressive justice thus stand in normative contrast. Viewing corrective justice as one overarching category of justice for allocating back would obscure the importance of a *wrongdoer's* corrective conduct.[62]

Responsibility for the outcomes of our actions is closely tied to who we are.[63] Indeed, it may be a fundamental part of our personal identities.[64] Yet, ascription of responsibility for wrongs is not the only way that our identities are shaped by our actions; our further actions after a wrong occurs are also ascribed to us. Someone who commits an act of negligence that harms another is responsible for that act. If this same individual voluntarily fixes the consequences of this negligence, he is responsible for the act of correction. His status is changed for the better: he is not just responsible for committing a wrong. If instead someone else fixes the consequences of his negligence, that other party is responsible. Corrective justice and redressive justice have very different

[60] An authorship problem may also arise under other categories of justice, depending on how the relevant category is theorized. For example, there is a question whether, under certain approaches to retributive justice, the punishment involved must be inflicted by the victim, or may instead be inflicted by the state. *See* Jean Hampton, 'Correcting Harms Versus Righting Wrongs: The Goal of Retribution' (1992) 39 UCLA L Rev 1659, 1692.

[61] As Gardner indicates, we cannot ever cancel out the fact that we have committed a wrong, even if afterwards we have undone the effects of that wrong. Cf. Gardner, 'What Is Tort Law For?' (n. 8) 35–7 (discussing rational remainders and corrective justice). On the other hand, we can have fewer reasons for regret if we tried to fix what we did.

[62] There may also be a parallel aspect to a right holder's redressive conduct. Stephen Darwall has suggested that right holders have a special authority when it comes to responding to wrongs committed against them. *See* Stephen Darwall, *The Second-Person Standpoint* (HUP 2006) 18. From this perspective, a right holder has done something different from a third party when she acts pursuant to this authority.

[63] *See* Tony Honoré, *Responsibility and Fault* (1999) 29 (noting that '[i]f actions and outcomes were not ascribed to us on the basis of our bodily movements and accompaniments, we could have no continuous history or character').

[64] Arguably, outcome responsibility is one of the most basic features of our identities. *See* ibid. 40 ('Our responsibility for what we do and for its outcome is inseparable from our status as persons. We cannot disclaim outcome responsibility without undermining that status; and outcome responsibility is therefore more fundamental than moral and legal responsibility, which are species of it.').

implications for duty bearers and right holders because they have very different authors.

It bears emphasis that authorship also matters from the right holder's end, albeit in a different way. Right holders who have fixed the wrongs they suffered (whether directly by their own hand, or indirectly through a private right of action) have now accomplished something important that would be lost if they were merely a passive bystander. They have stood up for themselves, and they may feel differently about cases in which they were self-reliant or in which they at least bear a causal relationship to the undoing of a wrong. Their life's narrative may be shifted by authorship just as much as the wrongdoer's is.

The fact that the remedies involved may appear identical in their material effects should not obscure the differences between allocation back when authored by a wrongdoer and allocation back when authored by a right holder.[65] Both types of allocation are meaningful but in different ways. Wrongdoers, right holders, and also third parties can quite plausibly care whose choice it is to undo a transaction, and see it as a different *kind* of justice depending upon which party brings this about.

IV. Differentiating Redressive Justice from other Types of Justice

It is now worth considering whether redressive justice is truly distinct from other types of justice.[66] Unquestionably, redressive justice resembles other types of justice in important respects. The prior parts indicate why corrective justice and redressive justice merit distinct categories. Even if one agrees that corrective justice and redressive justice contrast significantly, however, one might conclude that redressive justice is sufficiently similar to other types

[65] Along similar lines, retributive justice and corrective justice may overlap substantially in terms of the remedies they support, yet this possibility does not bridge the gap between retributive and corrective responses to a wrong. Cf. Hampton, 'Correcting Harms' (n. 60) 1663, n. 10 (suggesting that 'correcting a loss can sometimes play a role in annulling the wrongdoing, and therefore can be a partial response to the wrongdoing').

[66] A similar concern besets corrective justice theories, since corrective justice could be seen to share the same space as distributive or retributive justice. It should be noted, however, that not all theorists consider differentiation to be a concern (or, at least, not all theorists face an identical differentiation challenge). Some theorists suggest that retributive justice is a subset of corrective justice. *See*, e.g. Wright, 'Right, Justice' (n. 29) 175. Others appear to treat preventive justice as a form of corrective justice. *See*, e.g. Ernest J Weinrib, *The Idea of Private Law* (HUP 1995) 144, n. 41 (suggesting corrective justice allows for 'injunctions that prevent unjust harm'). And yet others conclude that corrective justice is in fact a type of distributive justice. *See*, e.g. Wojciech Sadurski, 'Social Justice and Legal Justice' (1984) 3 Law and Philosophy 329.

that it lacks a suitable boundary line. This part will therefore analyse whether redressive justice is truly differentiated from its neighbours.

An initial candidate for overlap is preventive justice: the type of justice that covers self-defence and other-defence. Redressive justice clearly has a close relationship to preventive justice, as both address permissible conduct by right holders in relation to wrongs. But preventive justice is concerned with the adjustment of harms ex ante. Redressive justice involves ex post concerns. Preventive justice and redressive justice thus address a distinct type of problem. To put the point another way, preventive justice is not concerned with allocating back, and redressive justice is. And, notably, there are cases of necessity where ex ante preventive justice would be improper, yet redressive justice would still plausibly apply.[67]

Retributive justice is another potential candidate. We might think that redressive justice is about acting against someone who has wronged you, in a retributive manner. Here, the difficulty centres on the remedy and its basis. Redressive justice is concerned with the undoing of transactions rather than the undoing of wrongs as such.[68] Its purpose is not punishment, vengeance, or even holding someone accountable for their misconduct. This is not to deny that retribution has relevance for private law. For example, compensatory damages in tort may be redressive, while punitive damages may be retributive. Yet it is to deny that redressive justice and retributive justice are the same thing.

Lastly, redressive justice differs from distributive justice. Distributive justice is concerned with allocation across a group (even a group of two).[69] Redressive justice, like corrective justice, is concerned with allocating back. As a legal matter, it is also characteristic of redressive justice that it may apply even in cases where the status quo ante is distributively unjust. The very rich plaintiff may, under private law norms, successfully seek compensation from a very poor defendant based on that defendant's tortious actions.[70] Distributive

[67] As Jeff McMahan notes, there is an asymmetry between preventive and corrective justice. *See* McMahan, 'Self-Defense' (n. 59) 279 (discussing a necessity case where preventing a harm would not be legitimate, but correcting its effects after the fact would be). This asymmetry is similarly applicable when we compare redressive and preventive justice.

[68] This distinction has been significant for some theories. Jules Coleman has historically viewed the annulling of wrongs as a retributive concern, and in *Risks and Wrongs* he rejected this view of tort law. *See* Coleman, *Risks and Wrongs* (n. 5) 325. There are, however, theorists who contend that tort law is precisely about holding people accountable for their wrongs. *See* John CP Goldberg & Benjamin C Zipursky, 'Torts as Wrongs' (2010) 88 Tex L Rev 917 (analysing and critiquing loss allocation theories of tort law).

[69] *See* Gardner, 'What Is Tort Law For?' (n. 8) 12–13 (noting the possibility of local distributive justice between two parties).

[70] In this respect, redressive justice shares features with corrective justice, which may similarly involve the restoration of an unjust ex ante distribution. Cf. Coleman, *Risks and Wrongs* (n. 5) 304–5 (describing corrective justice as a type of justice that permits distributive injustice). This resemblance

concerns can still be relevant to the availability of legal redress, and bankruptcy cases attest to this.[71] Distributive justice is nevertheless a distinct norm of justice.

There is a possibility of overlap between categories, both in law and in morality. In individual cases, private law might simultaneously achieve more just distributions, provide retribution against wrongdoers, provide corrective justice on behalf of wrongdoers, and also provide redressive justice on behalf of right holders. The overlap, however, is by no means guaranteed, as the concepts are genuinely distinctive.

V. Redressive Justice and Continuity

Yet even granting their distinctiveness, other norms of justice can also offer important lessons if we are trying to understand the justice in redress. In particular, we can learn a great deal by focusing on the norms that govern self-defence and other forms of preventive justice. One way this might occur is through the deterrent effect of redress. In some cases, ex post examples of redress could be legitimized as examples of self-defence, and this in turn could have bearing on the content of legal rights of redress. But I will suggest a different linkage here.

While the above analysis rejected the Continuity Thesis as a way of justifying the reversal of wrongs in private law, the Continuity Thesis is nonetheless a powerful model for a reason. That thesis underscores the way that private law remedies often echo primary rights and obligations. Furthermore, the Continuity Thesis allows us to locate a more general principle in support of such remedies, rather than rely on case-by-case intuitions. Redressive justice cannot draw on the Continuity Thesis, but it often can draw on a similar principle for support—and in studying this aspect we will see a profound connection between redress and the justice involved in self-defence. Redressive

should be unsurprising. While redressive justice and corrective justice are distinct, they are both separable from distributive justice as norms of allocation back.

[71] Distributive justice might also play a part in legal reasoning in spheres that are primarily concerned with redressive or corrective justice. Cf. Anthony T Kronman, 'Contract Law and Distributive Justice' (1980) 89 Yale LJ 472 (suggesting that rules of contract law can be used to implement distributive goals). In addition, we can coherently speak of the just distribution of redressive justice in those legal systems where some individuals have an opportunity for redress and others do not. Cf. John Gardner, 'What is Tort Law For? Part Two. The Place of Distributive Justice' in John Oberdiek, (ed.), *Philosophical Foundations of the Law of Torts* (OUP 2014) 335.

justice and preventive justice are not the same thing, but they are related in important ways.

A. The Persistence Thesis

Self-defence cases lead us in the right direction, even though ex post remedies are not necessarily a form of self-defence. A promising avenue for understanding ex post coercion is to look into the basis for coercive conduct in the pre-wrong setting. The same interests that justify the enforcement of rights prior to a wrong may also justify the enforcement of rights after the fact. In other words, the same interests that support ex ante protective acts may ground moral norms of redressive justice. Ex ante, these interests (such as the interest in bodily integrity) have sufficient importance that right holders can often legitimately exercise preventive force—at least under the right circumstances and in the right manner. By extension, these interests may explain the legitimacy of coercion after a wrong has occurred. This view allows us to locate a moral norm of redressive justice capable of underpinning the legal norm of redressive justice with a wide breadth of application.

In order to pursue this line of reasoning, we cannot rely on the Continuity Thesis (according to which the reasons that support primary obligations pre-wrong will support new, 'next best thing' obligations post-wrong). Recall why the Continuity Thesis will not adequately ground norms of redressive justice. Even if the Continuity Thesis supports a right-in, right-out principle, the existence of a remedial moral right need not entail a corresponding right of redress; it need not entail a right to enforce.[72] The example of an ordinary promise demonstrates the difficulty. It is commonly thought that promisors will, all else equal, owe duties to do the next best thing to their promised performance when they breach. It is also commonly thought that promisees have a moral right to receive the next best thing. It in no way follows that promisees can legitimately *force* performance of the next best thing in the ordinary case. If I promise to have lunch with you and then break my word, you will have a moral right to my having lunch with you on the next available occasion. But you cannot legitimately force me. The remedial moral right need not entail a moral enforcement right.

Yet as noted the Continuity Thesis is compelling, in part because ex post remedies often do echo a wronged party's rights prior to the occurrence of a wrong.[73]

[72] *See* section II.C.

[73] Cf. Gardner, 'What Is Tort Law For?' (n. 8) 29 (suggesting that a breached obligation 'seems to leave some traces of itself, some echo, behind for later').

Remedial moral rights frequently reflect the content of a claimant's primary rights, and legal remedies roughly parallel this structure. For example, contractual remedies in cases of breach frequently reflect the content of the originally promised performance. A private right of action often enables a plaintiff to seek expectation damages that approximate the originally promised performance. Thus, even though a right holder's privilege to enforce her remedial rights does not follow from the Continuity Thesis, some form of continuity (moral and legal) appears to operate in the enforcement realm. How can we account for this continuity if the Continuity Thesis is insufficient to support enforcement rights?

One answer is to develop a thesis that *is* concerned with enforcement. To avoid confusion with Gardner's Continuity Thesis, I will call this new thesis the 'Persistence Thesis'. The Persistence Thesis takes the following form: those reasons that support the recognition of a right holder's primary right of enforcement will also support the recognition of a secondary right of enforcement when the opportunity to exercise the primary right is no longer available.[74] In other words, if someone holds a moral right to enforce her rights ex ante—and then suffers a violation of those rights—she will, all else equal, also deserve the next best thing with respect to enforcement. She will deserve a right to undo the harmful transaction: a right to enforce her remedial rights ex post. An elaboration of this idea follows below.

Suppose that we start with the pre-wrong environment. From this perspective, a right holder's primary enforcement right is a familiar one. In many circumstances, an individual possesses rights of self-defence or defence of property that may be legitimately exercised to prevent a wrong. These primary rights are at the core of preventive justice and they are generally considered to be appropriate means for individuals to enforce their rights. Redressive justice can be linked to these well-recognized moral principles.[75] Self-defence, however, involves the ex ante enforcement of rights, before a wrong happens. Redressive justice occurs ex post, and this poses a conceptual challenge.

Imagine that a wrong has already occurred, either because the victim of the wrong did not choose to act in self-defence, or because any such acts failed to protect him. Suppose also that the type of wrong was one that would have

[74] One could express a related idea in terms of duties. The reasons for a potential wrongdoer's duty of non-interference when a primary right of self-defence is exercised will, all else equal, also support a duty of non-interference when a secondary right to allocate back is exercised. These latter duties, however, are not the same thing as duties to allocate back (which may or may not also exist).

[75] For a different linkage between self-defence and rights of action, see Benjamin C Zipursky, 'Civil Recourse, Not Corrective Justice' (2003) 91 Geo LJ 695, 735 (suggesting that 'a right of action in tort, focused on the right to respond to a legal wronging in the past, may be compared to self-defense in the criminal law, which recognizes the right to preempt an anticipated wrongdoing by another'). Zipursky's account in this paper appears to link self-defence with a right to hold someone accountable.

legitimately supported self-defence under the circumstances, if the right holder had managed to protect himself in time. For example, suppose that Brian realizes that Charles is about to punch him. He could legitimately prevent this from happening by hitting Charles first, but he hates violence and decides not to. He doesn't want things to escalate. Brian lets Charles hit him (albeit without consenting) and now faces some minor medical bills. Can we still draw on Brian's original right of self-defence to justify an allocation back? Not necessarily.

As John Gardner indicates, obligations pick out particular acts and, when the opportunity for performing those acts has passed, the obligation as such no longer exists.[76] Enforcement rights are similarly individuated. A right to enforce a right may pick out a particular set of acts as legitimate, prior to a potential wrong occurring. For example, a right holder may engage in certain legitimate acts of self-defence to protect against a threat of imminent harm that would violate her right to bodily integrity. The right holder may thus enforce her primary rights through ex ante defensive measures. But once the threatened harm has occurred, it makes no sense to say that she still has a right to protect against that very harm. One cannot exercise a right to protect against a future event when that event is now in the past.

Here is where the Persistence Thesis comes into play. In many cases, the reasons for recognizing a primary right of self-defence can continue in effect even when the exercise of that primary right is no longer an option. In this respect, these reasons are much like the reasons for a primary obligation, reasons which can continue in effect even when that primary obligation can no longer be met. The very reasons for holding a right to prevent an injury can also be reasons for holding an ex post right to undo that injury, to the extent possible. Whether we look to autonomy, human dignity, or other basic values, certain interests can legitimize coercive conduct to prevent a breach of an individual's rights. On this account, the reasons for primary rights to enforce a right pre-wrong have a continuity, or persistence, which justifies secondary rights to undo a wrongful transaction.

The Persistence Thesis thus holds that if all else is equal, the reasons for recognizing a primary enforcement right prior to an injury are also reasons for recognizing a secondary enforcement right after the injury has occurred. Under this thesis, the secondary enforcement rights that arise after a wrong are justified by the same reasons that undergird the right holder's primary right to stop the wrong before it occurs.[77] Where certain interests are at stake, both

[76] *See* Gardner, 'What Is Tort Law For?' (n. 8) 29 (discussing the manner in which obligations are individuated according to the action that they make obligatory).

[77] It is beyond the scope of this chapter to develop an account of which types of interest merit protection by means of self-defence or defence of property. Much depends on the theory of self-defence that

preventive and redressive justice may apply: preventive justice beforehand and redressive justice afterwards (although, as will become clear, in some cases only one of these types of justice will be appropriate).

To use a concrete example (and to return to our earlier theme), assume that Allen wishes to steal Beth's coffee mug right out of her hands. She is trained in martial arts and she expertly blocks each of his assaults, keeping the coffee mug for herself. She causes no injuries to Allen, but successfully stops his theft. This would be an example of property defence, possibly also self-defence, and Beth's conduct would be legitimate.[78] But what if Allen succeeded in taking the coffee mug? If we think Beth should now be able to take the coffee mug back, the Continuity Thesis will not be enough on its own to support Beth's conduct. Her remedial right to have the mug back is distinct from her right to retrieve the mug, and especially so if force is needed. Yet the Persistence Thesis could justify Beth's conduct in retrieving the mug, if we think her interest in the coffee mug is the right type of interest to merit a pre-wrong right of enforcement.

There are intimations of this idea in Gardner's work, although his ultimate account differs. In a recent paper, he describes a case called *Blind or be Blinded*.[79] In this hypothetical case, his enemy wrongfully attacks him and, under the circumstances, 'only one of us can possibly emerge with functioning eyes'.[80] He then notes a widely accepted norm of distributive justice under which, 'I enjoy moral latitude to defend my own eyesight against my enemy's attack by transferring the loss of eyesight to him.'[81] This is the familiar territory of self-defence, or, under a different wording, preventive justice.[82] But the next point in the discussion is striking:

> Now suppose that, in spite of my efforts to defend myself, my enemy still manages to blind me and thereby to save his own sight. Surely the norm of

we adopt. For recent (and differing) justifications for self-defence, see Shlomit Wallerstein, 'Justifying the Right to Self-Defense: A Theory of Forced Consequences' (2005) 91 Va L Rev 999; Boaz Sangero, 'A New Defense for Self-Defense' (2006) 9 Buff Crim L Rev 475.

[78] Additional facts may be required, depending on one's view of legitimate property defence. If the reader is concerned that a coffee mug is not important enough to merit forceful defensive measures, we can change the object to a priceless family heirloom or a wedding ring. Likewise, we can assume that, if she had not defended herself in this fashion, Beth would not have been able to prevent the theft.

[79] *See* John Gardner, 'Corrective Justice, Corrected' (2012) 12 Dirrito & questioni pubbliche 9, 17.

[80] *See* ibid.

[81] *See* ibid.

[82] Following Jeff McMahan, I prefer to call this ex ante category 'preventive justice' rather than 'distributive justice'. Gardner does not use that terminology, but for present purposes the distinction is not significant.

> distributive justice that already gave me the moral latitude to defend myself . . . still regulates the aftermath. The norm says that, as the wrongful attacker, he is the one to bear the loss of sight, all else equal. If that cannot literally be done (either because it is now impossible or because it is morally impermissible on some other ground) then surely he must now bear the cost of lost sight, the bills for treatment and care . . . .[83]

A norm of justice can give us a moral latitude in just this way. We often think of norms of justice as sources of duties, but they may also be sources of rights and privileges. Likewise, the suggestion that something carries over after the wrong was committed is compelling. It is easy, in fact, to feel as if the same norm of justice is involved pre-wrong and post-wrong. As Gardner asks: 'How are we going to explain the fact that when the gains and losses were still in the future we happily regarded the norm as a norm of distributive justice, but that applying it retrospectively we now think of it as typifying a different form of justice, *viz*. a corrective form?'[84] Even so, a different form of justice is implicated here, for in the latter case allocation back is involved.

Gardner thus comes close to describing the continuity I have in mind; his reference to a moral latitude is exactly on point, as is his concern with allocation back. Notice, however, that there is something unusual in viewing *corrective justice* as an ex post version of the original norm of distributive (or preventive) justice. Ex ante, the pre-wrong norm of justice gives a would-be victim the moral latitude to prevent the attack. The target can permissibly shift the impending blindness to the attacker and this would presumably be done on the target's own behalf. Yet, assuming symmetry between ex ante and ex post, the ex post norm of justice should then be giving the victim the moral latitude to allocate back on his own behalf. That, however, would not plausibly be a case of corrective justice on Gardner's account, because the victim would not be acting on behalf of his attacker when he seeks payment for his medical bills. Corrective justice governs parties with duties to correct their own wrongs, and it governs those who act on a wrongdoer's behalf. The kind of justice that gives us the moral latitude to enforce our rights raises a different concern from corrective justice.

In *Blind or be Blinded*, the attacker must pay the medical costs ex post, and if he does so voluntarily, this is corrective justice. But if the attacker doesn't feel

[83] Ibid. 18.
[84] Ibid.

like complying, can the victim force a payment? On the approach suggested here, the answer is yes (subject to certain limitations yet to be discussed). According to the Persistence Thesis, the basis for your having a moral right to prevent certain wrongs persists after those wrongs are committed. Your moral enforcement rights, however, cover different conduct once a wrong is completed. Just as many primary obligations can no longer be performed after their breach, and are replaced by secondary obligations that echo them, so too with moral enforcement rights. The primary enforcement right that permits one to prevent a wrong is replaced by a secondary enforcement right to allocate back, all else equal. The same reasons that ground preventive justice retain their force, grounding redressive justice ex post.

Naturally, the above discussion does not demonstrate that the Persistence Thesis is valid. The contexts for legitimate self-defence and property defence are controversial, and the same is true for rights of redress. If the Persistence Thesis is valid, moreover, it will only be applicable for a subset of legally enforceable rights. For example, unjust enrichment cases do not implicate the Persistence Thesis, as they involve primary rights and duties in the absence of wrongs. To the extent redressive justice applies in such cases, it will be on a different basis. Yet, the Persistence Thesis has significant explanatory advantages: it allows us to better understand why rights of redress should echo underlying rights of prevention, and it allows us to draw a deep connection between redressive justice and preventive justice. All else equal, the reasons for recognizing a moral right to forcibly prevent a wrong ex ante seem quite capable of supporting a moral right to forcibly undo that wrong to the extent possible.

VI. The Legitimacy of Redressive Justice in Particular Cases

Thus far, we have focused on the legitimacy of redressive justice in the abstract. There is another way to approach the legitimacy of redressive justice, for the legitimacy of redressive justice may also be assessed for specific categories of cases in which a right holder wishes to allocate back. To this end, many of the considerations relevant to the legitimate exercise of self-defence are also relevant to the exercise of rights of redress. As Jeff McMahan notes, there is a moral presumption against shifting of harms that applies in the self-defence setting.[85]

[85] *See* McMahan, 'Self-Defense' (n. 59) 252–3.

Redressive justice implicates this same presumption. Redressive justice involves conduct designed to undo transactions that have already happened; it also involves conduct designed to shift harms from one party to another.[86] More generally, the Persistence Thesis gives us reason to expect that the classic constraints on legitimate acts of preventive justice will have analogues in the redressive justice domain.

Redressive justice is not an ex post mirror image of preventive justice, and so caution is called for. There are cases where preventive justice would be inapplicable ex ante, yet redressive justice may be entirely appropriate ex post.[87] Necessity cases, like the famous tort case of *Vincent v. Lake Erie*,[88] are good examples. In these contexts, one individual commits a wrong against another as a way to protect herself or her property in an emergency. In *Vincent*, a boat owner damaged another party's dock in order to protect his boat during a storm. Ex ante, the emergency not only excuses the commission of the wrong, it precludes the victim from legitimately preventing that wrong. Ex post, a redressive remedy for the resulting damages is still fitting in the light of the wrong that was committed.[89]

We can also imagine a reverse scenario where prevention makes sense but redress does not. Suppose an individual perceives a severe, imminent danger, under circumstances where she is legitimately able to defend herself. Suppose that David has launched a projectile at Ellen (who is innocent of any wrongdoing), but that Ellen has the ability to divert the object so that it will instead bounce back and hit David. Let's say that Ellen fails to defend herself and the attack proceeds harmlessly. The projectile just misses its would-be victim and no measurable damage results; the anticipated injury did not come to pass. Preventive justice would have been appropriate under these circumstances given the very high risk of significant harm, but ex post redressive justice would not be appropriate given what actually happened. Under this hypothetical fact pattern, there would be nothing for the right holder to allocate back. Other

[86] *See* ibid. 253 (suggesting that, while a harm that has already occurred cannot literally be redistributed, 'it nevertheless counts as shifting the harm if a new harm is imposed on another person as a means of cancelling out the initial harm by fully compensating the victim').

[87] *See* ibid. 279 (arguing for the view that 'one cannot infer the permissibility of preventing a harm from the fact that the harm wrongs the victim and imposes on the injurer a duty ex post to compensate the victim for the harm').

[88] 109 Minn. 456, 124 N.W. 221 (Minn. 1910).

[89] The point here is not solely legal, but also moral. The right holder may legitimately deserve damages, even if he or she could not legitimately prevent the harmful conduct. For helpful discussion of such necessity cases in moral terms, see Joel Feinberg, 'Voluntary Euthanasia and the Inalienable Right to Life' (1978) 7 Phil & Pub Aff 93, 102.

variant fact patterns may hinge on differences in urgency or on a wrongdoer's apparent readiness to correct.

As these examples indicate, the 'all else equal' qualifier matters for the Persistence Thesis, just as it matters for the Continuity Thesis. All is not always equal ex ante and ex post. Despite such asymmetries, the constraints on an individual's permissible actions under a preventive justice rubric will ordinarily be important constraints when assessing the soundness of redressive justice for particular fact patterns. As we would expect if the Persistence Thesis is correct, similar concerns should apply in both settings. These concerns include the severity and type of harm caused by the right holder's conduct in enforcing her rights, the necessity of the enforcement selected, and the proportionality of the right holder's response to a perceived threat or committed wrong.

For example, in self-defence settings it is commonly thought that the defending party should not do more harm than necessary to successfully defend against a given threat.[90] It makes sense for the same constraint to apply ex post. Assume that a victim of theft (or the state acting on the victim's behalf) has to break a cheap lock on the thief's garage in order to retrieve a stolen bicycle. This minimal harm—the broken lock—could be permissible as a legitimate step towards redress, depending on the circumstances. In contrast, tearing down a garage wall and destroying the thief's entire house might not be morally acceptable if this level of harm would not be required to retrieve the property. Only a limited amount of harm or likely harm to the duty bearer will be permissible under a sound norm of redressive justice.

Or, suppose that the victim of a wrong will shortly receive a remedy from the wrongdoer, a remedy that will compensate the victim as fully as possible for the consequences of the wrong. It would arguably be wrong for the victim to enforce her remedial rights, if she could just as readily receive a voluntary act of corrective justice from the wrongdoer instead. Redressive conduct is not necessary to bring about an allocation back in this case.[91] The legitimacy of the right holder's conduct can thus be contingent on the duty bearer's post-wrong

[90] Cf. McMahan, 'Self-Defense' (n. 59) 277 (suggesting that 'self-defense is in all cases subject to a requirement of minimal force—namely, that one must not cause a greater harm if one can defend oneself equally effectively by less harmful means').

[91] Although there are differences, this suggestion roughly parallels a necessity requirement in self-defence cases. For example, we may not kill an attacker in self-defence if we could easily prevent the attack by less harmful means. Note that for present purposes, necessity and proportionality are treated as distinct concerns. For a recent suggestion that necessity is a feature of proportionality in the self-defence setting, see Larry Alexander, 'Self-Defense' in Andrei Marmor, (ed.), *The Routledge Companion to Philosophy of Law* (Routledge 2012) 222.

decisions. Indeed, in some cases redressive justice is a second-best type of justice. Corrective justice may be morally preferable when it is available, and redressive justice then becomes appropriate as a backstop when corrective justice is not forthcoming.

As noted, proportionality may also be a relevant limit on redressive justice. Suppose, for example, that we return to the Contract for Personal Property case described earlier in this chapter. If Allen has wrongly refused to give Beth's coffee mug to her as promised, and if she has a legitimate claim to take the coffee mug, redressive justice would not countenance Beth's killing Allen as a convenient way to acquire the mug. Irrespective of her privilege to take the mug, the means used would constitute an independent wrong against Allen, and a disproportionate wrong as well. Indeed, even if the bare minimum of harm required to successfully take the coffee mug would involve killing Allen, this would not be sufficient to justify doing so.[92] If killing Allen would be a necessary step in order to allocate back, it would not consequently be a legitimate act to kill him for that end.

Additional constraints will also apply.[93] There are a variety of criteria that delimit a sound norm of redressive justice, and the plausibility of redressive justice as a genuinely moral response to wrongful transactions will be context dependent. The above discussion is intended to outline some of the issues that need resolution and to point the way for further inquiry. Focusing on these considerations suggests that redressive justice, if it is to be legitimate, will involve an interlocking set of normative concerns. It also suggests that there is a substantial benefit in turning more of our attention to redressive justice as a category of study. Many of the above normative problems can be obscured by an emphasis on corrective justice (the other major form of justice in allocating back). Figuring out how and when someone should fix their own wrong does not adequately tell us how and when other parties should fix that wrong. Given the frequency of recalcitrant wrongdoers, the latter question takes on significant practical importance.

***

[92] Thomson makes a similar point in the preventive setting. *See* Judith J Thomson, *The Realm of Rights* (HUP 1990) 114 ('You have a claim against me that I not smash your flamingo; all the same, it is not permissible for you to prevent me from doing so if the only means you have of preventing me—shooting me—are unacceptably drastic.').

[93] For example, some interests are not apt for redressive justice. We saw an example of this concern earlier, when we considered breaches of ordinary promises. The above discussion is not intended to provide an exhaustive list of constraints, but rather to illustrate how these constraints will often parallel the constraints on legitimate acts of preventive justice.

Justice in the undoing of transactions is a fundamental form of justice, but this form of justice need not involve a voluntary choice by a wrongdoer to correct his wrongdoing; it may not involve any conduct by the wrongdoer at all. Right holders can undo transactions as well, acting on their own behalf. The moral questions raised by a right holder's choice to enforce a remedy are important ones and they cannot readily be subsumed within questions of a wrongdoer's remedial obligations. It is this difference that motivates recognition of redressive justice as a category of justice worthy of elaboration.

When allocation back is brought about on behalf of a right holder, this has a unique significance. Redressive justice is notable in part because it implicates an asymmetry in private law disputes. Not every transaction that merits reversal is fitting for redressive justice, and not every such transaction is an appropriate case for corrective justice. And, even when both types of justice are fitting, it may turn out that the remedies suited to corrective justice are different from the remedies suited to redressive justice. Moreover, the moral significance of each type of justice is distinctive: authorship matters. If a wrongdoer undoes a wrong, his moral ledger now includes that effort to fix what happened. If a right holder undoes a wrong instead, the result is distinctively just.

There is also an explanatory payoff to this shift in focus from the corrective to the redressive. A variety of legal settings are at best an awkward fit for corrective justice norms, given their focus on a wrongdoer's remedial conduct. Yet the standard alternative categories of justice are, if anything, an even more awkward fit. Redressive justice deserves a place alongside corrective, distributive, retributive, and preventive justice; in mapping out our norms of allocation, we will capture substantially more if we recognize that this type of justice has a distinct role in our legal reasoning. In turn, recognizing this role may help us to better address the moral questions raised by private law adjudication. With that concern in mind, Chapter 3 will turn to the value in redress. Chapters 4 and 5 will then consider the relationship between redressive justice and two central private law fields: contract law and tort law.

3

The Value of the Justice in Private Law

I. Introduction

The value of a right of redress is separable from the interpretive questions we have considered so far. Legally recognized rights of redress could be valuable even if no existing legal system has ever provided for them; likewise, if rights of redress are undesirable, we should oppose them even if they offer the best explanation of current doctrine. From an interpretive perspective, it helps to know whether a given set of legal concepts could be considered moral or just by legal actors; concepts that are morally beyond the pale are less plausibly the concepts judges have adopted. Still, there is an important difference between a theorist's assessment that private law participants *could* see a legal concept as moral or just, and the conclusion that it actually *is* moral or just.

Much of this book is devoted to questions of private law interpretation—with the conclusion that rights of redress are central to private law—but that interpretation invites the question whether rights of redress are a good thing. This chapter will assess the value to a right of redress. Some of the observations are tentative, in part because the benefits that rights of redress offer may be contingent on the primary rights and duties recognized in a given legal system.[1] But with that caveat, I will suggest a range of ways that rights of redress are important, with particular emphasis on the ways that they enable people to exercise authorship over their actions and lives.

Rights of redress have very substantial value for their possessors, and not just as a mechanism for undoing wrongs. I will begin with several of the more salient benefits that a redress-centred private law provides; some of these benefits are shared in common with a corrective justice-centred approach, but not all of them. I will then indicate how a broadly Lockean understanding of

[1] While these observations are tentative, the benefits at issue should be robust in most settings. One might conclude that certain legally recognized primary rights are sufficiently unjust or evil that there is no value in a right of redress with respect to their violation. We should bear in mind that this is likely to hold true (if it does) only in the most extreme cases; there can be value in redressing violations of primary rights even where those primary rights are poor policy or undesirable all things considered. I thank Nick McBride for raising the concern that some primary legal rights are sufficiently misguided that redress is valueless.

The Right of Redress. Andrew S. Gold, Oxford University Press (2020). © Andrew S. Gold.
DOI: 10.1093/oso/9780198814405.001.0001

redress offers further benefits—that is, I will indicate why it may matter if legal rights of redress are grounded in pre-legal entitlements to undo a wrong. In particular, this view allows people to understand their enforcement rights to belong to them as individuals, and to see their exercise as not being 'by the grace of another'. I will conclude by situating rights of redress within a broader pattern of private sovereignty. So understood, rights of redress allow individuals to exercise a valuable form of self-authorship and, in the process, to reinforce other private law values. Indeed, rights of redress allow for multiple types of authorship to co-exist, and these types may be valuable both on their own and in combination.

II. Shared Benefits and Unique Benefits

Why exactly should we value a right of redress? The most basic answer, implicit throughout this volume, is that exercising this kind of right accomplishes a certain kind of justice. Redressive justice is unique in that it arises when a right holder exercises her enforcement rights to undo a wrong, or someone acts on her behalf for the same end. To the extent this kind of justice is legitimate, we also have a basis for thinking it valuable. That conclusion, however, is only one of the reasons for considering rights of redress to be a worthwhile thing. Why else should we value a right of redress?

One prominent answer draws on expressive values. Civil recourse theories develop an account of the private right of action (i.e. civil recourse) as a means for a wronged party to act against the party who wronged her. A leading justification looks to expressive effects. For example, Jason Solomon suggests that civil recourse may constitute 'the best of both worlds'. As he argues:

> [P]erhaps we enjoy the best of both worlds when, instead of acting alone, we act against the wrongdoer through a state apparatus (like tort law): being the one to call a wrongdoer to account might affirm our self-respect, while the state backing our impulse by giving us a forum to do so affirms our moral worth in the community.[2]

On this view, private rights of action may simultaneously express a valuable recognition by the state that our rights matter, and express the self-worth and independence of the plaintiff who acts on her own behalf in bringing suit.

[2] *See* Jason M Solomon, 'Equal Accountability Through Tort Law' (2009) 103 Nw U L Rev 1765, 1795.

Where a private right of action provides a right of redress, rights of redress could partake of this benefit.

Of course, rights of redress don't always have this particular expressive effect. Recall the example in Chapter 1 of a thief stealing your bag; if you recover the bag on your own by chasing down the thief, that is an exercise of a right of redress. In a case like this one (a case that involves recaption of chattels), a private individual gets to affirm her self-respect through her own conduct, but the state's role will at best be hidden. This is a version of redress that does not make use of a private right of action, and accordingly its meaning is necessarily somewhat different. In the recaption setting, the opportunity to act is fleeting, and a failure to obtain redress on one's own could amount to a failure to obtain redress at all. We can't always have the best of both worlds, even if we want to. On the other hand, it might be that the expressive value of acting without any assistance (except indirectly) has its own unique significance. With this exception noted, I will focus here on redress that occurs by means of a private right of action.

Expressive effects are not the only potential benefit to redress through private rights of action. Some assess private rights of action in terms of efficient outcomes, with the lawsuit mechanism providing desirable incentives for both plaintiffs and defendants to act efficiently. We need not focus solely on the impact of sanctions on defendant behaviour, or of financial rewards on plaintiff behaviour. As Stephen Smith has emphasized, scholars concerned with incentive effects should also be thinking about the guidance function of law.[3] Private law provides guidance for how the parties ought to act, both at the ex ante pre-wrong stage and at the ex post stage after a wrong has already been committed. Rights of redress can provide sanctions (or financial rewards), and also bring about further judicial guidance. In the process, they might induce more efficient behaviour overall.

In some instances, the benefit of a private right of action may emerge most clearly in specific subparts of private law. The desirable consequences, however, can cut across legal systems in general even if their most typical context is in a subfield. Here is an example that starts from a local perspective, but quickly extends its influence further. In tort law, John Goldberg and Benjamin Zipursky note that civil recourse can play a role in creating and sustaining various loci of responsibility.[4] As they argue: 'Through the law, and in the law, a locus of

[3] *See* Stephen A Smith, 'The Normativity of Private Law' (2011) 31 Oxford J Leg Stud 215.

[4] *See* John CP Goldberg & Benjamin C Zipursky, 'Accidents of the Great Society' (2005) 64 Md L Rev 364.

responsibility is crystallized into a public reality. This public reality then becomes a basis for reliance on others, for trust, and for education of those who step into the scenario.'[5]

The ability to seek redress in tort settings may thus contribute to greater determinacy of individuals' obligations, which may in turn support other benefits, such as greater trust within a society. Naturally, greater levels of trust may produce yet other benefits (and also costs). Again, where a private right of action is a means to obtain redressive justice, a similar pattern of effects is possible.

It is worth asking whether a redress-centred approach to private law doctrine helps achieve benefits that might not otherwise be available through civil recourse. There is certainly reason to think so. Civil recourse is often (though not inevitably) seen as a means to hold someone accountable or to get satisfaction. But redress in the current sense—redress by means of enforcement rights—could offer a different type of self-reliance and a different expressive significance from holding someone accountable or getting satisfaction. This is particularly so if plaintiffs are sometimes motivated to enforce their rights and, at other times, motivated to get satisfaction. For example, if the victim of a broken contract seeks redress, she may be uninterested in holding someone accountable; she may be content as long as the deal is enforced. Likewise, if the victim of a vicious battery seeks to hold someone accountable, she may care much more about getting satisfaction than about having her medical bills paid. In such cases, substituting one idea of recourse for the other would not helpfully empower plaintiffs, but would instead limit their options.[6]

Other benefits span the various types of civil recourse, applying to each of them. For example, I will suggest below that there is another important advantage to rights of redress that can be applicable to any form of civil recourse, at least if authorship is attributed in a certain way. Rights of redress can be more fully private when they do not represent an omnilateral will, or the will of the state, or private parties acting as stand-ins for public actors. Such rights may instead be understood to originate with private parties, and this too can be valuable in several ways.

[5] Ibid. 404.

[6] There is also a basis in justice for giving rights of redress a place in private law. In some cases, exercising a right of redress might give someone what they are owed, while 'getting satisfaction' would give them more than they deserve. In those contexts, a shift from one type of remedy to another could result in a misallocation.

III. Towards a More *Private* Private Law

Private law can be *private* in a distinctive way, and this adds to the significance of rights of redress. When the parties to a dispute seek to enforce their remedial rights, those parties may exercise a type of private sovereignty that is not otherwise available because we lack other opportunities to enforce on our own behalf. It is not simply that private parties get to choose whether to sue a tortfeasor or a contract breaker. The authority involved in rights of redress may be attributable to the private individual herself. She is not then a stand-in for the state or the community, nor is she occupying a public office; she is exercising her own authority to enforce her own rights, on her own behalf.

This perspective may sound surprising as applied to the exercise of a *legal* power, but the core idea resonates with private law doctrine, and versions of it emerge, often unheralded, in various settings. For expressive reasons—and for reasons of self-constitution—this legal understanding is significant.

I will begin with the question whether attribution matters in general. As we will see, the view that it does is quite common both in private law theory and elsewhere. After a brief discussion, this chapter will adopt the idea as an assumed premise. Even those who doubt whether attribution matters at a deep level should be willing to concede that it matters for expressive purposes. The question on which this chapter will focus next is the more specific question whether private attribution has arguments in its favour. I believe it does, and for more than one reason.

I will consider the possibility that enforcement rights are not only legally attributed to right holders, but are understood to involve a residual, non-delegated authority. This view is not an inevitable component of private enforcement or of private law, but it resonates with a particular understanding of civil recourse theory. So understood, part of the value in attributing our acts of redress to ourselves is that it gives us the ability to exercise an important right without having to act 'by the grace of' another. And, as we will see, even if that attribution is rejected in a given legal system, there is much to be said in favour of such an attribution.

A. Why care about attribution?

The problem of attribution may seem somewhat abstract, and there are readers who may find it an odd area to focus our attention. Isn't the important thing whether a party gets to seek redress, and not how we ascribe authorship? The idea may seem counterintuitive to those who focus on end results, yet there is nothing unusual about the view that the attribution of a legal power matters. Otherwise divergent private law perspectives care about this, and there are good reasons why. Attribution concerns appear repeatedly, characteristically in settings where it is considered important that a power be attributed to the public, or to the state. In this section, I will suggest reasons to think that attribution matters in the redress setting. The primary difference in the account below is the party to whom attribution is made.

Kantian private law theory focuses heavily on attribution questions. Conduct that we might think involves the power of a specific judge, or the power of the majority in a given community, is conceptualized as an exercise of power by an omnilateral will; it is attributed to everyone, thus avoiding what the Kantian sees as a problematic exercise of unilateral coercion. From this perspective, the importance of attribution to an omnilateral will is that, without it, the coercive force of a judge's orders or a legislature's commands would inevitably be illegitimate. Note, however, that the coercive acts at issue might be identical in outward appearance to acts of unilateral authorship, but for the key question of the authorship itself.

Kantianism is not the only approach that cares about the possibility of attributing legal acts to all citizens. This view is also linked to a certain understanding of what a democracy should be like when it is working properly. As Seana Shiffrin argues in her analysis of contract law:

> [U]nderstanding the law's rationale should not present a conflict for the interested citizen qua moral agent. This is not merely because the agent is subject to the law and that to which she is subject should be justifiable to her. *Within a democratic society, the law should be understood as ours—as authored by us and as the expression of our joint social voice.*[7]

On this account, having a democratic society means we should be able to attribute our laws to ourselves; this in turn has a bearing on what those laws should express to moral agents as their rationale. Laws with the wrong rationale are harder for us to experience as truly 'ours'.

[7] *See* Seana V Shiffrin, 'The Divergence of Contract and Promise' (2007) 120 Harv L Rev 708, 718 (emphasis added).

Alon Harel provides a different take in his account of criminal law. From his perspective, attribution has a bearing on which parties should get to make certain legal decisions. As he argues:

> Our dignity dictates that only an agent that is superior to us can make authoritative normative judgments concerning the wrongfulness of our behavior and inflict criminal sanctions. Given that only the state can justifiably claim such superiority, it is therefore only agents *whose acts are attributable to the state*, namely public officials that can inflict criminal sanctions.[8]

Here, there is a subtle difference in the attribution of authorship. It is the state that should hold the authorial position; the state has a distinctive claim it can make, and it is therefore important that criminal sanctions are inflicted by parties whose conduct is attributable to the state.

As will become apparent in later chapters, I doubt that the Kantian view on private law is correct. This is not to deny that public attribution may be vital to legitimacy or perceived legitimacy. Harel may be right that criminal sanctions should only be attributable to the state, for example. Democratic theorists may be onto something in their assessment of how public authorship makes a difference. But none of the above examples is offered for an assessment of their merits on how attribution should work; they are offered instead to indicate how widespread attribution concerns are, and how important they can be for legal theory. Attribution is noteworthy for law and for political theory, even in cases where outcomes otherwise seem identical.

Whether it is the Kantian idea that coercion should be attributed to an omnilateral will, or Harel's view that criminal law should be attributed to the state, or Shiffrin's democratic approach to contract law's authorship, these approaches to attribution share a feature in common. These theories suggest a theory of rights and powers that focuses on authorship. That suggestion is very much on the right track, especially if our concern is with functional questions. What a legal system expresses has consequences for how it works, and this includes what it expresses concerning the authorship of legal coercion. Indeed, concerns with ascribing authorship are on the right track even if we think the appropriate way to handle attribution differs from what the above theorists suppose. An emphasis on attribution can be correct even if we endorse a different kind of authorship than these theorists suggest.

[8] *See* Alon Harel, *Why Law Matters* (OUP 2014) 61 (emphasis added).

Attribution arguments can cut in the opposite direction from a public-oriented approach. This chapter suggests a picture that contrasts with many of the private law (and some public law) approaches to attribution. Theorists who care about authorship often take great care to show how a power that appears to be exercised by a private individual is better seen as exercised by an omnilateral will or by the state. It is considered valuable for a legal system to attribute laws and legal rights to everyone within a polity (in aggregate), or to the polity itself as a unit. I suggest something very different: sometimes it is valuable for a legal system to attribute rights, privileges, and powers to private parties, *qua* private parties.

There is cause to attribute the exercise of many rights, privileges, and powers to ourselves in our individual capacity. In part, this is for psychological reasons; we may feel better about ourselves. Yet, this is not just a psychological point about how we might relate to our rights from our own individual perspective. There is an additional reason for legal systems to attribute some of our rights, privileges, and powers to ourselves, including our enforcement rights. The very unilateral coercion that Kantians oppose offers a kind of dignity for the individuals who engage in it.

B. The import of residual sovereignty

One way that private attribution could be meaningful is if civil recourse theorists are right in the Lockean version of their account. That is, attribution could matter if there is value in thinking that private rights of action reflect residual, pre-legal rights. After all, if authorship is attributed to the state, it will no longer make much sense to say that private rights of action are a mechanism for private parties to exercise their pre-legal rights. Indeed, the idea that private rights of action are a basis for the exercise of residual, private rights dovetails with a more general (albeit contested) picture of individual rights within legal systems. I will begin with examples of this perspective, and then turn to its import. In some cases, this residual rights view emerges in public law settings; in other cases, it is a private law phenomenon. In either instance, the idea of residual rights is a recognizable and well-established view on certain legal rights and their origination.

If we bracket cases in which someone is a judge, or a legislator, or otherwise holds a recognized public office, the contexts in which individuals directly participate in sovereign acts are still wide-ranging. Some of these cases have been interpreted as cases of residual sovereignty. One prominent example is the popular referendum. Many understand it to involve a legislative power that originates with citizens, rather than the state. Juries occupy a similar role, if we believe the jury system involves a form of residual sovereignty.[9] In each case, a pre-legal sovereignty is thought to operate through publicly provided venues.

Turning to private law, there are various legal powers that are likewise understandable as exercises of residual sovereignty. Contract law supports this view, if we take the power to enter into contracts as a power that originates with individuals rather than the state. Chief Justice Marshall expressed the core of this idea in his dissent in *Ogden v. Saunders*.[10] As he argued: '[I]ndividuals do not derive from government their right to contract but bring that right with them into society; that obligation is not conferred on contracts by positive law, but is intrinsic, and is conferred by the act of the parties.'[11] So long as a legal system adopts this understanding, the power to enter into contracts is a residual power.

Self-defence offers another example. There are theorists who contend that self-defence simply involves private parties acting as stand-ins for public officials.[12] But that is by no means an obvious implication of the common law precedents, and there is evidence that cuts in the other direction. A similar interpretation is available for recaption of chattels (where private parties take back items that were stolen from them). As John Simmons notes, Locke held the view that citizens retain a private right to reparation for wrongful injuries.[13] Recaption of chattels *can* involve private parties acting as stand-ins for public officials, but it need not—and it is more plausible to see recaption as a case of private parties acting for themselves. As with self-defence, recaption can be a residual form of sovereignty, not something delegated by the state.[14]

Civil recourse theory has at times extended this understanding of residual rights to a new context. Benjamin Zipursky has elaborated on the Lockean social contract to suggest that private rights of action are owed to us by the state, in light of its proscription of self-help alternatives. That view prominently suggests private rights of action involve an exercise of residual sovereignty. Indeed,

[9] *See* Robert P Burns, 'The Jury as a Political Institution: An Internal Perspective' (2014) 55 Wm & Mary L Rev 805, 808 (describing the view that juries possess some of the pre-constitutional sovereignty of the people).

[10] 25 U.S. 213 (1827).

[11] *See* ibid. 346 (Marshall, C.J., dissenting).

[12] For extended discussion of this view, see Chapter 7.

[13] *See* John Simmons, *On the Edge of Anarchy: Locke, Consent, and the Limits of Society* (Princeton University Press 1993) 176 ('Given these claims, Locke is not only consistently able to, he is obliged to assert that private individuals, even in civil society, "have a right to defend themselves and to recover by force what by unlawful force is taken from them."') (quoting John Locke, *Two Treatises of Government*, ¶ 208).

[14] That isn't to deny that acting in self-defence or engaging in recaption of chattels is, in an important sense, to be an institutional actor. Cf. John Gardner, *From Personal Life to Private Law* (OUP 2018) 215.

John Goldberg has suggested that private rights of action involve a partial delegation, *from* private individuals. As he explains: 'Individuals do hand over completely their right to act as judge and executioner; but they do not give up their right of self-preservation or their related right to redress wrongs.'[15] On this Lockean view, the delegation to the state 'is incomplete'.[16] While I will suggest a different, fiduciary account of this relationship in Chapter 6, the idea that residual rights are at stake is an important contribution.

When civil recourse theorists suggest that the principle of civil recourse draws on pre-legal rights, they are invoking a wider tradition. They are also making a point that merits further inquiry (and has received less attention than it deserves). What does it mean to say that rights of redress are only partly delegated to the state? It ultimately means that, in some form, the right at issue still resides with its holder—the private party—and implicitly that an exercise of this right is attributable to the plaintiff. Were it otherwise, civil recourse theorists would have a more difficult case to make when they argue that recourse involves a wronged party's right to act against another. Notably, a full delegation to the state suggests that civil recourse involves the state's right to act against another, instead of the wronged party's right.

This isn't to say that attribution to private parties calls for a recognition of residual rights. We do not have to see private rights of action in terms of a residual private sovereignty in order to conclude that redress belongs to individual plaintiffs. Powers can be delegated by the state to individuals and still count as private, through and through. Powers can sometimes be delegated such that they are no longer possessed by their delegor. For example, as John Gardner notes, certain powers delegated by the British Crown to Parliament now count as Parliament's inherent powers.[17] Parliament's powers in these contexts are no longer delegated powers at all from the legal perspective. The same can be true for private rights of action, as long as those rights belong to their holders, rather than indirectly belonging to the state.[18]

[15] *See* John CP Goldberg, 'The Constitutional Status of Tort Law: Due Process and the Right to a Law for the Redress of Wrongs' (2005) 115 Yale LJ 524, 543.

[16] *See* ibid.

[17] *See* John Gardner, 'Can There be a Written Constitution?' in *Law as a Leap of Faith* (OUP 2012) 89, 98–103.

[18] If the value in private attribution is sufficiently important, however, we may have reason to hope that accounts of private law fields that see right holders as office holders are incorrect. If our rights are held through offices, we may not as readily attribute their exercise to ourselves as private individuals. Cf. Dennis Klimchuk, 'Equity and the Rule of Law' in Lisa Austin & Dennis Klimchuk, (eds), *Private Law and the Rule of Law* (OUP 2014) 247, 259. For examples of such accounts in the property setting, see Christopher Essert, 'The Office of Ownership' (2013) 63 U Toronto LJ 418; Larissa Katz, 'Governing Through Owners: How and Why Private Property Rights Enhance State Power' (2012) 160 U Pa L Rev 2029.

There is nonetheless reason to care if private rights of action draw their basis from pre-legal rights. I will suggest below that a residual sovereignty account genuinely matters, for part of the value in private rights of action may hinge on whether they instantiate (or are seen by a legal system to instantiate) pre-legal rights of redress. To the extent legal systems adopt this perspective, it fits in with the view that individuals exercise residual sovereignty in various spheres (e.g. referenda; contract formation; self-defence). Such residual sovereignty also adds value to rights of redress that they would not otherwise have.

C. Not by the grace of another

Sometimes, it is not enough to have a right; we also need to have a certain relationship to that right. Republican theories of freedom firmly emphasize this point, and in a way that has bearing here. If we have a wide range of rights but live in constant fear that we will have those rights taken away, we are dominated by whomever calls the shots. That insight about freedom has bearing on many of the rights we hold, including our private rights of action. Yet there is another insight that can be drawn from this understanding, and it gives us a reason to care if our rights of action are a residual sovereignty. We shouldn't always have to feel deference or gratitude for possession of our rights, and there is a different, more dignified standing vis-à-vis the state when our rights are understood to belong to us from the start.

This insight can be traced to republican accounts, if they are read expansively. For example, consider Phillip Pettit's account of a state of non-domination. As he recognizes:

> You do not have to live either in fear of that other, then, or in deference to them. The non-interference you enjoy at the hands of others is not enjoyed by their grace and you do not live at their mercy. You are a somebody in relation to them, not a nobody. You are a person in your own legal and social right.[19]

Note that there is more at stake on this picture than just the avoidance of fear in the exercise of rights; someone who exists in a state of non-domination is also able to avoid being lower on the hierarchy than someone else.

This status is a fundamental benefit of non-domination. It is significant if our exercise of our rights is taken to be 'by the grace' of another. Note, however,

[19] *See* Philip Pettit, *Republicanism: A Theory of Freedom and Government* (OUP 1999) 71.

that Pettit's phrasing captures something important beyond the absence of fear regarding interference. Granted, a key limit on freedom is the possibility of interference in our rights, whether or not that interference ever transpires. That is Pettit's central point. The idea that exercising our rights should not be 'by the grace' of another can nonetheless be taken in a different direction (indeed, in a different direction from what Pettit may have in mind).

To make the point more cleanly, suppose that we remove any possibility of interference in the exercise of our rights. In this hypothetical world, *that* concern is set to one side. The standard republican worry is that someone should be free from the arbitrary will of another. As republican theorists note, this is a problem even if that will is never exercised; the reality that it could be exercised is enough to render someone unfree. In our hypothetical world, however, this limit on our freedom is not at issue. Even so, it could still be significant whether our rights are taken to be ours by the grace of another.

Being able to enjoy one's rights without having to think that it is by the grace of another is important because it produces a different relation between one's rights and another party. It matters whether, in possessing a right, we should take ourselves as owing gratitude because someone else granted us that right, or instead may simply conclude that this right is ours, no gratitude necessary. In the latter case, the right comes to us without strings attached, and exercises of that right are more exclusively attributable to us rather than our benefactor. Pettit's original point about being 'a somebody', or a person 'in your own right', is just as compelling in this scenario as it is in cases involving fear of interference.

Some variation on this idea may be at work when people think of a popular referendum as a non-delegated power. Why care whether sovereignty begins with the state or its people in such a case, as long as the referendum is available? A similar intuition may help explain why some have historically viewed the power to enter into contracts as a pre-legal power. Lon Fuller has suggested that it shouldn't matter from an autonomy perspective whether the power to contract originates with the state or with the contracting parties.[20] It could very well matter for other reasons. Likewise, rights of redress can offer a special kind of value for right holders if they allow people to enforce their rights without having to feel that the right to enforce is by the grace of another. Viewing private rights of action in residual terms allows for this possibility, and attributing their exercise to provide parties helps make this possible.

[20] *See* Lon Fuller, 'Consideration and Form' (1941) 41 Colum L Rev 799, 807 n.9 ('The principle of private autonomy has nothing to do with the ancient controversy whether the binding effect of a contract derives from "the law" or "the contract".').

IV. The Value of Private Attribution, Revisited

A. The authorship value

While it is important whether a legal system takes private rights of action to reflect a residual, pre-legal set of rights, attribution concerns are not dependent on that perspective. It would be a mistake to focus solely on the problem of delegation or the existence of residual rights in private law as a basis for recognizing right holders as the authors of redress. In some cases, rights of redress may allow us to enforce our remedies without acting 'by the grace of' another. But we have additional reasons to care whether rights of redress can be exercised by private parties, acting on their own behalf. There is another value at stake in that attribution.

Autonomy theorists suggest we should get to be part authors of our own lives.[21] In adopting this view, they often focus on the large-scale cases, such as career choices, decisions to marry, or comprehensive goals in life. Authorship may bear on the ground projects that give our life its meaning.[22] With this in mind, rights of redress may seem too small-scale to count for much, unless those rights of redress happen to correct a wrong that sent our life off course. Even then, the emphasis may be on successful rectification of the wrong, or fixing the relationship the wrong damaged, rather than the right of redress itself. From a self-authorship perspective, rights of redress may seem like a means to an end, without much need to worry about their import beyond that.

There is some merit to this view, but a focus on end results can easily obscure the full value in rights of redress. Just as it matters for our moral ledger whether we have corrected the wrongs we commit against others, it matters as well whether we redressed the wrongs we suffered. As Christine Korsgaard indicates, our individual actions are part of how we constitute ourselves. And each action contributes: 'For an action is attributable to an agent as its author—whenever you take control of your own movements—you are constituting yourself as the author of that action, and so you are deciding who to be.'[23] Authoring redress (as opposed to just benefitting from correction of a wrong) has bearing on who we are, for our lives are different when we have acted to undo a wrong on our own behalf.

[21] *See* Joseph Raz, *The Morality of Freedom* (OUP 1986) 369 (noting that 'the autonomous person is a (part) author of his own life').

[22] For seminal accounts of ground projects and their significance, *see* JJC Smart & Bernard Williams, *Utilitarianism: For & Against* (CUP 1983); Bernard Williams, 'Persons, Character and Morality' in *Moral Luck* (1981) 1, 13–14.

[23] *See* Christine M Korsgaard, *Self-Constitution: Agency, Identity, Integrity* (OUP 2009) xi.

Notice that this consideration is independent from any concerns with acting by the grace of another. Even in a state of nature, with no state yet in existence, it is significant if we can personally fix the wrongs we suffer. This was part of the lesson drawn in Chapter 2. If someone wrongfully grabs your coffee mug, the moral state of each actor is different based on whether you have taken that coffee mug back or instead had it returned to you. The state's presence provides an important variation on this theme, but your exercising a right of redress has bearing on your self-constitution with or without the state's imprimatur. To be sure, acting on your own behalf to redress a wrong will not always be a positive thing, but it does contribute something if it helps to constitute you as a self-reliant individual.

Some might agree that private authorship is valuable, yet argue that the legal system's point of view on attribution is irrelevant to the central moral concerns. The morality of rights enforcement might vary little regardless of whether enforcement is performed by a private party or a public office holder. Perhaps public office holders are governed by moral obligations much like the obligations that govern the rest of us, except that their obligations are more stringent given the powers they possess.[24] Extending this perspective, the sceptic might think the moral significance of redress is largely unchanged whether or not we are stand-ins for the state. A successful private right of action would have the same moral import regardless.

I would not go that far. The legal system's perspective can help support a moral relationship that alters the meaning of a right holder's actions. If the state takes me to be a stand-in for a public office holder, *and I also take myself to be a stand-in*, then I really may be acting on behalf of the state in these settings. This principal–agent relationship is not a fiction. We have a voluntary relationship where I am acting on the state's behalf with its permission, and these are circumstances under which a principal–agent relationship comes into existence (in law, and also in morality). Moreover, there will be practical effects to this relationship. My deliberations will be different if I understand myself to have an agent's responsibility, and the moral significance of my redressive conduct will change because my choices now incorporate public, systemic considerations.

And, even if we reject the above perspective on our deliberations, private authorship can have psychological benefits. If our enforcement rights are

[24] Cf. John Gardner, 'The Supposed Formality of the Rule of Law' in *Law as a Leap of Faith* (OUP 2012) 195, 213–14 (suggesting judges and other officials may have asymmetrical moral obligations to uphold the law).

attributed to the state, we may understandably perceive ourselves as agents of the state in fixing wrongs. That is a different way of seeing ourselves from one in which enforcement rights belong to us as individuals, and it results in a different self-conception. The resulting self-conception could be desirable in some respects (we have the imprimatur of the state when we act, and it suggests the state respects us enough to give us the relevant authority). Yet, this self-conception may also be impoverished, for we may not see ourselves as capable of enforcing on our own behalf when we don't get to directly attribute our enforcement actions to ourselves. The result is that we may not feel like we have fully stood up for ourselves when another has wronged us, even if the wrong was ultimately remedied through the court system.

Things can be taken too far if attribution is our central concern as right holders. There may be settings where it helps for people to seek distance between their acts and others' contributions—great poets often seek to avoid debts to their predecessors, and perhaps this distance helps them to write.[25] But redress is generally not one of those settings. A person who obsesses over whether he can exercise his enforcement rights without assistance—or over whether those rights originate with him—is not worrying enough about more important things. Overemphasis on attribution is unwise at best. But it doesn't follow that the private attribution of our enforcement rights is without value, as it can add something substantial with respect to both our self-constitution and our self-perception.

V. The Judicial Agency Challenge

It is a contingent matter whether our enforcement rights belong to us as individuals, for it is an open question whether a legal system endorses that view. Yet, if the above discussion is right, we have reason to hope our legal system will offer us a genuinely private law in this sense. The value of a more *private* private law should thus matter to us in part because it is an institutional choice.[26] The features of private law that make it more or less private are dependent on the law at issue.

Private law is often considered private because it resolves disputes between private parties, rather than disputes where the state is a litigant. A right of civil

[25] *See* Harold Bloom, *The Anxiety of Influence: A Theory of Poetry* (2nd edn) (OUP 1997) (developing this point and indicating how poets seek to achieve separation).

[26] Cf. John Gardner, 'Justification Under Authority' (2010) 23 Canadian J L & Juris 71, 95 (noting that the law of self-defence 'has its legal source, its legal derivation, in whatever case law and statute law is currently authoritative in the legal system under scrutiny').

recourse is a core part of this understanding. Such features are not inevitable. As the oft-discussed New Zealand example should remind us, it is not mandatory that private law provides for civil recourse through private rights of action. But the same contingency holds true for attribution questions. Even if private individuals are taken to be acting on their own behalf when they bring suit, it is not inevitable that private law will understand this power to originate from ourselves, as individuals. Likewise, it is not inevitable that legal systems will attribute authorship to private parties. The state, after all, could view private parties as stand-ins for public officeholders, in an effort to more efficiently prosecute actions on behalf of those private parties.

Moreover, not every contingent possibility for a legal system is a readily feasible possibility. A critic might argue that attribution to private parties is not a plausible choice in the modern era. After all, many of our most important private rights are now the product of legislation, and even in areas where the common law occupies substantial space there is often a statutory overlay. How much room is there today for enforcement rights that belong to private individuals? The available domain could seem quite small, perhaps limited to self-defence, recaption of chattels, and other forms of self-help. The structure of private law today may suggest that attribution of redressive acts to private parties is unrealistic.

A concern with statutory origins seems overblown. Statutes often codify pre-existing common law doctrines without displacing the idea that those doctrines are continuous with the common law. Statutory codification of rights of redress does not inherently preclude the idea that those rights belong to their holders. The same point applies in the public arena where statutes govern popular referenda; these referenda can still be conceptualized as exercises of sovereignty by members of the public, rather than as delegated exercises of state authority. Indeed, even when authority originates with a delegation it can belong to the party that ultimately exercises that authority. All is still contingent on a legal system's individual approach.

Judicial agency poses a more profound challenge. It might be argued that civil recourse is in the end a matter of judicial enforcement, not private enforcement. For example, Ori Herstein questions whether the powers that civil recourse theorists identify aren't ultimately best understood to belong to the courts that adjudicate and enforce plaintiffs' rights.[27] Herstein notes that there are multiple ways private rights of action 'empower' plaintiffs, but he contends

[27] *See* Ori Herstein, 'How Tort Law Empowers' (2015) 65 U Toronto LJ 99.

that plaintiffs are generally not empowered—in either a practical or a legal sense—in the way civil recourse theorists suppose.

As Herstein suggests, civil recourse theorists could understand private rights of action to empower plaintiffs by giving them a de facto power to act on the legal rights of defendants, using the courts as a vehicle. He describes a 'vending machine' theory that could support this view; on this theory, plaintiffs who bring meritorious claims are effectively able to change the legal rights of tortfeasors through the workings of the judicial process.[28] Courts on this view act mechanistically once a viable suit is brought, invariably enforcing plaintiff's rights in a predictable fashion. Just as a vending machine provides the selected snack or drink when quarters are dropped into the coin slot, so too courts provide the requisite remedy when a properly filed suit is pursued by an aggrieved plaintiff.

In Herstein's view, the shortcomings of the vending machine theory quickly emerge when we look at how courts actually function. As he notes, on occasion courts fail to correctly follow the law.[29] This means that even when a plaintiff has the law right, she may not be able to exercise a legal power over the rights of defendants. In addition, and perhaps more importantly, courts possess a form of judicial agency. In performing their responsibilities, they must exercise 'interpretation and judgment'.[30] As Herstein emphasizes: 'The law is often vague, general, under-determined, and filled with principles and standards requiring interpretation.'[31] Indeed, courts not only create norms, they render pre-existing norms more specific—they 'crystallize' them.[32]

Herstein effectively shows that the civil recourse account of a plaintiff's powers is not inevitable. On the other hand, he does not successfully rule out that account as an option. It is surely right that courts exercise discretion in crystallizing the content of legal rights and remedies in individual adjudications. It is also sadly apparent that courts err with some frequency. Neither of these facts is sufficient to defeat the idea that private parties can act against wrongdoers while using courts as a vehicle to do so. To see why, it may help to compare some key features of agency relationships.

Zipursky perceptively notes in the civil recourse context that, 'it is almost as if the state acts as an agent of the plaintiff'.[33] Nothing demonstrated by Herstein's

[28] *See* ibid. 115–18.
[29] *See* ibid. 117.
[30] *See* ibid.
[31] *See* ibid.
[32] *See* ibid. 111. *See also* John Gardner, 'Torts and Other Wrongs' (2011) 39 Fla St U L Rev 43, 56.
[33] *See* Benjamin C Zipursky, 'Philosophy of Private Law' in Jules Coleman & Scott Shapiro, (eds), *The Oxford Handbook of Jurisprudence & Philosophy of Law* (OUP 2002) 623, 633. For a stronger claim, *see* John Gardner, 'What Is Tort Law For? Part 2: The Place of Distributive Justice' in John Oberdiek, (ed.),

argument should prevent this conclusion. Contra Herstein, an agency analogy does not require that the court's 'capacity to alter the legal rights and relations of tortfeasors to obtain redress is somehow derived from the plaintiff'.[34] The important feature of an agency relationship for present purposes is that the agent's conduct can count as the conduct of the principal. A court's acting in the interest of another party is not enough to support the civil recourse theorist's view.[35] But a court's acting on another's behalf, pursuant to their expressed wishes, is a different story. Person A does not have to command Person B for an agency-*like* relationship to exist between them; it is enough if A requests B to act in a certain way, and B predictably does so acting on A's behalf. In such cases, we can conclude that A is acting by means of B's conduct.

What of errors and interpretive discretion? Notice that real-life, actual agents make mistakes in carrying out their tasks. Notice also that such agents exercise discretion in following the instructions of their principals (indeed, this may be a central reason agents are properly considered fiduciaries).[36] If A asks B to run an errand and pick up widgets on her behalf, B may have some choice as to the timing, method of transportation, and widget type. The agent must interpret these instructions, and the principal may be bound by a reasonable interpretation. We do not hesitate in attributing authorship of an agent's conduct to her principal in such cases, despite the existence of discretion as to the exact mode of obedience.

Now, Herstein is correct to note that private parties can't order the courts around.[37] Plaintiffs are not like agency law principals in that regard and courts do not resemble agents in this way. That is a reason for understanding agency to be an analogy rather than a template. What we want to know, however, is whether it makes sense to understand the conventional case of civil recourse as a case in which private parties are exercising an indirect, mediated power over the legal rights of defendants. That reading is available to us even if other readings are conceivable, and an agency analogy is useful for seeing why.

Philosophical Foundations of the Law of Torts (OUP 2014) 340 (suggesting that plaintiffs have the right to 'conscript the court').

[34] *See* Herstein, 'How Tort Law Empowers' (n. 27) 115.

[35] *See* ibid. 115 ('[A]cting in the interest of another does not entail that the "fiduciary's powers are controlled, held, or derived from the beneficiary".').

[36] *See* Paul B Miller, 'The Fiduciary Relationship' in Andrew S Gold & Paul B Miller, (eds), *Philosophical Foundations of Fiduciary Law* (OUP 2014) 63, 80 ('[V]irtually all agents have discretion in the exercise of powers notwithstanding the presence of instructions. This may be so even where instructions are quite detailed, insofar as they are subject to interpretation by the agent.').

[37] *See* Herstein, 'How Tort Law Empowers' (n. 27) 119 ('Simply put, litigants do not order courts how to rule in their matters.').

The possibility that courts get to put their own fingerprints on the outcome, and in some cases just misconstrue the law, is not a reason to deny that redress can be attributed to plaintiffs. It is a reason to recognize that the power at issue is a fallible one, subject to various intervening difficulties; much as the powers that principals exercise through agents can be thwarted by various agent choices. There is no conceptual obstacle to attributing conduct to a principal in cases where an agent acts on behalf of that principal while exercising discretion as to her precise manner of advancing the principal's objectives. Courts are not agents, but the analogy can still be useful for purposes of understanding how one party can act in another's place for attribution purposes.

Indeed, the agency analogy has a long pedigree respecting judges themselves. Judges are often seen as 'faithful agents' of legislatures when they engage in statutory interpretation.[38] While that analogy is controversial (perhaps judges act more like partners in a partnership?), it resonates for a reason. The idea that legislatures act through courts is not usually considered problematic at the conceptual level. Here, too, judges make errors, and here, too, judges fill in gaps in a way that crystallizes textual indeterminacies or even deviates from the legislature's intended or expressed meaning. Likewise, legislatures are not ordinarily in a position to order courts around. Legislatures can nonetheless exercise a de facto power over regulated parties through judicial readings of statutory text.

Furthermore, if we turn back to litigants, private parties can be *part* authors of redress, and this holds true even if that authorship is shared with a court. There are multiple illustrations of the part-author phenomenon in legal settings. Congress counts as an author of legislation, even if the President must sign a bill into law before it is enacted. A contractual promisor is an author of a contract, even though the promisee may share in that authorship. Authorship does not cease to exist when it is shared, even if the fact of sharing is important in its own right. Indeed, just as an actor may be individually culpable for conduct that is also collectively brought about, an actor may claim individual authorship of something that is simultaneously part of a joint endeavour.[39]

There are a lot of nuances in play here, many of which fall outside the current topic. Sometimes, the party that drafts a text is not the party to whom that text is attributed; politicians give speeches that are appropriately ascribed

[38] *See*, e.g. John F Manning, 'Textualism and Equity of the Statute' (2001) 101 Colum L Rev 1, 7 ('[T]extualism also starts from the faithful agent premise—that a federal court is responsible for accurately deciphering and implementing the legislature's commands.').

[39] Cf. Christopher Kutz, *Complicity: Ethics and Law for a Collective Age* (CUP 2000) 105–6 (noting the possibility of both exclusive and inclusive (collective) authorship).

to the politicians themselves, not their speechwriters.[40] In other cases, the party that actually drafts a text will count as its sole author, even when another person utters its content. Similar concerns emerge in the civil recourse setting. Context is a major factor in assessing attribution, and the right answer may depend on conventions as much as on moral principles. Yet, the hard cases need not detain us here. Scholars differ on how much discretion courts exercise in deciding cases, but there are plausible readings that leave room for attributing redress to private parties.

In saying this, we shouldn't ignore the reality that plaintiffs often play a very hands-on role in bringing about legal outcomes. Zipursky nicely captures the mechanism by which a private right of action ultimately leads to redress:

> [T]he private party must prosecute the action at every step. Even if plaintiff obtains a judgment from the court, the judgment itself is not redress; the judgment creates a debt of the defendant to the plaintiff. It will still be plaintiff's job to enforce the payment of the debt. Hence, the picture of the state as *sua sponte* ordering wrongdoers to pay their victims is entirely incorrect. Courts judge that certain demands shall be granted, and accede to those demands.[41]

I would suggest a further gloss on this account; the authorship of redress can be legally ascribed to the private party without her being a component of a fictional omnilateral will. On this view, the private party brings about redress in a successful suit, and the right to do so belongs to her; she is not acting as a stand-in for a state actor. She is an author of the outcome. That authorship has value because it allows for a different kind of self-constitution for the right holder herself, and because it creates a different kind of relationship between that right holder, the state, and the wrongdoer who injured her.

VI. The Multiple Levels of Authorship

Authorship means many things, in both life and law. From a corrective justice perspective, it might seem that the remedial part of private law is concerned

[40] *See* Andrew S Gold, 'Reassessing the Scope of Conduct Prohibited by Section 10(b) and the Elements of Rule 10b-5: Reflections on Securities Fraud and Secondary Actors' (2004) 53 Cath U L Rev 667, 687 (indicating it is the President who makes the statements in his speeches, not the speechwriter). *See also Janus Capital Group v. First Derivative Traders*, 564 U.S. 135, 143 (2011) ('Even when a speechwriter drafts a speech, the result is entirely within the control of the person who delivers it. And it is the speaker who takes credit—or blame—for what is ultimately said.').

[41] *See* Zipursky, 'Philosophy of Private Law' (n. 33) 640.

with one kind of authorship in particular: the kind involved in undoing one's own wrong. A private right of action is a way of helping such wrongdoers succeed in this. Alternatively, we might emphasize the right holder's authorship of a redressive act that responds to a wrong. Both types of authorship are noteworthy, but they do not comprise the full set of important cases. A closer look at redress suggests that it cuts across various authorship types, each potentially valuable. And, importantly, it is the right holder's authorship that is at stake for each.

Notice, first, that our primary, pre-wrong rights may implicate authorship values. As Joseph Raz argues, autonomy involves part authorship of our lives.[42] The choices that private law institutions enable us to make may be an important part of pursuing that authorship. For example, the primary rights that property owners possess enable them to engage in various life choices, free from outside interference. It is possible to exercise ownership rights for just about any reason a property owner might fancy, and also for no apparent reason. Property owners may even destroy their property and, in some famous cases, artists have engaged in this very thing, eliminating priceless works of art.[43]

There is also more in play than happiness or preference satisfaction. In some cases, we can exercise our primary rights in ways that neither make us happy nor provide us with what we prefer. While this may reflect errors in our choices (or, alternatively, altruism), there is an additional possibility. The law of property enables us to advance what we find meaningful in life, and meaningfulness can be an imperfect match for standard measures of our best interests. As Susan Wolf has emphasized, meaningfulness is a non-derivative component of well-being: 'its goodness does not result from its making us happy or its satisfying the preferences of the person whose life it is'.[44]

But note what is at stake when we talk about rights and meaningfulness. When something is meaningful to us, it is commonly because there is a connection between that thing and our life's narrative. Since this meaningfulness is worthwhile, the value of authorship—as it relates to our lives—offers another justification for the broadly discretionary rights held by property owners.

Tort law reflects similar considerations. Gregory Keating has emphasized how tort law's primary rights protect autonomy.[45] As he notes, in cases of

[42] *See* Joseph Raz, *The Morality of Freedom* (OUP 1986) 204 ('An autonomous person is part author of his own life. His life is, in part, of his own making.').

[43] For discussion, *see* Lior J Strahilevitz, 'The Right to Destroy' (2005) 114 Yale LJ 781.

[44] *See* Susan Wolf, 'Happiness and Meaning: Two Aspects of the Good Life' in The Variety of Values: Essays on Morality, Meaning, and Love (OUP 2015) 108–9.

[45] *See* Gregory C Keating, 'The Priority of Respect Over Repair' (2012) 18 Legal Theory 293, 332–6.

sovereignty-based torts, various powers that we hold with respect to ourselves and our property are protected by tort law's primary rights. In cases of *harm-based torts*, serious physical injuries and severe pain can thwart 'one's control over the content of one's life'.[46] Tort law's primary rights are significant here as well. And his point is not limited to classic cases involving physical harm. As Keating indicates, the tort of fraud undercuts autonomy by means of deception; other torts border on private law fields like contract law, protecting the autonomy that those adjacent fields facilitate.[47] Tort law delineates primary rights in part to protect autonomy, and thus helps us to be part authors of our lives.

This set of insights might seem to lead away from rights of redress; such rights will only occasionally involve an enforcement of primary rights (as with unjust enrichment cases). Yet the enforcement of secondary, remedial rights can help reinforce the autonomy that primary rights advance. Consider a return of physical property that was tortiously converted, or damages that will enable the purchase of something equivalent to what was lost. The idea that private law remedies restore someone's means incorporates this insight.[48] The means that are restored by acts of redress enable people to be part authors of their lives, through the choices that will be facilitated down the line. There may well be other reasons to care about such restoration—we may value what we had pre-wrong, even if it was not the product of our own choice and even if we are not particularly autonomous[49]—but the import of autonomy still helps support redress.

This argument can be taken too far. Keating errs in suggesting that tort law prioritizes (or ought to prioritize) primary duties over remedial duties.[50] True, it is better not to have wronged someone at all than to have wronged them and fixed it, but this insight tells us little about whether private law should or does prioritize primary duties over remedial duties. Imagine a hypothetical world in which the state had an opportunity to either a) fix 100 existing wrongs or b) prevent 100 new wrongs from occurring. It is not at all clear that the state should choose to prevent the 100 new wrongs, even if part of the value in fixing the existing wrongs is that it restores autonomy that we would prefer had never been lost in the first place. (Maybe an uncorrected wrong is worse

[46] *See* ibid. 333.

[47] *See* ibid. 334–6.

[48] *See* Arthur Ripstein, 'As If It Had Never Happened' (2007) 48 Wm & Mary L Rev 1957, 1958 (contending that 'money can be understood as restoring to the wronged party the means he or she is entitled to').

[49] On the possibility that private law is not essentially about autonomy, see Gardner, *From Personal Life* (n. 14) 195–9. I think Gardner may be right in this claim, but it does not undercut the idea that private law can be valuable for autonomy-linked reasons.

[50] *See* Keating, 'The Priority of Respect' (n. 45) 309–10.

for expressive reasons than an unprevented wrong.) And, by extension, the importance of primary duties tells us little about whether legal systems should prioritize them (or their correlative primary rights) over rights of redress. Part of what makes redress valuable is that it restores, to some degree, the autonomy that our primary rights are designed to secure, but the implications of that insight should not be overstated.

Yet, redress also operates in relation to a larger scale application of autonomy principles. The selection of certain private law institutions, or relationships enabled by those institutions, can likewise assist us in being part authors of our lives. This is evident in Hanoch Dagan's elaboration of private law pluralism.[51] Private law offers various institutions (different kinds of property, different kinds of contracts, different kinds of fiduciary relationships), each with their own regulative principles and expressive significance. There is a menu of private law interactions that individuals or groups can choose among, and the resulting choices are a component of self-authorship. The reasons justifying this kind of authorship can likewise support the primary rights that go with those institutions and partly constitute them.

By extension, this picture of private law institutions can support redress (even distinctive kinds of redress) when the rights that are integral to a given private law institution are violated. For example, a disgorgement remedy is one reason why a sophisticated party might choose a fiduciary relationship over a non-fiduciary one. In doing so, she has selected a particular private law institution to govern her relationship with others. Even where the remedy itself is not a product of conscious choice, that remedy may also reinforce the attractive features of a private law institution. In cases where a wrongful transaction is undone—cases involving redress—this remedy may then reinforce the authorship involved in choosing the private law institution at issue, and not just the choices internal to the operation of that institution.

Each of the above examples suggests a derivative link to authorship. From this perspective, redress is the next best thing to the enforcement of primary rights, where those primary rights are directly or indirectly contributing to authorship our lives. In contrast, we might think the choice to engage in redress itself allows us to partly author our own lives; the undoing of a transaction is itself significant as an authorial choice. In this case, the authorship in redress is relevant in a non-derivative way. The narrative of our life looks different when, among other available choices, we have acted to undo the wrongs

[51] *See* Hanoch Dagan, 'Pluralism and Perfectionism in Private Law' (2012) 112 Colum L Rev 1409.

committed against us. We have chosen to stand up for ourselves when another person violated our rights.[52]

Examples of this latter kind of authorship show up in the types of situations emphasized in the civil recourse theory literature. When people get satisfaction against a person who wronged them, they are part authors of their own lives in a way that truly can matter to them a great deal, even if the primary rights at issue have little meaning for them. Imagine, for example, that Jane doesn't care much about a piece of property she owns; she owns several similar properties and there is no real attachment to this one. This particular property has no real bearing on her life's narrative. If, however, someone intentionally damages that property, her life's narrative might change depending on whether she does something about it.

On Stephen Darwall's account, responsive conduct can signify a kind of self-respect. Consider his suggestion: 'To acquiesce in the avoidable denial of one's rights is to fail to respect one's rights as a person.'[53] Remedying a wrong committed against us is a particular way in which we can show recognition respect towards ourselves. The value in showing this self-respect is not the same value (or at least not in an immediate way) that is at stake in recognition of the underlying primary rights that were violated by a wrong. While exercising rights of redress is not necessarily motivated by such things as self-respect—sometimes what we care more about is the outcome, and not how we get there—this should not obscure the reality that at times self-respect is precisely what makes rights of redress important to their holders.

Each of these types of authorship is concerned ultimately with the choices they enable private parties to make, such as the choice to use one's property in a certain way, or the choice to stand up for oneself when that property is encroached upon. The authorship that we get through redress can also be assessed along other dimensions. It can be assessed in light of its grounding, in that we might care to know if our authorship is legally attributed to us or to an omnilateral will. Alternatively, it can be assessed in light of other contextual features, such as a need to seek permission or a need to obtain agreement from other parties.[54]

[52] Note that even small-scale cases of authorship have bearing on large-scale authorship questions. *See* Christine M Korsgaard, *Self-Constitution: Agency, Identity, and Integrity* (OUP 2009) xi ('For an action is attributable to an agent as its author—whenever you take control of your own movements—you are constituting yourself as the author of that action, and so you are deciding who to be.').

[53] *See* Stephen L Darwall, 'Two Kinds of Respect' (1977) 88 Ethics 36, 47.

[54] In some cases, this sharing of authority can extend quite far. This is why contract obligations may partake of authorship in a much more complete way than legislation, even if in a democracy each citizen has an attenuated authorial role in a statute's enactment. Cf. Philip Pettit, *A Theory of Freedom: From the Psychology to the Politics of Agency* (OUP 2001) 160–1 (describing the authorial role of citizens in the policies put forward by public office holders).

And, if our choices are vulnerable to the choices of others, authorship can be seen as incomplete. The more diluted our authorship, or the more it hinges on a co-author's or supervisor's decision, the less we may understand it to be our own.

This is not to downplay the value of attribution to a group, or even to an omnilateral will (fictional as such wills may be). Some kinds of authorship are meaningful precisely because they are shared. This is implicit in Seana Shiffrin's argument that individuals should see contract law as their own. The chance to co-author the law can matter, and there is a lot to be said for citizens identifying with the laws in their polity. Moreover, individual authorship can co-exist with shared authorship under some circumstances. Applied to redress, this view dovetails with Jason Solomon's 'best of both worlds' hypothesis. If in authoring redress as individuals we can also feel that the state has an authorial role, so much the better.

Perhaps there are also tragic choices here, if genuine private authorship crowds out state authorship. Yet private law need not face such stark choices when the problem of authorship is viewed systemically. It can offer unilateral and multilateral categories of authorship, depending on what is at stake in expressive meaning, enforcement success, and also costliness. Individual settings may require a specific kind of authorship, but at a system level it is possible to offer a broader set of arrangements. For our purposes, what matters is that by offering legally supported rights of redress—and by recognizing that these rights originate with private parties—the state can offer individuals types of authorship that are quite hard for them to achieve in other settings. Wronged parties can effectively author coercive acts to remedy the wrongs they have suffered, acting on their own behalf in doing so and also acting from their own authority. To retain this right even outside the state of nature is to hold a valuable status both with respect to the state and with respect to those who may wrong us.

***

Rights of redress derive their value indirectly, from the significance of our primary rights. They also derive their value from the import of standing up for ourselves when we have been wronged. In addition, they may present the opportunity to attribute legal rights and powers directly to ourselves. Legal rights and powers are often thought to derive their legitimacy from an omnilateral will, or from attribution to the state, but we need not see redress in that way. And, if we are willing to let go of that public law image of authority, we can see that one of the greatest values to redress is found in the possibility that we can attribute redress to ourselves as individuals. Redress can be private, and that has a unique value. The justice in private law, then, is important not only because it is a matter of justice, but also because of the kind of authorship that it provides.

4
The Enforcement of Contracts

I. Introduction

Contracts show some of the key differences between focusing on redress and focusing on a wrongdoer's obligations. A redress-based theory also diverges from the conventional civil recourse approach, as redress is not about accountability but enforcement. As we will see, the differences here are more than just academic puzzles; they matter in a way that is fruitful for explanatory purposes. Recognizing when and how redress is appropriate can help to explain contract law doctrines that are otherwise difficult to explain, including not only contract law's emphasis on the expectation remedy, but also formation rules like the consideration doctrine.

Ever since Lon Fuller and William Perdue's famous paper on the reliance interest,[1] scholars have struggled to explain exactly why the expectation damages remedy is the standard contract law remedy, one which often pushes aside reliance damages, specific performance, and other potential remedial options. The challenges involve more than just legal doctrine. In addition, a contractual promisor's moral obligations do not straightforwardly match the expectation damages remedy. And, even if we turn to the right holder's side of the picture—focusing on what a right holder can legitimately demand of a promisee—expectation damages are not the obvious result.

For many, promissory morality lies at the heart of these concerns. True, not everyone sees a divergence between promissory and contract norms. Some, such as Charles Fried, see expectation damages as an implication of promissory morality. On his view, '[t]he expectation standard gives the victim of a breach no more or less than he would have had had there been no breach—in other words, he gets the benefit of his bargain'.[2] But others view the expectation damages remedy as a signal that contract law diverges from promissory morality. Revisiting this debate will be helpful, as an exploration

[1] See L L Fuller & William R Perdue, 'The Reliance Interest in Contract Law' (1936) 46 Yale LJ 52.
[2] See Charles Fried, *Contract as Promise: A Theory of Contractual Obligation* (HUP 1981) 17.

The Right of Redress. Andrew S. Gold, Oxford University Press (2020). © Andrew S. Gold.
DOI: 10.1093/oso/9780198814405.001.0001

of what promissory morality shows will indicate how rights of redress can illuminate contract law.

Critics contend that promisors owe something morally that is different from what a contracting party can legally insist upon. The wrongdoer may owe an apology for breaching, but the legal remedy will instead be measured in damages. In addition, third parties do not ordinarily get to sue. Turning to the right holder's perspective, what a promisee can morally insist upon will only sometimes qualify as something that a contracting party can legally insist upon. This suggests a gap between what promisees can morally demand and what they may use the law to bring about. Furthermore, even where enforcement is legitimate, it is still necessary to explain why a specific performance remedy isn't the conventional response. Arguably, expectation damages fall short in such cases.

By turning to rights of redress as a grounding for legal doctrine, these features can be explained. This chapter begins with those cases in which a promisor appears to owe something different from what a promisee can insist upon (e.g. an apology versus damages). It then assesses the problem of standing; not everyone gets to sue when a contractual promisor breaks her word. I will next consider cases in which a promisee can morally demand something that differs from what the law allows the contractual promisee to legally enforce. In some cases, a promisee can legitimately demand performance, but not legally obtain a remedy. In other cases, a legal remedy is available, but the standard remedy—expectation damages—is offered in place of specific performance. In each context, a focus on rights of redress can show why these features make sense. Finally, the chapter will conclude with a discussion of how contract formation doctrines fit in; legal doctrines like the consideration doctrine follow naturally under a redress-centred approach.

II. Is There a Divergence from Promissory Morality?

A. A promisor's obligations

Challenges for duty-centred accounts of contracts are often taken to be challenges for promissory accounts of contract obligations. Nathan Oman's recent book, *The Dignity of Commerce*, provides a compelling example. For Oman, the difficulty with promissory accounts of contract law is that a promisor's obligations are not even close to what contract law permits a right holder to claim. Drawing on several evocative examples, he raises doubts whether a promisor's obligations fit well with the expectation damages remedy.

Here is Oman's leading illustration, based on a husband's promise to pick up his wife from the airport:

> Suppose I promise my wife that I will pick her up from the airport. I fail to do so, and as a result, she must hire a cab to drive her home. In this situation, what is my moral obligation to my wife? I have clearly made a promise, and I have clearly broken the promise. It is very easy to determine my wife's expectation damages: the cab fare.[3]

The damages are easy to calculate, yet there is something that doesn't feel right about paying expectation damages. As Oman asks:

> Does my duty to keep my promise obviously imply a duty on my part to give my wife a sum of money equal to the cab fare? It would certainly be strange were I to do so. A much more natural response would be for me to apologize to my wife for my carelessness or to acknowledge the legitimacy of her feelings of resentment toward me.[4]

I think Oman is correct in these claims, and I suspect many readers will agree. As John Gardner puts it: '[W]hen we work out what do about the irreparable aspects of our everyday wrongs, we often prefer not to say it with money at all, but to say it with flowers.'[5]

There are several reasons why Oman could be right, and the context of his airport promise may help in determining which reason applies. It might be that an apology will suffice because the promisee, the wife in this example, has exercised a normative power by accepting an apology and choosing to dissolve any further remedial duties the promisor may owe. It might be that an apology will suffice because, all else equal, it is the next best thing to performance. For various reasons, remedies other than an apology might be less satisfactory than an apology alone. Or it might be that there are features of the relationship at issue, in this case a specific marriage, that include an implied term, so that an apology would be expected, but other remedies would not fit. In any of these cases, an apology will make more sense than a payment of expectation damages.[6]

[3] *See* Nathan B Oman, *The Dignity of Commerce: Markets and the Moral Foundations of Contract Law* (University of Chicago Press 2016) 117.

[4] Ibid. 117.

[5] *See* John Gardner, *From Personal Life to Private Law* (OUP 2018) 159–60.

[6] Cf. David Owens, *Shaping the Normative Landscape* (OUP 2012) 48 ('If I fail to show up to your wedding as promised, you might expect me to do something to make it up to you, but that something is not valued as *compensation* for the wasted place at the wedding breakfast, nor even for your sense

Suppose, however, that we turn to the right holder's side of the picture and consider what the promisee can legitimately demand in light of promissory morality. Now the analysis looks different. In many cases, an apology is enough from the promisor's point of view (and even from the perspective of a neutral onlooker, for apologizing will often seem sufficient to a third party bystander). In these cases, payment of damages may feel out of place, even where a sincere apology would have sufficed. In other cases, the promisor has a moral obligation to perform after the fact, and nothing less. This is often true for solemn promises, especially if they involve a performance that lacks easy substitutes. Often, the promisee and her decisions will also bear on these questions. To figure out whether an apology suffices to address a breach, we may need to know not only what the promisee can insist upon, but also what she has insisted upon.

Suppose that the promisor in Oman's example gives a sincere apology after forgetting to pick up his wife, and suppose that this is all he should have done, all else equal. It is still possible that he could end up owing an ex post performance (maybe picking her up at the airport next time?), in light of his wife's subsequent decisions regarding his promise. If she insisted on performance after the fact, he would likely owe performance after the fact despite the otherwise satisfactory apology. Imagine the wife in this example has responded to her husband's apology as follows: 'Of course I accept your apology, but you must pick me up from the airport next time I need a ride!' I expect that the promisor would owe more than the initial apology: he would need to pick her up from the airport next time.

Shifting our attention from the problem of obligation to what the promisee can demand thus offers a very different picture of the relation between contract law and the morality of promising. Significantly, in some cases a promisee's post-breach demand may alter or at least clarify the moral obligations of a promisor.[7] If it turns out that a contractual promisee's demand has this effect, then observing the initial post-wrong obligations of the promisor will not tell us all of what we need to know. Potentially, expectation damages match the morality of promising after the plaintiff has filed suit and made her case, for the legal demand has moral import.

Benjamin Zipursky has noted a similar phenomenon in the tort setting, and more generally in social contexts where one person has wronged another. He

of disappointment.'). Note that the selection of a marriage setting may alter the analysis. For a suggestion that friendship settings offer more helpful comparisons for relational contracts, see Ethan J Leib, 'Contracts and Friendships' (2009) 59 Emory LJ 649.

[7] There are important subtleties that distinguish between insisting on performance, demanding it, and rebuking a failure to perform. I am grouping this case in the demand category, but it could easily implicate one of the other types. For helpful discussion, see Margaret Gilbert, *Rights and Demands: A Foundational Inquiry* (OUP 2018) 21–3.

offers a provocative example. A boyfriend has cheated on his girlfriend with whom he is living, and she has responded with a demand: 'You cheated on me. Move out!' In this case, the boyfriend's obligations shift with her legitimate demand. As Zipursky argues: 'Let us suppose that it is justifiable for her to make this demand in response to his having cheated on her and that he ought to move out if she so demands under these circumstances. It would hardly follow from these statements that the boyfriend would have a duty to move out even if she did not so demand.'[8] On this account, the boyfriend's wrong results in a prerogative on the part of the wrong's victim.

In parallel fashion, there are promissory cases where remedial obligations diverge from ex post performance, especially in close personal settings where apologies are often best. Be that as it may, promisees can still retain the moral right to demand an ex post performance in such cases. This isn't to say that such a demand will be the most reasonable choice all things considered. Even where a promisee can legitimately demand an ex post performance, perhaps the promisee should forgive and forget (and maintenance of interpersonal relationships may likewise counsel against such demands). Still, if our aim is to assess divergence between promissory morality and contract doctrine, it helps to understand promissory morality from the right holder's perspective. Right holders may be able to demand something more than what promisors would otherwise owe.

B. The standing problem

Some question contract law's fit with promissory morality on other grounds; they focus on who gets to seek a judicial remedy. Ordinarily, only contractual promisees can sue. For some, this 'substantive standing' is a challenge to promissory accounts, since the promisor's obligation to perform is not linked in any obvious way to the promisee's choice to file a complaint.[9] Here, too, a focus on the right holder's perspective offers important insights. Mainstream theories of promissory morality suggest that promisees do have a special standing to make demands on promisors.[10] Private rights of action generally parallel this understanding of promissory morality.[11] Instead of showing divergence, standing

[8] *See* Benjamin C Zipursky, 'Substantive Standing, Civil Recourse, and Corrective Justice' (2011) 39 Fla St U L Rev 299, 332.
[9] *See* Oman, 'The Dignity of Commerce' (n. 3) 113.
[10] *See* Andrew S Gold, 'Consideration and the Morality of Promising' in Jason W Neyers, et al., (eds), *Exploring Contract Law* (Hart 2009) 115, 124.
[11] Cf. ibid. 116.

doctrine could thus indicate that promissory morality is central to contract law in another way.

For example, Margaret Gilbert's work on promissory morality suggests promisees have a special standing not shared with the general population.[12] She imagines a case in which she has made a promise to the reader. On Gilbert's view, 'If I were to allow that I owe you performance, then I would recognize that you have the standing to upbraid me for nonperformance, or to insist on performance. Before the fact you could pressure me, saying in effect: "Give me that! It's *mine*!"'[13] Third parties may have standing to respond, but she notes that their standing is importantly different:

> It is true that a bystander could say, 'Give her that! It's hers!' The case in which I command you to give me what is mine is special, however. The bystander's standing to command you to give it to me can be questioned. My standing surely cannot be questioned. In the bystander's case, the riposte 'It's none of your business!' makes sense. In my case, it does not.[14]

This phenomenon is easily recognizable, including the reaction that, for bystanders, 'it's none of your business'.[15] Social practices of promising incorporate the idea that a promisee has a special standing to insist on performance; promissory morality plausibly includes this same feature.

Stephen Darwall's account of the second-person standpoint in morality supports a similar conclusion.[16] Darwall's most famous example involves a foot-stomping episode.[17] When someone non-consensually stomps on your foot, this wrong has significance for anyone in the moral community, but it also implicates a specific relationship between the wrongdoer and the victim.[18] As Darwall explains:

> In addition to there being weighty reasons against others stepping on your feet, indeed, in addition to members of the moral community having the standing to demand that people not step on your feet, if you have a right, then you have standing to make a special demand against people who might

[12] *See* Margaret Gilbert, 'Scanlon on Promissory Obligation: The Problem of Promisees' Rights' (2004) 101 J Phil 83, 83.

[13] Ibid. 101.

[14] Ibid.

[15] Ibid.

[16] *See* Stephen Darwall, *The Second-Person Standpoint: Morality, Respect, and Accountability* (HUP 2006) 5.

[17] Ibid.

[18] Ibid. 8–9.

> step on your feet—you have the authority to resist, claim compensation, and so on.[19]

Since promises create moral rights in a promisee, it is not surprising that promissory morality should recognize this special standing in appropriate cases.

This is not to deny the complexity of a right holder's special standing when responding to a wrong. David Owens brings out some of the nuances for promissory breaches. As he asks: 'Shouldn't a bystander sometimes be able to insist that I keep my promise to John when it looks as if I am about to break it?'[20] Sometimes yes—the more interesting question will be when this is true. In fact, there are several different categories of standing that bear on a promisee's (or a bystander's) conduct. Sometimes promisees may possess a standing that is not shared by bystanders, in other cases multiple parties may have standing to do something about a promissory breach.

One area where promisees may share standing with others is when they blame. As Owens notes:

> There are occasions on which blame and indignation from all sides is apt, occasions on which nobody should blame (the wrongdoer has a good excuse), and finally occasions on which only third parties should blame. An instance of the latter is where the promisee has himself breached faith with the promisor on many previous occasions and is getting a dose of his own medicine.[21]

Blaming implicates a special standing that is limited (or potentially expanded) by multiple background features. Other types of standing, such as the standing to forgive, are more stable. Ordinarily, the only party that can forgive is the specific party who was wronged.[22] And, ordinarily, the wronged party will have this standing to forgive even if, as Owens puts it, he is 'getting a dose of his own medicine'. Such a person may be under added pressure to forgive, but he won't automatically lose standing to forgive simply because he has unclean hands.[23]

19 *See* ibid. 18. A related point is developed in Stephen Darwall, 'Law and the Second-Person Standpoint' (2007) 40 Loy LA L Rev 891, 891–2. This perspective also appears more broadly in Joel Feinberg's account of a claim right. *See* Joel Feinberg, 'The Nature and Value of Rights' in *Rights, Justice, and the Bounds of Liberty* (Princeton University Press 1980) 143, 150.

20 *See* Owens, *Shaping the Normative Landscape* (n. 6) 50.

21 *See* ibid.

22 Note that some suggest a third party can also have standing to forgive. *See* Nicolas Cornell, 'Wrongs, Rights, and Third Parties' (2015) 43 Phil & Pub Aff 109, 117.

23 *See* Owens, *Shaping the Normative Landscape* (n. 6) 50 n. 6 ('[a] bad record need not undermine the victim's ability to *forgive* the wrong').

Where does this leave the standing to demand performance after a breach? Perhaps there are specific settings where bystanders will share in this standing along with a wronged promisee; the urgency of a remedy could be a significant factor.[24] Yet the settings where bystanders have standing to demand performance are less widespread than settings involving blame. Promisees can legitimately demand a remedy even from people who are not blameworthy, and third parties will not always get to make such demands. If a third party insists that a breaching promisor keep her promise, she can plausibly ask the bystander, 'Who are you to tell me what to do?' In the ordinary case, a promisee is uniquely positioned to insist that the promisor perform. Standing to demand performance thus occupies a middle ground between standing to blame and standing to forgive.

Contract law may still diverge from promissory morality on some of the details, but this analysis suggests that it does not diverge in a way that calls into doubt a promise-centred reading of core contract law principles. For institutional reasons, the law may not be able to cost-effectively or accurately address the fine-grained moral questions that impact different types of moral standing.[25] It nonetheless can match the features of promissory morality by approximation. A contractual promisee's unique standing to bring suit is a plausible match for that party's special standing to demand performance in promissory morality. Correctly or not, judges could see a contract plaintiff's substantive standing to bring suit as consistent with promissory morality, for the plaintiff is usually the only party with the moral standing to demand performance.

To be sure, one might see morality in general, or promissory morality in particular, from a different perspective. But if we seek an interpretation of contract law that makes sense under principles of promissory morality, a promisee's unique standing to bring suit is well within the realm of interpretive plausibility. Indeed, a contract law that extended private rights of action more broadly could pose a greater risk of divergence.[26] Focusing on

[24] Cf. Andrew S Gold, 'A Moral Rights Theory of Private Law' (2011) 52 Wm & Mary L Rev 1873, 1906 n. 154 (indicating that urgency might impact the standing of third parties to enforce). One way that the law shows sensitivity to contextual concerns is through equitable doctrines. For further discussion, see Chapter 8.

[25] Cf. Seana V Shiffrin, 'The Divergence of Contract and Promise' (2007) 120 Harv L Rev 708, 733 (noting the possibility that there are distinctively legal bases for divergence between contract law and promissory morality).

[26] An interesting exception to the standing rule is the third party beneficiary doctrine. For an argument that third party beneficiaries of promises can be wronged by a breach, see generally Cornell, 'Wrongs, Rights' (n. 22).

compliance with promissory obligations has raised questions about a contract plaintiff's special standing to bring suit. The right holder side of the picture highlights how contract law could actually match promissory morality in that regard.

C. What is missing

Given the above discussion, emphasizing morally rightful demands might seem to solve the explanatory challenges posed by expectation damages, together with the standing to seek this remedy. In situations where an apology or some other behaviour is owed instead of ex post performance, the promisee can still legitimately demand performance or the next best thing. Since it is often impossible to perform after the fact in compliance with the terms of a breached promise, expectation damages may be a close substitute. On this view, the right holder's side of promissory morality could help make sense of promissory obligations that differ from what contract law provides. As we will see, however, the problem is more complex—what we actually need to figure out is whether a promisee has a *right of redress*.

The question to ask from a redress-centred perspective is not whether the promisor has an obligation to perform as promised, nor whether providing money will be just as good as an actual performance. Nor is the question simply whether the promisee can legitimately demand damages or ex post performance in the event of a breach. She may be able to demand a variety of things, and they could end up only imperfectly matching what was owed ex ante; regardless, not all of the things she has moral standing to demand will be things she has moral standing to coerce or otherwise bring about through force or the threat of force. The question from a redress perspective is this: when can the promisee or someone acting on her behalf legitimately enforce her rights, either through coercion or through other means?[27]

[27] I distinguish between coercion of a wrongdoer and other cases to take into account situations where a party may be able to legitimately take what is owed to her, without having to coerce a wrongdoer in the process. Such fact patterns are prominent in recaption cases, where a wronged party can sometimes take back stolen property without directly interacting with the individual who stole it. Other possibilities may arise if a remedy ultimately requires a third party's involvement, as may occur when an employer of the defendant is made to pay wages to a claimant. For discussion of such contexts, see Stephen A Smith, *Rights, Wrongs, and Injustices: The Structure of Remedial Law* (OUP 2019) 68.

III. The Enforcement Concern

A. Demands, complaints, and enforcement

We might think a closer look at a claimant's standing to demand performance (or the nearest equivalent) can solve our interpretive challenges. Or, perhaps, we may think that these puzzles are answered based on a moral standing to complain about how someone has treated us. Recent work in private law theory has brought both of these perspectives to the fore. Benjamin Zipursky emphasizes the standing to demand responsive conduct from a wrongdoer; Nicolas Cornell emphasizes the significance of a moral standing to complain.[28] In each case, adopting the right holder's perspective may allow us to sidestep gaps between a promisor's post-breach obligations and contract law's standard legal remedies.

Notably, when we lack standing to demand responsive behaviour from someone who has wronged us, we also generally lack standing pursuant to a private right of action. Zipursky rightly notes that private law has a 'substantive standing' doctrine that centres on a wronged party's standing to make demands, and he is right to note that it has an analogue in positive morality.[29] He has also extended his account of civil recourse to contract law, where a version of the same standing doctrine applies. As he argues: '[i]n contract, civil recourse is used, in the first instance, to demand performance or substitute performance—in any event, to demand the fulfilment of expectation legitimately rooted in a bargain.'[30]

And Cornell is right that the moral standing to complain about a wrong can be forfeited in ways that shed light on legal doctrine. He notes standing problems for people who have unclean hands, or who have created conditions of duress.[31] They can forfeit their moral standing to complain when they feel their rights have been violated, and arguably this forfeiture underpins analogous features of private law.[32] Cornell's account may also help to make sense of mitigation doctrine, which is arguably in tension with promissory morality.

[28] *See* Zipursky, 'Substantive Standing' (n. 8); Nicolas Cornell, 'A Complainant-Oriented Approach to Unconscionability and Contract Law' (2016) 164 U Pa L Rev 1131.

[29] *See* Zipursky, 'Substantive Standing' (n. 8) 325–7.

[30] See Benjamin C Zipursky, 'Civil Recourse and the Plurality of Wrongs: Why Torts are Different' [2014] New Zealand L Rev 145, 158.

[31] *See* Cornell, 'A Complainant-Oriented Approach' (n. 28) 1159–63.

[32] It is an interesting question whether these cases are better explained by a loss of standing to complain, as Cornell contends, or instead by a 'self-regarding' account of judicial conduct. Cf. Seana Valentine Shiffrin, 'Paternalism, Unconscionability Doctrine, and Accommodation' (2000) 29 Phil & Pub Aff 205 (developing a self-regarding account for unconscionability doctrine). The answer may depend on the fact pattern at issue. I discuss the self-regarding account further in Chapter 8.

We may have less standing to complain about a wrong if we have not sought to mitigate the resulting harms when they could easily have been limited.[33]

Standing to make demands and standing to complain likewise provide useful insights for understanding rights of redress. Sometimes we forfeit our standing to complain due to our own wrongful behaviour. We could even lack standing to make demands in the first place, if we have sufficiently damaged our relationship with a counterparty by wronging them ourselves. When we lack such standing, we will generally also lack a moral enforcement right. Standing to make demands, to complain, and to enforce are closely linked, and they appear to rise and fall in tandem.[34] In general, determining whether we have standing to demand something or standing to complain about a wrong should thus be incorporated into an analysis of rights of redress.[35] Yet, while the moral standing to make demands or to complain are helpful as a starting point, they cannot be our endpoint if we want to fully understand rights of redress. Rights of redress require something more.

As Herbert Hart perceptively noted, 'having a justification for demanding that a person shall or shall not do some action is a necessary though not a sufficient condition for justifying coercion.'[36] There are times when we should be able to demand something from others—sometimes in very strong terms—yet we still can't force them to do what their obligations require. And this is true irrespective of whether we have clean hands, and irrespective of the degree to which the wrong at issue has harmed us. The morality of promising is a good illustration.

Consider an ordinary promise to have lunch; let's say that I promise to have lunch with you tomorrow. This promise creates moral obligations and it gives you a special standing to make demands on me if the promise is broken. Indeed, you have a moral right that I now have lunch with you at the chosen time. You will also have standing to complain if I'm a no-show. Nevertheless, you don't get to force me to have lunch with you if I refuse.[37] The same point applies

[33] *See* Cornell, 'A Complainant-Oriented Approach' (n. 28) 1169. For the view that there is divergence, see Shiffrin, 'The Divergence of Contract' (n. 25) 724–6.

[34] Cf. Gilbert, *Rights and Demands* (n. 7) (describing a possible Hartian view that 'one is only justified in coercing someone to do something if one is justified in demanding that he do it'). I am not aware of a good counterexample where standing to enforce won't also mean standing to make demands, but this stage of the argument does not depend on a perfect correspondence between these types of standing.

[35] Though standing to complain won't always exist where there is standing to make demands. Unjust enrichment cases may implicate a right of redress, but in these cases there may be no standing to complain because there is no wrong to complain about.

[36] See Herbert LA Hart, 'Are There Any Natural Rights?' (1955) 64 Phil Rev 175, 178 n. 6.

[37] *See* Andrew S Gold, 'Consideration and the Morality of Promising' in Jason W Neyers, et al., (eds), Exploring Contract Law (2009) 115, 127 ('A moral right to performance of a promise could mean the possessor of the right has standing to demand the other party meet the obligation . . . or it could mean the possessor of the right has standing to demand performance and also, if performance is not

where property is involved. If I promise to give you my prized coffee mug, and then tell you I am repudiating the promise, you don't get to just take the mug off my desk.[38] The right holder must also hold a moral enforcement right, and this enforcement right can't be demonstrated merely by showing that something is owed to her, that she has good cause for complaint, or that she has standing to demand responsive conduct after the fact.[39] If I promise to have lunch with you, and nothing more occurs—no consideration, no reliance—you are not in a position to legitimately coerce performance or an equivalent remedy for my breach. You have standing to demand or rebuke, but little more.

But is this too strict a view of what standing to demand means? In her recent book, *Rights and Demands*, Margaret Gilbert argues that 'one might think of *justified* coercion as, in essence, an amplified demand, the possible amplifications of which include forms of physical constraint'.[40] Furthermore, she concludes: 'Having the legal standing to sue for an injunction to restrain the continued or further breach of a duty is analogous to having the standing to demand an action that is owed one outside the legal context.'[41] If Gilbert's view is accepted, standing to demand something may explain why we get a private right of action, and the important thing to figure out is when we have standing to make this amplified kind of demand. I think this potential argument fails, both because justified coercion is not an amplified demand, and because bringing a private right of action is not a legal analogue to making a demand.

First, demands are communicative and, while coercion expresses something, that expressive feature is not integral to coercive conduct. Demands involve a form of address that coercion does not. Suppose that someone has stolen your bag and you demand they return it. Now assume they refuse to return the bag. If you ultimately chase them down and pry the bag away, you are not making a demand when you take back the bag—you are no longer doing something that depends on their uptake. You are no longer seeking their agreement through your communicative acts. Coercion may substitute for a demand, but it is not an amplified demand (and this holds true even if standing to make a demand is a precondition for standing to coerce).

forthcoming, to physically coerce the other party to meet the obligation.'). See also Gilbert, 'Scanlon on Promissory Obligation' (n. 12) 89 ('Contemplating the exercise of 'force' in connection with everyday promises and agreements may seem to go too far.').

[38] Note, however, that in cases where you get to enforce your rights by simply taking something back, this type of enforcement will not involve a demand even though a demand would be apt. This is another respect in which demand-centred pictures of private law are not adequate.

[39] *See* Gold, 'Consideration' (n. 37) 124.

[40] *See* Gilbert, *Rights and Demands* (n. 7) 246.

[41] *See* ibid. 298.

Second, coercion takes the choice away from the other party. When someone takes back their bag from a thief, the thief no longer gets a say in the matter. It is perfectly sensible for someone to say: 'I'm tired of demanding he return what he stole; I'm taking it back now.' It is true that in some sense demands can be a means of enforcement, but it is not the same kind of enforcement involved in redress. A demand can bring about an outcome by exerting pressure on the other party, perhaps by convincing the other party to comply for moral reasons, or perhaps by making them feel guilt, or shame, or a risk to their reputation. But in the ordinary case, these effects are not at all the same thing as taking away the other party's choice in the way that physical force or the threat of physical force accomplish. This is not to deny that occasionally public shaming or reputation costs can have an overwhelming effect on their target, particularly if someone's occupation is put at risk. Even so, using force or the threat of force is a qualitatively different kind of enforcement given the way it characteristically removes the other party's choice—and standing to use force or the threat of force is thus different in kind from standing to make a demand.

Bringing a private right of action, in turn, is analogous to cases in which we get to use force or the threat of force to bring about a remedy. As such cases are quite different from cases in which we make demands, it is not true that standing to make a demand—of whatever type—will be analogous to bringing suit to seek an injunction, let alone damages. We have good reason to want to know whether standing to make a demand exists because such standing is likely a moral precondition for standing to enforce, but that is as far as the connection goes.

For redress to be legitimate, we need to locate a basis for thinking that a promisee holds more than a moral right to a given outcome (e.g. a right to a promised performance), and also that she has more than just the standing to make a demand for responsive conduct in cases of breach, or the standing to complain about how she was treated by the wrongdoer. These are first steps, but they do not get us far enough to explain contract law. If they did, a far wider range of promises should be enforceable than the ones that the law actually recognizes. For example, we might expect that you could force me to have lunch with you, as promised. A forced lunch, however, would be an untenable outcome, and this suggests that there are additional features at issue, beyond a simple standing to make demands or a standing to complain about a promissory breach.[42]

[42] Note that Zipursky recognizes demands made in the legal setting involve enforceability. *See* Zipursky, 'Substantive Standing' (n. 8) 336 ('The presence of courts and law permits plaintiffs to make enforceable legal demands for such responsive conduct.'). Yet this observation invites the question

B. Distinguishing contracts from ordinary promises

Standing to demand is an important part of understanding private law. As Zipursky notes, 'having been wronged by another generates not only a basis for complaining of having been wronged by the other, but also a basis for a demand for ameliorative conduct by the wrongdoer'.[43] We have now seen that having a basis for a demand will not be enough to justify a private right of action. Yet having been wronged can generate another moral consequence beyond the standing to complain or to make demands: it can generate a basis for the wronged party or someone acting on her behalf to legitimately reverse what was done by the wrongdoer. When does that happen? As we will see, by focusing our attention on this question, a redress-based analysis will not only shed light on the morality of promising, it will also help elucidate the conceptual structure of contract law.

If our goal is to make sense of contract law in redress-centred terms, we will need something that differentiates contractual promises from ordinary promises. This is not a minor concern for promise-based theories of contract law. The courts' general unwillingness to enforce my promise to have lunch with you is mysterious if we just focus on what promisors owe. It is just as mysterious if we focus on a promisee's standing to demand. On the other hand, contract law clearly does draw on promissory practices. What accounts for this gap between promissory obligations and enforcement? We can't answer this question just by focusing on the obligations side of the picture, but it is also not solved by shifting to the realm of demands and complaints.

There is, however, a discernible difference between legally enforced promises and other promises, and this difference extends beyond the fact that contract law simply chooses to enforce these particular promises. Note that contractual promises are not like ordinary, non-enforceable promises in that contractual promises are usually contingent on the actions of others.[44] In the case of a contractual promise, a performance obligation is not triggered *until the promisee has met the terms of the promise.* I will argue that this difference

why some demands are apt for enforceability and others not. That question is the concern of a redress-focused account like the present one.

[43] *See* ibid. 332.

[44] Raz has also emphasized this feature of promises in the context of agreements. *See* Joseph Raz, 'On the Nature of Rights' (1984) 93 Mind 194, 202–3. Raz suggests that the right to make conditional promises is 'derivative of the general right to promise.' Ibid. 202. *See also* Fried, *Contract as Promise* (n. 2) 47 ('Where the promise is conditional, . . . until the condition is fulfilled A is not bound in law by the obligation of a promise.').

is one we should care about and, in particular, that we should care about it because it helps explain the legitimacy of redress.

As developed below, contract law distinguishes enforceable promises from unenforceable promises in a way that broadly tracks the morality of redress, and this parallel treatment suggests that understanding rights of redress can help us to better understand contract law. The differences between contractual promises and ordinary promises reflect a particular aspect of promissory morality—the enforceability aspect. In short, we can explain the legal differences between promise types by turning to moral differences between promise types. Figuring out when there are moral rights of redress—and moral enforcement rights more generally—can then make sense of a doctrinal feature (the consideration doctrine) that has troubled a wide range of contract theories.

To begin, consider patterns of enforceability more generally. As Stephen Smith's work suggests, we can look to property or property-like concepts for assistance in legitimizing coercive remedies for breaches of contracts.[45] While there are various ways to ground enforceability, one way that promissory rights could be apt for coercive enforcement is if these rights are understandable as ownership rights, or at least as ownership-like. If we have a proprietary interest in contractual performance—or an appropriate analogue—this is the kind of relation that classically supports legitimate exercises of force.[46] People can legitimately use force to protect themselves in self-defence cases, and they can also legitimately use force to protect their property from external threats.[47] A similar logic applies ex post. If someone steals your wallet from you, you can chase after them and rightfully grab your wallet back—both as a matter of law and as a matter of morality.[48] Turning to the state's role, it is likewise a fitting exercise of state power when the state acts on our behalf to protect our property rights after they have been infringed. If contract rights are property rights (or

[45] Stephen Smith's concern is related but not identical to mine; he looks to property concepts as a response to concerns under the harm principle. *See*, e.g. Stephen A Smith, 'Towards a Theory of Contract' in Jeremy Horder, (ed.), Oxford Essays in Jurisprudence (Fourth Series) (OUP 2000) 107, 120–9; Stephen A Smith, *Contract Theory* (OUP 2004) 72 (suggesting the import of owning rights to performance).

[46] *See*, e.g. Andrew S Gold, 'A Property Theory of Contract' (2009) Nw U L Rev 1, 46 (discussing this possibility).

[47] *See*, e.g. Zoë Sinel, 'De-Ciphering Self-Help' (2017) 67 U Toronto LJ 31, 50–51 (discussing these types of self-help).

[48] This may depend, however, on whether one adopts a Kantian perspective on private law. Compare Arthur Ripstein, *Force and Freedom: Kant's Legal and Political Philosophy* (HUP 2009) 146 (describing the Kantian view on unilateral choices regarding the entitlements of others) with Victor Tadros, 'Independence Without Interests?' (2011) 31 Oxford J Leg Stud 193, 202–6 (critiquing this perspective). These issues will be discussed further in Chapter 7.

suitably analogous), that is a prima facie basis for thinking coercive enforcement is permissible.

Granted, there is controversy over whether contract rights can count as a genuine form of *property*, strictly speaking.[49] Yet the relevant moral principles should apply even if contract rights are merely property-*like* in the right way—for something can be understood to belong to us in the relevant moral sense even if we define this relation as something other than property ownership per se. The promisee can properly say in such cases: 'this performance is mine'. Where I refer to contract rights in proprietary terms, the reader should feel free to view this as an analogy that captures the sense that something now morally belongs to a promisee. With that caveat in mind, how can a promisee acquire such ownership of a promised performance?[50]

As will be developed below, contractual promises have the right features to support the acquisition of a property right (or a moral likeness) in performance. Theories of just property acquisition suggest multiple ways to justly acquire something, and several of these bear on promissory relations. Each of these avenues leads plausibly to a proprietary interest in performance of the promised acts (although they will not always converge on the details). While the terrain of property acquisition is contested, mainstream accounts of just property acquisition map onto the contractual setting in a way that supports rights of redress in the event of breach. Moreover, these principles help to differentiate the ordinary promises that the law refuses to enforce.

C. Theories of just property acquisition

Several prominent theories of property acquisition are adaptable to support acquisition of a promisor's acts of performance. Importantly, the promisee's relation to the promisor's expression of consent resembles other contexts in which individuals are thought to rightfully acquire property in a thing. The major difference in the contractual context is that the thing acquired is of an unusual type. As it happens, there are multiple justifications for viewing contracts as legitimately enforceable, each of which converge to some degree. This is an unconventional setting, but the principles at issue should be just as relevant for

[49] *See* JE Penner, *The Idea of Property in Law* (OUP 1997) 91, 112–14. For a response, see Gold, 'A Property Theory' (n. 46) 48–9.

[50] Cf. Smith, 'Towards a Theory of Contract' (n. 45) 120–9 (discussing theories under which a property-like interest in contract performance could be created by drawing on an analogy to property acquisition theories).

contract-based acquisition as elsewhere, and more than one potential basis for acquisition can apply.

To begin, the process of meeting the terms of a contractual promise sometimes resembles the initial acquisition of physical property through an individual's labour. Where a contract is binding, the promisee has acted to meet the requirements of a promise (in some cases by providing a promise herself), creating the conditions under which the other party's promise has force as an obligation. Until the contract's conditions are met, the promisor has not bound herself to perform (she has bound herself to perform only if certain events transpire). The conditional promise thus requires the promisee to labour or at least engage in a specified action in order to bring about the promised performance. On this view, the promisee justly acquires this performance through her actions taken to bring the other party's promise into effect.

John Locke has propounded the best-known labour-desert theory of acquisition. Locke describes how a person can acquire property through this process as follows: 'Whatsoever . . . he removes out of the state that nature hath provided . . . he hath mixed his labour with, and joined to it something that is his own, and thereby makes it his property.'[51] One way of explaining our sense that the promisee deserves the promised performance is to note that the promisee's labour, aimed at attaining the promised act, merits recognition of ownership in performance because his labour has been joined together with the acquired property. Notwithstanding the debates over labour-desert theories and their overall merits, that approach is a natural fit here.

Other examples resemble a capture, which is also a classic mode of acquisition. In cases of unilateral contracts, the conditional promise is usually open to the world. In such instances, the successful promisee has brought the promise under her control by complying with its terms first.[52] By acting to meet a condition precedent, the promisee obtains the promisor's consent—it is no longer open to the whims of the promisor and no longer subject to withdrawal without infringing the promisee's rights. To illustrate, consider a unilateral contract, where the first person to meet the terms of an offer has a right to $100. If Jane meets those terms before anyone else, she can claim that this is now 'her' promised performance, that it has been brought under her control.[53] She is the one

[51] John Locke, 'The Second Treatise of Government' in David Wootton, (ed.), *Political Writings of John Locke* (Penguin Books 1993) ¶ 27.

[52] Cf. Richard Epstein, 'Possession as the Root of Title' (1979) 13 Ga L Rev 1221, 1224–5 (describing a first-possession theory of property acquisition); Carol M Rose, 'Possession as the Origin of Property' (1985) 52 U Chi L Rev 73 (discussing a first-possession theory). The classic case is *Pierson v. Post*, 3 Cai. 175 (N.Y. Sup. Ct. 1805).

[53] For a similar insight, see Benjamin L Fine, Comment, 'An Analysis of the Formation of Property Rights Underlying Tortious Interference with Contracts and Other Economic Relations' (1983) 50 U

described by the promise's terms, by making its language applicable to the facts under consideration. Its terms can no longer cover anyone else.[54]

Alternatively, the actual 'thing' the promisee changed by her labour may be the conditional promise itself. Contracts could thus involve a form of acquisition through property *creation*.[55] On one view, the promise represents an interest in the underlying performance, and this future action is (arguably) transferred from the promisor, not created. That is the core idea underlying transfer theories of contract. But on another view, a successful contract—one in which the terms of a conditional promise are met—is brought into existence in part by the intentional acts of the promisee. According to this understanding, the process of contractual drafting and acceptance gives the promisee a proprietary interest in performance as co-author of a binding promise; in turn, owning that promise is effectively to own the actions that the promise calls for.

In addition, it is possible to borrow from principles of acquisition developed by Hegel. A fully Hegelian theory of contract law is distinct from the one suggested here in several major respects.[56] That said, Hegel has described the acquisition of property in a different way from the above accounts, and his theory may likewise assist in conceptualizing why it is just for an individual who meets a promise's conditions to have rights to performance. From this perspective on acquisition, a thing has been acquired if it is now intelligible only in light of the acquirer's will.[57] This is another angle on acquisition, and we too might share the intuition that property is acquired when the acquirer's will is, in a sense, embodied in the relevant thing.[58]

Chi L Rev 1116, 1142 (comparing the obligee in a contractual relationship to 'the pursuer of a wild animal who has significantly advanced towards capture'). Fine's view of the relation between contracts and property is distinct from the present one, but the intuition that capture norms apply is suggestive.

[54] Note that contracts under seal are not addressed by the theory developed here. I agree with the suggestion that such contracts 'are creations of positive law, which for instrumental purposes makes available a means of juridically binding oneself.' *See* Ernest J Weinrib, *The Idea of Private Law* (HUP 1995) 138 n. 30 (discussing Hobbes's view).

[55] For further discussion of this type of acquisition theory, see Jeremy Waldron, *The Right to Private Property* (1988) 198–201.

[56] For explanations of modern legal doctrine in light of Hegel's contract theory, see Peter Benson, 'Abstract Right and the Possibility of a Nondistributive Conception of Contract: Hegel and Contemporary Contract Theory' (1989) 10 Cardozo L Rev 1077; Alan Brudner, 'Reconstructing Contracts' (1993) 43 U Toronto LJ 1. Cf. GWF Hegel, *Elements of the Philosophy of Right* (Allan W Wood (ed.), 1991) (1820) ¶ 44, at 75.

[57] *See* Waldron, *The Right of Private Property* (n. 55) 365 (discussing this idea); cf. Stephen R Munzer, *A Theory of Property* (CUP 1990) 69 ('To grasp the importance of causing physical changes in external things it is necessary to see why Hegel requires that the embodiment of a person's will be recognizable by others. The root idea . . . is that property is an intersubjective concept.').

[58] *See* Margaret J Radin, 'Property and Personhood' (1982) 34 Stan L Rev 957, 960 ('Once we admit that a person can be bound up with an external "thing" in some constitutive sense, we can argue that by virtue of this connection the person should be accorded broad liberty with respect to control over that "thing." ').

Jeremy Waldron provides helpful examples of this idea in cases where an acquirer has brought about a physical change in an object:

> If the object is inanimate (say, a piece of marble formed into a statue) then the aspect of the object which may be understood only by reference to my will is one of its physical properties—its shape, for example. If the object is organic, then maybe it is not merely some property which is understood in this way but also some ongoing process in the object. . . .[59]

As Waldron notes, a principle of acquisition along these lines has certain advantages over Locke's labour theory: 'We do not have to insist (as Locke has to) that the willed actions are actually present *in* the product, only that the condition (and, of course, the value) of the product is such as to be intelligible only by reference to the will that shaped them.'[60]

This idea can be extended to the contractual setting, for the promisee's meeting of the promisor's conditions alters the nature of the promise. A conditional promise with its conditions unmet is only binding in a hypothetical world. Once the conditions are met, the promise becomes binding according to its own terms. A promisee can thus embody his will in the promise by working to change it from a contingent moral obligation to an actual, noncontingent duty. The meaning of the promise is now only fully intelligible in light of the promisee's having met its conditions. Where contractual conditions are met, the promise shifts from something that might oblige to something that does oblige, just as an unsigned law has a different force when you add a president's signature. A promisee may think of the promise as 'his' now that he has met its requirements because these efforts are what made the promise binding.

There are a number of contending theories for a principle of just acquisition of ordinary, physical property, and the above theories are sketched in their bare outlines. With adaptations for context, these principles of acquisition suggest how contractual promises may result in proprietary or at least property-like interests in performance.[61] The fit may not be perfect. Yet it is not necessary

[59] Waldron, *The Right to Private Property* (n. 55) 364.

[60] Ibid. 365; *see also* ibid. 364 ('Notice again that we are not required to believe here that my actions or my will literally enter into or become part of the object on which I work. In Hegel's account, the important thing is that the gap between the subjectivity of the will and the perceived externality of the objects of the world has been bridged.').

[61] An objection still might be raised: these theories of just property acquisition all tend to involve unilateral or original acquisition. Contract is characteristically bilateral or multilateral, involving a special relationship between the parties. This objection, however, is less forceful once we focus on the ambition of this part of the argument. Just as theories of property acquisition are not intended to explain promissory morality (on which they partly depend in this case), they are also not intended to explain the

to accept any of these theories in their precise shape, so long as the case can be made that a promisee deserves to own a contractual performance under conventional contracting conditions. What we are looking for from a redress-centred perspective is a reason to think that the promisee holds a moral enforcement right. Various theories of acquisition can support this view.

IV. The Specific Performance Question

The reader may now wonder if a focus on redress really has offered insight into the standard contractual remedy. Isn't it the case that specific performance is much closer to enforcement of a contractual promise than expectation damages? While courts do sometimes order specific performance, expectation damages are the more common result, and this is true even in cases where the plaintiff has a strong argument that the defendant breached.

This challenge raises concerns which will be developed further in Chapter 8. Redress is subject to various limits within the law, and the case for the legitimacy of enforcement rights does not argue for absolute enforcement rights. The fact that one has an enforcement right does not mean that one can always enforce by any means available, and the morality of enforcement must take into account questions of necessity, proportionality, and perhaps moral standing to complain. It is a strength of a redress-centred account that it focuses our attention on the morality of enforcement under the specific factual circumstances of a given dispute. Just as self-defence may be legitimate in general but not in those cases where a defensive response is disproportionate or unnecessary, so too rights of redress are sensitive to moral constraints. When we turn to the problem of specific performance, we have a concrete example of this sensitivity.

Here is the basic concern: accepting that valid contracts give a promisee a moral enforcement following a breach, it may appear that ex post contractual performance should be mandated by the courts whenever a promisor breaks her word. Especially if our understanding of contract obligations is premised on proprietary concepts, injunctive relief would appear to be an obvious remedy rather than an exceptional case. Instead, courts frequently provide expectation damages, rather than specific performance.

special relationship within contractual agreements. A given part of contract law may be explicable in light of a particular moral phenomenon even if the rest of contract law is not explicable in light of that moral phenomenon. In my view, principles of just property acquisition work in this fashion, as they can help explain the legitimacy of enforcement (but do not explain all features of contract law). I thank Nick Sage for noting this concern about theories of property acquisition and their relevance.

This poses a challenge for contract theories that assert an ownership interest in the promised performance. As Dori Kimel notes:

> [S]pecific performance is the remedy that aims at granting the innocent party precisely what she bargained for, whereas expectation damages merely aim at compensating her, albeit fully, for not receiving what she bargained for. At best, excuse the pun, it is a second best. So why not opt for the best?[62]

Indeed, a contract theory that emphasizes the justice in allocation back would seem to call for the remedy that best makes the promisee whole, rather than a more distant substitute.

It might be argued that contracts actually involve disjunctive promises to either perform the promised acts or to pay damages for a failure to perform. Certainly, contracting parties can enter into such disjunctive obligations. But, as a general description of what parties intend, or even as an interpretation of the public meaning of contract language, this explanation seems inadequate.[63] Frequently, agreements do not assert that damages may be substituted for performance, and there is a common belief among both courts and contracting parties that promisors owe a duty to perform the promised acts.

Some explanations for why courts choose damages instead of specific performance can be squared with a redress-centred framework, if that framework is sensitive to administrative costs. For example, it may be that monitoring and implementation of a specific performance remedy against a noncompliant defendant would be quite costly and even ineffective in a wide range of cases.[64] The institutions set to administer justice may offer second-best measures, given a legal system's limited budget and time constraints. In such instances, it is still plausible to view the court's approach in aspirational terms. The end is redressive justice between the parties, but the means are constrained by pragmatic considerations.

It appears there is more involved, especially if we are concerned with the internal point of view. Courts evince a genuine distaste for forcing the promisor to perform a service contract, and this may be included in legal reasoning.

[62] Dori Kimel, *From Promise to Contract* (Hart Publishing 2003) 95.

[63] *See* Smith, *Contract Theory* (n. 45) 402 ('It just seems implausible, as a matter of fact, to regard contracting parties as having agreed, in the typical case, to disjunctive obligations to perform or compensate.').

[64] *See* Anthony T Kronman, 'Specific Performance' (1978) 45 U Chi L Rev 351, 373 ('There is another common explanation for the reluctance of courts to enforce private injunctive agreements: the specific enforcement of contracts . . . entails special administrative costs which normally can be avoided under a money damages rule, and private individuals should not be allowed to shift the special costs associated with this form of relief to the taxpayers who subsidize the legal system.'). Note, however, that Kronman questions this view. Ibid. 373–6.

As Anthony Kronman describes one version of this understanding: '[E]ven a contract of short duration that calls for the performance of routine and unobjectionable tasks is a contract of self-enslavement and therefore legally unenforceable if it bars the employee from substituting money damages for his promised performance.'[65] Many commentators, myself included, are uncomfortable with the idea that an individual could be forced to perform services she does not want to, absent criminal forfeiture of rights.[66]

Administrative cost concerns are thus only a partial explanation for the manner in which contract obligations are enforced. Are additional explanations available? Kimel has suggested an additional possibility. He adopts an extension of the harm principle to questions of remedies.[67] In its standard meaning, the harm principle precludes coercion except to prevent someone from harming others.[68] Kimel discerns the following additional norm:

> [W]hen it comes to remedies for breach of contract, the harm principle, assuming that it is compatible in the first place with the imposition of legal obligations in order to prevent or redress the harm which is loss of bargain, counsels against the employment of the more intrusive remedy whenever the award of a less intrusive remedy could redress this harm just as effectively.[69]

Applying this premise, he suggests that 'accepting the harm principle entails that specific performance should be awarded only when the less intrusive remedial measure, the award of (expectation) damages, could not fully redress the harm caused through violation of the right.'[70]

Yet, assuming the harm principle extends this far, Kimel's response does not cover all cases in which courts refuse to require performance. The difficulty with Kimel's argument is that, in practice, damages are not truly equivalent to specific performance for all contracts.[71] Suppose, for example, that the services

[65] Anthony T Kronman, 'Paternalism and the Law of Contracts' (1983) 92 Yale LJ 763, 779.

[66] *See* Smith, *Contract Theory* (n. 45) 401 (noting 'the idea, common to both common and civil law regimes, that directly enforcing personal service contracts is undesirable because it is intrusive of personal liberty').

[67] Kimel, *From Promise* (n. 62) 103–9 (suggesting that the harm principle can be applied to the selection between expectation damages and specific performance).

[68] See John S Mill, *On Liberty* (1859) (David Bromwich & George Kateb, eds., Yale University Press 2003) 80). For a recent formulation, see Joseph Raz, *The Morality of Freedom* (OUP 1986) 412 ('Mill's harm principle states that the only justification for coercively interfering with a person is to prevent him from harming others.').

[69] Kimel, *From Promise* (n. 62) 104.

[70] Ibid.

[71] *See* Kronman, 'Specific Performance' (n. 64) 366 ('When the subject matter of a contract is unique, the risk is greater that the promisee's money damage remedy will be undercompensatory.').

called for by the contract are unique services, only capable of being performed by one individual. A standard market valuation might undercompensate the promisee. Courts may still refuse to mandate specific performance in these circumstances, yet Kimel's version of the harm principle would not apply to such cases.

Recognizing limitations on the means of legitimate redress offers a more comprehensive approach. When an individual promisor's autonomy will fall below a certain level, or is limited in a certain manner, it can be morally unacceptable to enforce an agreement, period. But respect for autonomy can also circumscribe legitimate enforcement even in cases where enforcement in some form is acceptable. In these cases, if a promisor concludes that she is simply unwilling to perform the act owed to the promisee, she may change her mind and deny the promised performance—subject to liability for her wrong. The right to reassert control over one's actions is inalienable in some contexts, and where that holds true the promisee's claim to performance must give way to the promisor's interest in performing different acts. Legitimate acts of redress may still be available, but they are bounded by this constraint and accordingly their form must be different.

This does not mean that the promised future act was never successfully contracted for, nor that the obligation imposed by the contractual promise is anything less than full performance. Instead, it means that the autonomy interest of the promisor is strong enough that she should be permitted to effectively reclaim her actions from the promisee, breaking her word. Just as the public's need can justify eminent domain if the government pays compensation, the importance of autonomy can justify the promisor's assertion of will over her own body if the promisor pays damages. This does not mean that the promisor disjunctively owes performance *or* payment of damages; she owes performance and nothing less. Even so, the promisee can only legitimately enforce where the resulting limitations on the promisor's autonomy fall within a bounded range.

In contract cases where the promisor decides not to perform despite having successfully transferred a property interest in performance to the promisee (or despite the creation of a proprietary interest in performance now held by the promisee), this breach is an infringement of the promisee's rights. The promisor has committed a wrong, and justice calls for the promisee's loss to be redressed (or subject to redress). Yet there is an autonomy principle at stake that restricts the morally acceptable means of redress even though it does not preclude redress altogether. Payment of damages represents an exercise of redressive justice within limits set by respect for this principle of autonomy. It is wrong for the promisor not to recognize the promisee's ownership of the promised act; at the enforcement stage, it would also be wrong to mandate specific performance.[72]

V. Explanatory Payoffs

The breadth of legal doctrine that matches a redress-based account is substantial, as the conceptual inferences extend well beyond the remedial moment itself. Recall that redress as understood here involves *enforcement*—this means that there must be underlying rights to enforce. In the contract setting, this also means redress will hinge on features of promissory morality that govern the underlying rights and obligations; for example, those parts of promissory morality that determine when a promisee has a genuine remedial moral right. With that in mind, various contract formation doctrines, such as offer and acceptance, are a match for a redress-based explanation. Likewise, doctrines such as duress or fraud are a good fit. Under circumstances that undercut the validity of a contractual promise, the promisee can no longer claim a right to performance, and in the absence of a legitimate promissory claim the possibility of redress based on promissory breach is no longer viable.

As understood here, redress is also a better fit for contract law than the accountability or satisfaction that civil recourse theories often emphasize for tort law doctrine. Civil recourse theories commonly view recourse as a means for a tort victim to respond to the affront of a wrong; recourse is a means for her to hold someone accountable, or to 'get satisfaction'.[73] Yet contract law is famous for imposing strict liability and that means in some cases it imposes liability on parties who have done their best to meet the terms of a contract, without any negligence or misfeasance.[74] There is very little basis for feeling an affront in many of these cases. Furthermore, the victims of a contractual breach are often just focused on getting what was promised to them. Only occasionally are they looking to 'get satisfaction' and, in many circumstances, it would be inappropriate to seek this kind of accountability. What the promisee may want is simply that the contractual promise is kept, or the closest equivalent.

[72] In a different context, compare Jules Coleman, *Risks and Wrongs* (OUP 1992) 298 ('The underlying moral claims may be that the injurer is justified under certain conditions in appropriating another's property *and* the victim is entitled in justice to repair in the event she suffers a loss as a consequence of the injurer's conduct.').

[73] *See* John CP Goldberg & Benjamin C Zipursky, 'Tort Law and Moral Luck' (2007) 92 Cornell L Rev 1123, 1162; Jason Solomon, 'Equal Accountability Through Tort Law' (2009) 103 Nw U L Rev 1765, 1814.

[74] Curtis Bridgeman, 'Reconciling Strict Liability and Corrective Justice in Contract Law' (2007) 74 Fordham L Rev 3013.

This isn't to deny that some contractual breaches are egregious and intentional. The victims of these breaches quite properly feel an affront, and no doubt they wish to get satisfaction. The egregious case supports a different kind of recourse in limited contexts, but we should recognize that these contexts are genuinely narrow. Some scholars do build a civil recourse picture of contract law that centres on retaliatory impulses.[75] Still, the reality of many contractual breaches is that civil recourse is an appropriate option, yet not for 'getting satisfaction' or anything that would approach vengeance or retaliation. Enforcement rights are frequently the most reasonable inference in these cases, and the only basis for civil recourse that courts should find appropriate for lending their assistance.

Note also how remedies are not variable in the way we would otherwise predict from a conventional civil recourse perspective. A civil recourse approach is often taken to be superior to corrective justice theories of tort on the basis that holding someone accountable is consistent with the great remedial flexibility of tort law.[76] And, no doubt tort law does evince a wide range of remedial outcomes, suggesting an interest in providing more than one kind of compensation. If, however, remedial flexibility is support for an accountability-based picture of tort law, it should follow that the remedial standardization in contract law suggests a different picture. That picture—with its tendency towards expectation damages—is a better fit for enforcement rights than accountability.

Finally, a redress-centred approach can help explain contractual doctrine beyond those components that are linked to the validity of ordinary promises as such. Where a promisee has provided the contractually required form of consideration, the promise has been made binding through the promisee's conduct. Its terms have been met. This change in status does something more than simply activate a promise because it also has bearing on the set of rights held by the promisee.[77] It means that the promisee has an interest in performance that is different from the interest held by an ordinary, non-contractual promisee; the promise is legitimately enforceable at her option.[78] Consideration doctrine is a reflection of what it takes to justify enforceable promissory rights.[79] This too is an explanatory strength of the redress-centred approach, as many theories of contract stumble over the consideration doctrine.

[75] *See* Nathan B Oman, 'Consent to Retaliation: A Civil Recourse Theory of Contractual Liability' (2011) 96 Iowa L Rev 529.

[76] *See* Benjamin C Zipursky, 'Civil Recourse, Not Corrective Justice' (2003) 91 Geo LJ 695, 710–13.

[77] *See* Gold, 'Property Theory' (n. 49) 40.

[78] *See*, e.g. Gold, 'Consideration' (n. 37) 126.

[79] *See*, e.g. Gold, 'Property Theory' (n. 49) 62.

It still might be wondered whether this picture fits one of the most common types of contracts: the bilateral executory contract. Here, a contract is binding from the moment the agreement is formed, prior to the promisee providing any labour in the normal sense, and seemingly prior to the kinds of action described earlier as supporting a capture or an embodiment theory. Yet the ability to explain bilateral executory contracts is also a strength of a redress-centred picture of contract law.

Critics of promissory theories of contract—and by extension theories like this one—make their strongest case in the context of bilateral executory contracts.[80] With such contracts, there may be no reliance whatsoever, and the harm in non-enforcement appears slight if not non-existent.[81]

Charles Fried has provided a good example of such an agreement:

> I enter your antique shop on a quiet afternoon and I agree in writing to buy an expensive chest I see there, the price being about three times what you paid for it a short time ago. When I get home I repent of my decision, and within half an hour of my visit—before any other customer has come to your store—I telephone to say I no longer want the chest.[82]

A contract of this type might be enforced even if the breach occurred just moments after formation. Such contracts resemble liability on a mere promise.

The executory contract has thus raised a difficult challenge for various theories of contract. Executory contracts raise concerns that contract enforcement violates the harm principle. Unlike the situation where one party has performed their promised half of a bargain by, for example, delivering an object, the executory contract is seemingly binding prior to either party physically providing the promised thing. It is understandably debated whether consideration exists in these instances.[83] Furthermore, the longstanding legal enforceability of contractual promises cannot be used to show that there is adequate consideration in cases of executory contracts. Since the whole point is to figure out if such contracts *ought* to be

[80] *See* PS Atiyah, *The Rise and Fall of Freedom of Contract* (OUP 1979) 4 ('The protection of mere expectations cannot (it is suggested) rank equally with the protection of restitution interests . . . or reliance interests . . . . A person whose expectations are disappointed, but who suffers no pecuniary or other loss from the failure to perform a promise, has surely a relatively weak claim for complaint or redress.').

[81] In addition, as Joseph Raz notes, many promises that are relied upon would be considered binding prior to the existence of the reliance. *See* Joseph Raz, 'Promises in Morality and Law' (1982) 95 Harv L Rev 916, 924 (book review).

[82] *See* Fried, *Contract as Promise* (n. 2) 18.

[83] *See*, e.g. PS Atiyah, *Essays on Contract* (OUP 1986) 28.

enforceable in the first place, the legal enforceability of a promise is unavailable as a supporting premise.[84]

In fact, executory contracts can be consistent with the doctrine of consideration without falling into circular reasoning. Yet this challenge is an important one. To the extent the binding force of an agreement is to be explained without the invocation of pre-existing legal conventions, the promise itself must merit treatment as consideration. An explanation of how this can occur was suggested over a century ago by James Barr Ames. Ames noted that there is 'a difference between the act of a party and legal result of his act'.[85] A promise is sufficient as an act—a change of position—separate and apart from its legal consequences (the promise has substantial moral consequences that are also recognizable to the parties). Viewing promises as consideration is thus consistent with the theory suggested in this book. Although the obligatory force of a mere promise is different from the force of a legally enforceable contract term, it is still a type of obligation and, more importantly, it represents a change of position for the promisee. Promises create moral duties of performance and as such can be a type of consideration, and, importantly for present purposes, their provision in this context can be sufficient for just property acquisition.

In turn, this account suggests how a theory based on principles of just property acquisition can gain purchase in the executory contract setting. Each party's promise acts upon the other party's promise by meeting its conditions, thus giving it promissory effect. Mutual promises can thus result in a transfer of property interests, akin to the transfer that occurs in cases where the promisee has physically accomplished his half of an agreement.[86] Granted, in such cases we are at the outer boundaries of the principles of just property acquisition described above, but we are still within those boundaries.

[84] *See* Peter Benson, 'The Unity of Contract Law' in Peter Benson, (ed.), *The Theory of Contract Law* (CUP 2001) 118, 160 n. 52 (describing the vicious circle that arises if the promise is required to be legally binding in order to count as consideration); cf. Smith, *Contract Theory* (n. 45) 181 ('The usual explanation given by those who defend the promissory model is that a contract in which each party agrees to do something for the other party is a pair of conditional promises. . . . The difficulty with this suggestion is that if each promise is conditional on the other, neither party is under an obligation to do anything.').

[85] *See* James B Ames, 'Two Theories of Consideration' (1899) 13 Harv L Rev 29, 32.

[86] Several commenters have suggested that the theory described here could also extend to promises that are merely conditioned on acceptance, as long as the promisee accepts the promise. However, others question whether acceptance alone can enable an act of appropriation by the promisee. *See* Benson, 'The Unity of Contract Law' (n. 84) 156 ('The consideration would consist here simply in the promisee's evaluation of and reaction to the promise; it represents nothing more than the effect which the promise, with its anticipated benefit, has upon the promisee.'). The difficulty is that promises may require acceptance in order to be morally obligatory. *See* Fried, *Contract as Promise* (n. 2) 43 (discussing the importance of acceptance to promising). I suspect there is an arbitrary cut-off point here (regarding what it takes to acquire a promised performance), but I also suspect that arbitrary dividing lines may be inevitable with principles of just property acquisition.

For transfers of physical property, the process is simpler. The transferor can place the object in the transferee's possession and abandon his own interest. This ease of transfer reflects the ability of the transferee to take possession of a physical object.[87] For example, one can do more than promise to transfer a hat to another person, one can physically hand the hat over. This does not work for future actions, which by their nature do not exist at the time of promising. Absent consideration (or provisions of positive law), a promisee cannot ordinarily attain an interest in another person's future actions in the same manner that he can attain an interest in a physical thing.[88] That is to say, the interest is not the right kind to ordinarily support private enforcement rights. But in cases where consideration is provided—*even in the form of a promise*—the promisee acquires an interest sufficient to support rights of redress.

Admittedly, there is a potential irony in suggesting that an account of the consideration doctrine is an explanatory strength, as incorporating the consideration doctrine into a theory of contracts could also be seen as a weakness. For example, Seana Shiffrin contends that consideration doctrine is in tension with promissory morality.[89] And perhaps such normative concerns suggest an interpretive concern. Perhaps, but they need not. We should not assume that whatever explanation suggests the most moral version of contract law will be the best explanation of the contract law we have. When interpreting a private law field, a vital consideration is doctrinal fit and, in the United States and other common law countries, the consideration doctrine is unquestionably a part of the doctrinal landscape. Even so, if a theorist is concerned that the consideration doctrine is a mismatch for promissory morality, the account offered here suggests a different possibility.

If the redress-centred account is correct, then promissory theorists who are troubled by the consideration doctrine are focusing on the wrong aspect of promissory morality. From the right holder's side of the picture, promissory morality grounds a promisee's standing to complain about a breach, her standing to demand rectifying conduct, and her standing to blame the wrongdoer. Promissory morality does not ground an enforcement right except under limited circumstances (or, if one maps the conceptual landscape of promising

[87] Cf. Peter Benson, 'The Idea of a Public Basis of Justification for Contract' (1995) 33 Osgoode Hall LJ 273, 296 ('For there to be a completed gift or exchange, something more is required than just the transferor's act of alienation. The transferee must also take possession of the transferred object for there to be acquisition.'). *See also* Benson, 'Unity of Contract Law' (n. 84) 129 (noting distinctions between physical transfers and contracts).

[88] Promissory estoppel represents a special case (and a different kind of claim); I would not rule out the possibility that rights of redress are also justified in some estoppel settings.

[89] *See* Shiffrin, 'The Divergence of Contract' (n. 25) 709–10. *See also* Fried, *Contract as Promise* (n. 2) 29–39 (questioning the coherence of the doctrine).

more narrowly, promissory morality does not ground an enforcement right, but is consistent with enforcement rights when additional moral principles come into play). Rather than a divergence between contract law and promissory morality, the consideration doctrine becomes an extension of promissory morality or at least sensitive to the way a promisee's moral rights are structured in a given context.

Then again, a theory that views the consideration doctrine as an integral part of contract law is inevitably subject to the following objection: civil law jurisdictions do not have a consideration doctrine. True, they do not. And civil law jurisdictions do not have defective contract law, nor are they necessarily mistaken to offer the kind of contract law that they provide. Legal systems on either side of this divide can still lay claim to a mainstream and reasonable version of contract law. On the other hand, this jurisdictional variation does not represent a genuine challenge to the idea that rights of redress are integral to contract law in an important sense. The consideration doctrine may be integral to norms of contract law that build on norms of interpersonal morality—in the manner of the common law—even if other contract law finds its basis for enforcement in a different place.[90]

There is an additional explanatory benefit to note, but it will only gradually become visible during the course of this book. Explaining the features of contract law in this way enables us to find continuities that extend through other private law spheres. The insights that a redress-centred approach offers for contract law are available in other parts of private law, such as fiduciary law. Questions of when private parties should be able to enforce their rights appear and reappear in various settings, with interesting new variations depending on context. In short, the type of analysis we engage in when we seek to distinguish enforceable promises from ordinary promises is a template for the analysis of other private law fields—in each case, we will want to figure out whether the moral rights at issue are such that moral enforcement rights will also be appropriate.

Indeed, we will want to figure out the contours of these moral enforcement rights as well. In the fiduciary setting, for example, we will want to know what it is about a beneficiary's claims that makes her legitimately able to insist not only on compensation for losses, but also on disgorgement of profits from a conflicted fiduciary. If, as Paul Miller suggests, beneficiaries have an ownership-like interest in their fiduciary's exercise of fiduciary power, we can start to see how redress will be appropriate in this field as well, and even why this type

[90] Cf. n. 54.

of redress will include disgorgement of profits as a standard remedy.[91] There is reason to think that a beneficiary has the right kind of property-like relationship to some of her rights, and in turn that those rights have the right content, to justify enforcement in this manner. The rights of redress in contract law represent one instance of a much broader phenomenon that runs throughout the private law; in this way, rights of redress offer new perspectives on multiple private law fields.

***

The above analysis suggests how rights of redress and the contexts in which they are legitimate can help to explain fields like contract law. While the range of interpretive insights is expansive, there is also cause for explanatory modesty; we should notice that certain components of private law doctrine do not have the right features to fit this model. That will be a topic for Chapter 5. What contract law demonstrates, however, is that moral enforcement rights have explanatory purchase on a set of problems that are hard to explain simply by focusing on the moral standing to make demands or to complain about a wrong. Rights of redress and their proper scope enable us to differentiate ordinary promises from contracts, to explain the expectation remedy and the consideration doctrine, and to avoid concerns that contract law is in serious conflict with promissory morality. A focus on moral enforcement rights helps make sense of contract law's legal enforcement rights, and in doing so it shows how the justice in redress is well-established in private law.

[91] *See* Paul B Miller, Justifying Fiduciary Remedies (2013) 63 U Toronto LJ 570.

5

Tort Law and Redress

I. Introduction

We have focused thus far on examples from the law of contracts, with some discussion of fiduciary relationships and unjust enrichment. I will now turn to the law of torts. In some cases, redressive justice is a clear match for tort law, particularly in settings involving the return of property or its equivalent. The remedy for conversion is readily explained in redress terms. As we will see, rights of redress can also explain compensatory remedies for torts in which people sustain serious and, in some respects irreversible, injuries. The analysis in these settings is more complex, but again allocation back accounts for the legal doctrine. That said, there are also difficult areas, most notably injunctive relief, nominal damages, and punitive damages. Not everything in tort law involves allocation back and it is best for theorists to recognize this fact. This chapter will elaborate on these problematic contexts, and indicate their significance for redressive justice as a core principle of private law.

This chapter will begin with a discussion of remedial fit, starting with make-whole remedies. There are areas of tort law for which redressive justice is not only a good fit, but a compelling explanation of legal doctrine. Tort law's make-whole remedies are readily explained in these terms, even in those cases where it is impossible to ever fully compensate a victim for her loss. Other remedial features do not easily match an allocation back structure, and these features are properly explained by different approaches. I will develop the view that at least some remedies—such as punitive damages—are central components of tort law but are difficult to account for in redress terms. The chapter will then assess the significance of these divergent remedies.

Contrary to many leading private law theories, I will suggest that a pluralist explanatory approach is appropriate. In doing so, I will also offer a distinctive perspective on the interpretive criteria for a successful private law theory. A coherence criterion should be more modest than it is usually thought to be, and this premise leaves room for pluralist explanations of private law fields. On the other hand, although this chapter will endorse pluralism, a pluralist approach need not involve an ad hoc balancing of private law goals. As will be developed,

The Right of Redress. Andrew S. Gold, Oxford University Press (2020). © Andrew S. Gold.
DOI: 10.1093/oso/9780198814405.001.0001

several distinctive private law principles can co-exist within tort law, operating in independent spheres. On the view developed here, redressive justice is a central feature of tort law, but it is a feature that comfortably shares space with other private law aims.

II. The Remedial Fit Question in Make-whole Settings

A. Torts with proprietary remedies

Let's begin with the most clear-cut cases. The most easily recognized applications of redressive justice involve a claim to something that belongs to the plaintiff, or to its equivalent in value. As a mode of justice concerned with allocation back, redressive justice readily accounts for the enforcement of a contract, the return of an unjust enrichment, or the disgorgement of profits by a fiduciary. These are cases that involve proprietary or property-like remedies, in which something that belongs to an individual is returned to her, or the next best thing. As developed in Chapter 4, in these contexts allocation back typically applies in a straightforward manner: the plaintiff is seeking something that she effectively owns, whether the remedy calls for return of an object, for losses to be undone, for performance to be provided, or for profits to be disgorged.

For similar reasons, property-related torts can often be explained within a redressive justice rubric. In the case of a conversion, the redressive justice picture is a particularly good fit. Suppose, for example, that Jack wrongfully converts Jane's book. Jane has a property interest in the converted object, which is now in the possession of the wrongdoer. Where Jane formerly held a primary right to retain the converted object without interference, she now possesses a secondary, remedial right to the object's return. Barring the return of the book (say it was sold and is no longer recoverable), she has a remedial right to the book's value. Indeed, she possesses an enforcement right as well. She not only has a right to allocation back, she can legitimately force an allocation back.[1]

This remedial fit is an important strength of a redressive justice rubric. Conversion is a core example of a broader category of torts—strict liability torts. As Gregory Keating has recently emphasized, strict liability torts are a central component of tort law and it is important for a tort theory to be able to

[1] The fit between conversion cases and allocation back is recognized even by scholars who otherwise critique allocation back accounts. *See*, e.g. Scott Hershovitz, 'Tort as a Substitute for Revenge' in John Oberdiek, (ed.), *Philosophical Foundations of Tort Law* (OUP 2014) 86, 90.

explain them.[2] As he also notes, strict liability torts come in two categories that pose conceptual challenges: harm-based liabilities that are imposed on justified conduct; and rights-based liabilities that are imposed on innocent conduct.[3] Both categories can be challenging for corrective justice approaches, at least if corrective justice is conceptually linked to reparative duties that arise following a wrong.[4] Yet these are not insurmountable obstacles, depending on how we define wrongs (and on some views wrongs may be justified). As Keating and others have shown, there are ways to square innocent conversions with the existence of a wrong.[5]

Such innocent conversion cases can also be squared with the civil recourse picture, although the ease of doing so will depend on the type of civil recourse at issue. Civil recourse theory seeks to explain private rights of action in light of the principle that a wronged party should be able to act against the party that wronged her, through the state. While civil recourse is a capacious enough category to cover the enforcement of rights,[6] in many applications civil recourse involves holding someone accountable. The latter version of civil recourse is problematic in this setting. If civil recourse is about holding someone accountable, or about 'getting satisfaction', what it takes to hold that person accountable or to get satisfaction will often vary with context.[7] Yet, in the case of a conversion, damages characteristically reflect the value of the converted object. This makes perfect sense if the aim is to make the victim whole by reversing the effects of a transaction, but does not readily track norms of accountability. Why should it be the case that precisely this amount of damages will equal accountability, and nothing more? Why, for that matter, would it make sense to hold an innocent party accountable?

[2] *See* Gregory Keating, 'Strict Liability Torts' in John Oberdiek, (ed.), *Philosophical Foundations of Tort Law* (OUP 2014) 294–5.

[3] *See* ibid. 295.

[4] *See* ibid. 293 ('Moral theorists of torts are generally committed to the idea that torts are wrongs. Moral conceptions of torts, therefore, take it as fixed that there are no justified torts.'). It is not clear that a justified wrong is a contradiction in terms, however. *See* John CP Goldberg, 'Inexcusable Wrongs' (2015) 103 Cal L Rev 467, 471 ('To plead a *justification* is to claim that one's conduct was permissible, all things considered, even though it meets the definition of a wrong.').

[5] For recent analysis of strict liability and its relation to duties, see John Gardner, 'Some Rule of Law Anxieties about Strict Liability in Private Law' in Lisa M Austin & Dennis Klimchuk, (eds), *Private Law and the Rule of Law* (OUP 2014); Stephen A Smith, 'Strict Duties and the Rule of Law' in Lisa M Austin & Dennis Klimchuk, (eds), *Private Law and the Rule of Law* (OUP 2014). One can also find wrongfulness in a failure to return something even if it was not wrongfully acquired. *See* John Gardner, 'What Is Tort Law For? Part 1: The Place of Corrective Justice' (2011) 30 L & Phil 1, 23.

[6] For example, Zipursky has endorsed the view that civil recourse can involve enforcement rights in the contract setting. *See* Benjamin C Zipursky, 'Civil Recourse and the Plurality of Wrongs: Why Torts are Different' [2014] New Zealand L Rev 145, 158.

[7] Cf. Benjamin C Zipursky, 'Civil Recourse, Not Corrective Justice' (2003) 91 Geo LJ 695, 710–13.

In conversion settings, it is entirely possible that the converting party was completely lacking in harmful intent. The defendant may not even have been careless. If the aim is for plaintiffs to have a means to 'get satisfaction' (an aim which some, though not all, forms of civil recourse involve), there is something counterintuitive about civil recourse. It is prima facie odd to apply this notion here, without at least varying the quantity of damages to reflect the fact that some defendants are good faith actors who exercised due care. And, just as in the contract setting a plaintiff may be much more concerned with having a promise kept than she is with holding the wrongdoer accountable, so too in the conversion setting a plaintiff may be much more concerned with having the property (or its value) returned than she is with getting satisfaction. Recourse as a way to hold accountable, to get even, or to get satisfaction is a questionable way to explain conversion law.

As noted, the allocation back picture works well in explaining conversion torts. From a redressive justice perspective, it is also unnecessary to find a wrong as a starting point (although if these cases do implicate wrongs, that understanding has the advantage of fitting the general view that tort law is a law of wrongs). As with unjust enrichment cases, the important question is simply the question of whether the right holder can legitimately reverse the transaction at issue. If the transaction was wrongful, so be it. But if the defendant's conduct was innocent, and if we are unable to accept the idea that innocent conduct can result in a wrong, it is still entirely possible that the right holder can legitimately insist on the return of her property or its equivalent. From a redressive justice perspective, the key conceptual and normative inquiry concerns the enforceability of a plaintiff's right to the property at issue, or the next best thing.

As an allocation back account, the redressive justice approach thus has significant explanatory power. It explains the standard make-whole remedy, without requiring us to be troubled by the defendant's potential innocence. There is, however, an objection that now emerges: the objection is that allocation back *only* works well in this type of case. Scott Hershovitz has made a claim roughly along these lines, with an emphasis on cases involving personal injury. Accordingly, I will turn next to negligence law. Negligence law includes cases of damage to property that can readily be undone; in some cases the resemblance to torts like conversion is notable. Yet negligence law also includes cases of serious bodily injury that can never fully be reversed. These latter cases present an important challenge for the allocation back picture.

B. Torts and accident law

For theories of tort law, negligence law typically takes pride of place.[8] If allocation back did not fit in this setting, this might call into question the plausibility of an allocation back account. To be sure, there are negligent wrongs that are easily addressed by the theory. Sometimes, negligently caused harms are largely fixable; they can effectively be undone, as if the tort had not occurred. A torn piece of clothing, for example, might be repaired with no sign of the harm it suffered. A broken toy can be glued together. Frequently, however, negligent wrongdoing results in destruction of property, or injuries to people, such that an appropriate remedy is no longer going to resemble the return of property or a clear equivalent. There is a continuum in these cases, with some remedies that resemble a full-fledged reversal of a transaction, and other remedies that are further afield. I will begin with the simpler cases, and then work towards more difficult examples.

Suppose we start with negligent damage to property. In some cases, allocation back will enable the damaged property to be fixed so that it is 'like new'. For example, a scratched car can be repainted, perhaps in a way so that no one could tell the difference. Allocation back is not hard to conceptualize in this type of situation. True, it will always be the case that a wrong occurred—for something to be like new is not the same as it actually being new.[9] Yet in many contexts we are able to get a very close approximation to the undoing of a wrongful transaction. This is a comparatively easy type of case. To make the case more difficult, assume that the property at issue cannot be restored to its original state. For example, consider negligence that causes loss of property through its destruction.

For these purposes, we can begin with an example used by Arthur Ripstein. Suppose that you possess a vase that I negligently destroy.[10] For Ripstein, the original rights and duties with respect to the vase stay in place; they remain in existence after the negligent wrong has occurred.[11] Unlike Ripstein's account, the redressive justice account does not say that you get a remedy because you

[8] Some would suggest that accident law is overly emphasized in tort theory. Cf. John CP Goldberg & Benjamin C Zipursky, 'Torts as Wrongs' (2010) 88 Tex L Rev 917, 917 (suggesting an overemphasis on accident law in the teaching and theorizing of torts). This may well be right, but for present purposes it is valuable to show that redressive justice can fit negligence cases.

[9] *See* Gardner, 'What Is Tort Law For?' (n. 5) 35–7 (discussing the remainder after a wrongful transaction has been reversed to the extent possible). As Gardner notes, there is always cause for regret if one has committed a wrong, even if the wrong is corrected.

[10] *See* Arthur Ripstein, 'As If It Had Never Happened' (2007) 48 Wm & Mary L Rev 1957, 1980.

[11] *See* ibid.

still have a right to the original vase (a distinction that will be discussed further in section III.A). The original obligation to leave the vase unharmed can no longer be complied with, as the vase is now shattered. Instead, a secondary remedial obligation has taken its place. Corresponding to this secondary obligation is a secondary remedial right. In this case, the wronged party also holds a right to enforce this remedial right and it is the enforcement right that is crucial on the redressive justice picture.

Under the present account, the key feature with which the law is concerned is the right holder's right to undo the wrongful transaction. In ordering compensatory damages, the court acts on behalf of the right holder in allocating back, and this action is determined, indirectly, by the right holder's choice to pursue the claim.[12] Although it is no longer possible for the right holder (or the court) to return the vase to its original, pristine condition, it is nonetheless possible for the right holder to seek the next best thing—to wit, the value of the vase. This is not to say that the value of the vase is truly equivalent to an un-smashed vase; the vase may have had sentimental value, or it may be one of a kind. Likewise, the fact that a negligent wrong occurred in the first place has not been erased. Even so, compensatory damages function as a 'next best thing' remedy, returning us to a state as close as reasonably feasible to the pre-wrong state of affairs.

Notice that on this account the remedy is not designed to hold the negligent party accountable or to get satisfaction. Instead, the aim is to get the right holder back to the pre-wrong state to the extent that is an option. If possible, the vase would be returned in its original condition. Since it cannot be, its value is provided instead. If getting satisfaction were the aim here, we might expect the damages award to regularly exceed the value of the vase in cases of great negligence, or to commonly fall under that value in cases of very slight negligence. Similarly, if the aim were to 'get even', we would expect more significant variation in the available damages awards than we actually see. What the law ordinarily appears to be doing, instead, is trying to make the plaintiff whole to the extent possible. The legal remedy is an attempt at undoing the wrongful transaction.[13]

[12] While the court acts on behalf of the successful litigant in ordering damages, this may also be understood as a component of the court's obligation to advance more abstract, justice-related purposes. For development of the latter view in fiduciary terms, see Paul B Miller & Andrew S Gold, 'Fiduciary Governance' (2015) 57 Wm & Mary L Rev 513.

[13] While rejecting the allocation back account, Goldberg and Zipursky recognize that, as a default, the make-whole remedy sets an outer boundary for compensation in cases of non-willful wrongs. *See* Goldberg & Zipursky, 'Torts as Wrongs' (n. 8) 947. My point is that this outer boundary makes sense on an allocation back picture, but is harder to account for when we have a focus on getting satisfaction.

C. The problem of incomplete reversals

Yet critics of allocation back theories can point to more difficult fact patterns. For example, Scott Hershovitz has argued that allocation back accounts are well suited to explain property-related torts, but poorly suited to explain a variety of other tort scenarios. Consider Hershovitz's illustration:

> Tom steals Jerry's ball. What does Tom owe Jerry? His ball is an obvious answer. But what if Tom breaks Jerry's leg? Jerry still has his leg, so it can't be allocated back. If Tom could unbreak Jerry's leg, that would seem in order, and we might think of it as an allocating back of sorts. Healing Jerry's leg restores what he started with. But already we are one step removed from an allocation of a good back from one person to another. Repair is not the same as return.[14]

As this example suggests, allocation back requires further analysis when extended to personal injuries.

An initial concern raised here involves the type of transaction involved. The classic case of corrective justice governs a wrongdoer's return of a wrongful gain to the victim of a corresponding loss. Not all cases look like this. There is a well-recognized difference between cases in which a wrongdoer has acquired a gain at the victim's expense, and cases in which a wrongdoer has simply damaged a victim. As Aristotle noted, there are situations in which corrective justice addresses losses that do not literally correspond to another party's gain.[15] It is, arguably, a fiction to claim that a wrongdoer gains something when she damages the interests of another.[16] Still, these fact patterns are not overly difficult for allocation back theories to address. Allocation back involves the reversal of transactions. In some cases, a transaction has inflicted damages on someone with no corresponding benefit to the party who caused the injury. The transaction between these two parties is nevertheless capable of being reversed—to the extent feasible—when a wrongdoer is forced to pay damages that undo costs imposed by a wrongful injury that she caused. A wrongful transaction is

[14] Scott Hershovitz, 'Corrective Justice for Civil Recourse Theorists' (2011) 39 Fla St U L Rev 107, 110.

[15] *See* Aristotle, 'Nicomachean Ethics' in Jonathan Barnes, (ed.), *2 The Complete Works of Aristotle* (Princeton University Press, 1984) 1132a10-13 ('For the term "gain" is applied generally to such cases, even if it be not a term appropriate to certain cases, e.g., to the person who inflicts a wound—and "loss" to the sufferer; at all events when the suffering has been estimated, the one is called loss and the other gain.'). For a helpful analysis of this fact pattern in allocation back terms, see John Gardner, 'Corrective Justice, Corrected' (2012) Diritto e questioni pubbliche 14, 29–30.

[16] But cf. Ernest J Weinrib, 'The Gains and Losses of Corrective Justice' (1994) 44 Duke LJ 227 (describing a normative gain in such cases).

in an important sense being undone when the wrongdoer engages in actions that reverse the effects of her earlier conduct.

The challenging part of Hershovitz's argument is not that we can't have allocation back where there is no gain to be returned to a tort victim. Instead, it is that the injury at issue is often of a type that cannot be completely fixed by payment of money. Serious physical injuries may result in chronic pain and other life changes that are not fully resolved by a damages award. Fortunately, responses are available. First, we need to recognize that a full allocation back is an aspiration.[17] The core idea in seeking the 'next best thing' is to get as close as one can to undoing a transaction, given the limitations of legal institutions, the possibility of intervening moral concerns, and the inability to turn back the clock. In some cases, allocation back might be exorbitantly expensive, or it might involve the creation of new harms that may be worse than the original injury. Even then, a partial allocation back can still be measured against the goal of complete reversal of a wrongful transaction.

Second, any amount of allocation back is still an allocation back. As Gardner describes the setting of an allocation back, '[s]omething has already shifted between the two parties',[18] and allocation back involves a reversal of this prior shifting of whatever that something is. One implication of this idea is that there is a distinctive allocative event whenever any quantum of this initial shifting is reversed. We can readily see this in cases involving conversions. If A wrongly converts five apples from B, the return of two of those apples would still be an allocation back. Suppose that A has lost the remaining apples and has no other possessions. It is still allocation back when the two apples are returned, even if the return of just those two apples is the only feasible remedy. A similar point obtains in cases where there have only been losses suffered and the wrongdoer has not obtained any corresponding gains.

Unsurprisingly, corrective justice theorists are aware that the complete reversal of a transaction can be difficult or impossible. Ernest Weinrib argues that tort law 'places the defendant under the obligation to restore the plaintiff, *so far as possible*, to the position the plaintiff would have been in had the wrong not been committed'.[19] Gardner argues that '[c]orrective justice . . . is rendered rational, all else being equal . . . by the residual possibility of restoring things, *at*

[17] Cf. Robert Stevens, *Torts and Rights* (OUP 2007) 59 ('Where the defendant is required to make good the claimant's consequential loss . . . this is the law's attempting to reach the nearest approximation of the wrong not having occurred.').

[18] *See* Gardner, 'What Is Tort Law For?' (n. 5) 9.

[19] *See* Ernest J Weinrib, *The Idea of Private Law* (HUP 1995) 135. *See also* Arthur Ripstein, *Private Wrongs* (HUP 2016) 13 ('Sometimes the remedy will be a near equivalent; in many others it will be deficient, but the best that can be done.').

least in some measure, to where they would have been had one not occasioned their loss'.[20] These explicit qualifiers are important recognitions that corrective justice does not completely reverse the effects of a wrong. No one, in other words, is actually claiming that wrongful transactions can be fully reversed in all cases (or even in any cases).

Yet Hershovitz contends that these qualifiers are insufficient, given the frequent inadequacy of the legal response to a wrong. As he argues: 'in an awful lot of cases, we can't do anything like put the plaintiff in the position she would have been in had the wrong not been committed, so if we are doing that insofar as possible, we are doing it not at all'.[21] His point about the degree of deficiency rings true. There are numerous examples in which we cannot come close to putting someone back in the position she would have been in had the wrong not been committed. Post-defamation, we may not be able to restore someone's reputation. Money damages will not be adequate after a rape, and negligence that results in death is impossible to undo in any substantial way. Some torts result in losses that the law cannot even come close to fully reversing.

While this inadequacy of remedies claim is clearly correct, there is still a flaw in Hershovitz's argument. The inadequacy of an allocation back does not mean that the idea of allocation back is inapplicable to the fact pattern. To conclude that we cannot put the plaintiff back in the position she would have been in but for the wrong she suffered is quite different from concluding that we are not allocating back at all. Moreover, if we accept the idea that norms of justice are norms that govern allocations, then the norms that govern a partial reversal of a transaction are still norms of justice.

Allocations back can thus qualify as a form of justice even if they are not the justice we would hope for, all things considered. It can also make sense to say that such allocations are truly allocations back even when they fall short of their aim of making someone whole. In this regard, an allocation back conception is different from some other proposed understandings of justice between individuals. For example, Hershovitz's own account of corrective justice suggests it involves a form of 'getting even'.[22] Suppose that we use this account as a template. Notice that, on a 'getting even' view of corrective justice, there will be many cases in which there is no way to ever be precisely 'even'. Does one ever 'get even' in a case where negligence resulted in death? Perhaps we can still

[20] Gardner, 'What Is Tort Law For?' (n. 5) 37 (emphasis added).
[21] Hershovitz, 'Corrective Justice' (n. 14) 116.
[22] Ibid. 118 (describing a tradition of thinking about corrective justice that involves getting even).

talk of 'getting even' in such cases despite the inability to ever fully do so. One might nevertheless think that if the plaintiff has not become *fully* 'even', then the plaintiff simply hasn't 'gotten even', full stop.

In contrast, allocation back need not face this concern. We can readily talk of allocation back despite an inability to ever completely undo a transaction. Even a tiny bit of allocation back is still allocation back. Unlike 'getting even'—which may imply that one needs to actually be 'even' after the responsive conduct occurs—the notion of allocation back does not imply that someone is fully made whole. To make this concrete, imagine a very poor tortfeasor who negligently breaks his victim's leg and cannot afford to pay full compensation. If the only feasible compensation after this wrongful injury is the defendant's payment of one quarter of the medical bills, this would still be an allocation back—it would be a partial undoing of the wrongful transaction. It would also still be a form of justice, albeit a disappointing one. The case might be different if an allocation back conception meant that an individual must successfully be made whole, but that is not something that this conception requires.

III. Injunctions, Nominal Damages, and Punitive Damages

Partial allocations back are still allocations back—and they can still qualify as redressive justice. Not every tort law remedy, however, is explicable in these terms. Some remedies apply ex ante and cannot be described as allocations back under any plausible explanation. The basic justification for these ex ante remedies may be very closely tied to redressive justice concerns, but they are not examples of redressive justice. Other remedies, such as nominal damages, are difficult to describe as a form of allocation back (although the task is not impossible). Yet other remedies, such as punitive damages, are a very poor fit. In general, the idea of punishing someone is not about reversing transactions by allocating back.

Faced with remedies that are at best an imperfect match for a given unifying theory, private law theorists have several potential responses. One is to carve out the offending area of law, and suggest that it is not truly a component of the subject matter under discussion. Another possibility is to downplay its importance. I do not think either approach is viable here. Punitive damages, for example, are definitely a part of tort law, and in the United States they are definitely a core part. This book will instead develop a third possibility: private law advances multiple values, and private law remedies constitute several distinct types of justice. Redressive justice is central to private law—and private law cannot be adequately understood without understanding its role—but it is not the only type of justice that private law incorporates.

I will begin with a discussion of the remedies at issue and will then turn in the next section to an analysis of pluralism as a response.

A. Ex ante injunctive relief

Injunctive relief presents a distinctive challenge. Here, a remedy is awarded *prior* to a tortious wrong occurring, which raises the natural question of how the remedy counts as corrective, or, for present purposes, how the remedy counts as an allocation *back*. In response, some corrective justice theorists attempt to unify ex post and ex ante remedies under a single theory. One might seek a solution along these lines, yet as we will see, such solutions are problematic. The alternative is to recognize that injunctive relief involves a different type of justice from corrective justice, redressive justice, or other ex post approaches. I will begin with the first approach and then turn to the second.

An influential account that brings injunctive relief within the fold is to say that the parties' secondary, remedial rights and duties are simply transformed versions of their primary rights and duties. One of the most prominent supporters of this thesis is Ernest Weinrib. As Weinrib describes his position:

> Suppose that the defendant has tortiously destroyed an object belonging to the plaintiff. Prior to the tortious act, the defendant was under a duty of care with respect to the object... The defendant's breach of this duty destroyed the object as a physical entity, but it did not destroy the plaintiff's right as a normative entitlement.[23]

For Weinrib, the idea that the plaintiff's right continues to exist is significant. It provides a basis for remedies in corrective justice:

> Even after the object's destruction the plaintiff is linked to the defendant through a right that pertains to the object as an undamaged thing, so that the right now takes the form of an entitlement to the cost of replacing it. . . .

[23] *See* Ernest J Weinrib, 'Two Conceptions of Remedies' in Charles Rickett, (ed.), *Justifying Private Law Remedies* (2008) 3, 12.

> the right remains intact as the normative marker of the relationship between them with respect to that object.[24]

This type of theory has been called the 'unity approach' to private law remedies, as it unifies primary and secondary rights and duties.[25]

The unity approach has the advantage of tying legal remedies to a plaintiff's pre-wrong status. It can thus account for the measurement of certain damages awards, and more generally for the make-whole concept that governs many private law remedies. It also has bearing on the ex ante remedies that courts sometimes provide. Unsurprisingly, given the unity approach, Weinrib claims that injunctive relief *is* corrective justice.[26] The claim follows naturally from the view that ex post remedies involve transformed versions of primary duties: when a court enforces a remedial duty after a wrong, it is effectively doing the same thing that it does when it enforces a primary duty through injunctive relief prior to a wrong occurring.

One problem is that it is very hard to see *ex ante* injunctive relief as corrective.[27] Corrective justice presumably corrects things that have already happened.[28] Under the unity approach, moreover, corrective justice may even become a redundant category. Corrective justice norms may become unnecessary because there are already other norms that support judicial remedies. As Gardner suggests:

[24] *See* ibid. Arthur Ripstein's view of corrective justice takes a similar perspective, one in which primary rights survive their violation. As he puts it:

> [I]f I break your vase, all you have are shards. But you have a right to the intact vase. Only deeds to which you are a party can change your private rights; a deed of which you are simply the victim cannot. The deed is a datable event in the world, but one that is entirely without normative significance.

See Arthur Ripstein, 'As If It Had Never Happened' (2007) 48 Wm & Mary L Rev 1957, 1980. For further elaboration, see Ripstein, *Private Wrongs* (n. 19) ch. 8.

[25] Credit for this phrase goes to Zoe Sinel, 'Concerns about Corrective Justice' (2013) 26 Can JL & Juris 137, 143 (describing the unity approach to private law remedies).

[26] *See* Weinrib, *Idea of Private Law* (n. 19) 144 n. 41.

[27] Cf. Andrew S Gold, 'A Moral Rights Theory of Private Law' (2015) 52 Wm & Mary L Rev 1873, 1915 ('Injunctions are not a measure of corrective justice when they are designed to prevent a wrong that has not yet happened.'); Zipursky, 'Civil Recourse' (n. 7) 713 (noting that injunctive relief cases 'are not cases of defendants taking responsibility for the harm they have caused').

[28] Some suggest that a similar problem arises with ex post fact patterns. For example, as Stephen Smith argues:

> [I]t . . . seems odd to describe the idea that duties to pay damages are transformed primary duties as grounded in corrective justice. Damages, in this view, have little to do with correcting—they are just the original duty in a new form—and even less to do with reversing gains and losses and, more generally, with restoring equality.

See Stephen A Smith, 'Why Courts Make Orders (And What This Tells Us About Damages)' (2011) 64 Current Legal Problems 51, 82.

> [I]f it were true that the so-called secondary obligation is always the same obligation as the primary one, then there would be no norms of corrective justice. We would have no need of them. The norm creating the primary obligation would be the only moral norm we would need; the rest of the work would be done by logic (entailment).[29]

In other words, the unity approach provides a basis for corrective outcomes (grounded in the legitimacy of the parties' primary rights and duties), and it allows us to incorporate injunctive relief, but it does so in a manner that removes the need for corrective justice as a separate category. It should be enough on the unity approach to say that we have norms of enforcing primary rights and duties.[30]

Proponents of the unity theory might reply that these differences in approach are a matter of terminology.[31] Different definitions of corrective justice lead to different implications. That said, grouping almost everything in private law together under one umbrella notion of corrective justice—ex ante and ex post, primary rights and secondary rights—can obscure more than it clarifies. Just as there is a benefit in distinguishing corrective justice from distributive justice (despite the possibility of defining all forms of justice as distributive),[32] there is a benefit in adopting terminology that clearly captures the different conceptual steps from wrong to private action to remedy, the potentially distinctive normative questions courts and litigants face ex ante and ex post, and the characteristic variations in legal rationale when these contexts change. When we say that a remedy is corrective justice prior to a wrong occurring—prior to there being anything to correct—it is arguable that more phenomena are hidden than illuminated.

29 Gardner, 'What Is Tort Law For?' (n. 5) 49. *See also* Sinel, 'Concerns About Corrective Justice' (n. 25) 145 (describing how corrective justice can be redundant under a given theory of Kantian right); Nathan B Oman, 'Why There Is No Duty to Pay Damages: Powers, Duties, and Private Law' (2011) 39 Fla St U L Rev 137, 158 n. 121 (suggesting that Weinrib's approach 'does not seem to require any notion of corrective justice').

30 There may be other difficulties. Some argue that Weinrib's account suffers from a circularity problem. *See* Hershovitz, 'Corrective Justice' (n. 14) 114 n. 25; John Gardner, 'The Purity and Priority of Private Law' (1996) 46 U Toronto LJ 459, 469–70. For present purposes, I will focus on the redundancy concern.

31 *See* Ernest J Weinrib, *Corrective Justice* (OUP 2012) 334–7 (suggesting that Gardner's and Weinrib's different views on this question stem from terminological differences). Cf. Sinel, 'Concerns About Corrective Justice' (n. 25) 147 (suggesting that '[w]hat Gardner means by corrective justice is very different from Weinrib's intended usage', and accordingly that Weinrib's account is not vulnerable to one of the critiques Gardner develops).

32 *See* Gardner, 'What Is Tort Law For?' (n. 5) 9 (discussing the value in distinguishing corrective from distributive justice).

Regardless, as an allocation back theory, the redressive justice account is not able to make use of the unity approach. Taken as an ex post response to a transaction that merits undoing, redressive justice cannot be a fit for ex ante injunctive relief. Injunctive relief is hardly in tension with redressive justice, however. To the contrary, it fits a picture in which private law is concerned with enforcement rights—both ex ante and ex post.[33] It is quite coherent for private law to allow individuals to enforce their rights such that a wrong is prevented and to also allow individuals to enforce their rights such that a wrong is undone or alleviated to the extent feasible. On the allocation back picture, the ex ante and ex post phenomena are different, but the reasons that support legal enforcement ex ante and ex post may be the same.

What injunctive relief actually represents is preventive justice. Preventive justice is a pre-wrong counterpart to ex post allocation back norms. It is perhaps overlooked in tort law settings because it is so easy to think of tort law in ex post terms. For example, Jeff McMahan argues: 'While preventive justice is concerned with the *ex ante* redistribution of harm in accordance with liability, *corrective justice*, which is the goal of the law of torts, is concerned with the ex post redistribution of harm, or loss.'[34] McMahan is right to recognize that these types of justice are different. He is wrong to suggest that tort law is only concerned with 'after the fact' remedies or, for that matter, with corrective justice. Tort law is concerned with both the ex ante prevention of harm, and with ex post redress.[35]

As developed in Chapter 2, preventive justice and redressive justice are closely connected as a normative matter. They are often linked through a continuity of reasons, as the reasons for an individual's permission to defend herself or her property ex ante continue in existence after a wrong has occurred.[36] Post-wrong, it is no longer possible to defend her person or property. Yet there are new permissions that parallel the original permissions—the victim of a wrong now has, all else equal, a permission to do the next best thing to prevention.[37]

[33] For an account that emphasizes enforcement rights across both pre- and post-wrong contexts, see Gold, 'Moral Rights Theory' (n. 27).

[34] *See* Jeff McMahan, 'Laws of War' in Samantha Besson & John Tasioulas, (eds), *The Philosophy of International Law* (OUP 2010) 493, 499.

[35] It should be noted that preventive justice is not tort law's only ex ante concern. For example, tort law is also concerned with guiding behaviour. *See* Gregory Keating, 'The Priority of Respect Over Repair' (2012) 18 Legal Theory 293, 318.

[36] That said, I am not claiming that there is always symmetry in terms of the permissibility of ex ante and ex post enforcement. Cf. Jeff McMahan, 'Self-Defense and the Problem of the Innocent Attacker' (1994) 104 Ethics 252, 279 (indicating, based on a hypothetical fact pattern, that 'one cannot infer the permissibility of preventing a harm from the fact that the harm wrongs the victim and imposes on the injurer a duty ex post to compensate the victim for the harm').

[37] This is not the same as the right-in, right-out thesis Gardner defends, as it is concerned with enforcement rights, and not merely remedial rights. Cf. Gardner, 'What Is Tort Law For?' (n. 5) 46.

Where she once had enforcement rights with respect to her primary rights, ex ante, she now has enforcement rights with respect to her secondary rights, ex post. It is important nonetheless to recognize that ex ante injunctive relief is not an example of redressive justice as defined here. We have, then, our first major example of a tort remedy that does not match the redressive justice picture. Injunctive relief to prevent a future wrong constitutes a close relative of redressive justice, and it suggests an account in which private law is centrally concerned with enforcement rights, whether ex ante or ex post. Nonetheless, strictly speaking, this is not redressive justice.

B. Nominal damages

As noted, compensatory damages that do not fully compensate are explicable in allocation back terms. Nominal damages are a harder case, and allocation back approaches struggle to explain them. One possibility is to see nominal damages cases as an example of reparative damages, even in the absence of something that can be repaired. Another option is to rethink the nature of the transaction that will be subject to an allocation back—we might think of the transaction in expressive terms, subject to a reversal by expressive means. Each possibility will be considered in turn.

1. Repair 'when there is nothing to repair'

John Gardner takes the former path and I will begin with his account. On his view, a distinctive feature of tort law is that reparative damages take pride of place. Other remedies are available under the court's discretion, but reparative damages are a matter of right when a tortious wrong has been committed.

As Gardner argues:

> The courts do not regard themselves as legally free to deny reparative damages to the plaintiff even when there is nothing to repair. The court can, however, express the point that there is nothing to repair by awarding a symbolic sum. Indeed, the court can go further. It can award such a conspicuously trifling sum that it thereby expresses contempt for the plaintiff who was such

A promisee may have, for example, a remedial moral right to the reversal of a breach—correlative to a wrongdoer's remedial moral duty to correct—but without possessing an enforcement right. In the case of ordinary promises, there is a remedial moral right to performance ex post, but typically no enforcement right. The distinction is developed in detail at Andrew S Gold, 'A Theory of Redressive Justice' (2014) 64 U Toronto LJ 159, 179.

> a stickler for his rights that he insisted on upholding them expensively and painfully in court even when the defendant's violation of them caused him no loss.[38]

In other words, the court's hands are tied; if a tortious wrong has been demonstrated, the court must award reparative damages, and the award of nominal damages is the form that such damages accordingly take when no losses are suffered. On this account, reparative damages are present from a legal perspective even in those cases where the plaintiff has suffered no loss. As Gardner puts it, these are nominally reparative damages.

By extension, the nominal damages remedy could also qualify as an example of redressive justice. Along these lines, we might argue that the plaintiff is able to nominally enforce remedial rights, even where there is nothing for redress to repair. I do not think such a move is convincing. While this account is a conceptual possibility, it seems an interpretive stretch to view nominal damages as reparative in cases 'when there is nothing to repair'. Damages designed to repair losses that do not exist are not actually repairing losses. Instead, this view would suggest courts use a legal fiction to render something that is not truly subject to repair into something that is reparative for legal purposes. Private law does make use of legal fictions, and we cannot rule the possibility out; but if fictions are required to buttress a particular interpretation, we have cause to inquire whether non-fictional alternatives are available.

In addition, while Gardner does not argue that nominal damages are exclusively a means of demonstrating judicial contempt for a claim, it is worth emphasizing that nominal damages may occupy multiple roles. Nominal damages may go along with powerful punitive remedies, suggesting that nominal damages, even when they are trifling, are not always used as a means to demonstrate the poor regard in which a plaintiff's claims are held. A good example is the famous case of *Jacque v. Steenberg Homes, Inc.*[39] There, the defendant had ploughed a path through the snow on the plaintiff's land, in order to deliver a mobile home to a third party. Because of the snow, there was no harm whatsoever to the plaintiff's land, but there was a clear trespass. The Wisconsin Supreme Court found that, in a case of intentional trespass, nominal damages could support an award of punitive damages.[40] It does not appear that this award of nominal damages was intended to express contempt for a stickler

[38] John Gardner, 'Torts and Other Wrongs' (2011) 39 Fla U St L Rev 43, 57.
[39] 209 Wis.2d 605 (1997).
[40] Ibid. at 621.

whose claim ought not to have been brought. The nominal damages here do not seem to express any negative inferences about the underlying claim itself.

2. Reversal of an expressive transaction

It is worth asking whether an alternative account is available: an account in which a transaction is genuinely reversed by nominal damages. Whether or not contempt is involved, how is it that a remedy that primarily communicates something could qualify as an allocation back? Barring the use of legal fiction, the answer to this question remains unanswered. Yet there is a way to view communicative acts in allocative terms, and this suggests an additional gloss on nominal damages. Suppose that we take nominal damages to have a very basic message: nominal damages may simply express that party A committed a wrong against party B. As we will see, this view offers another manner of interpreting the type of justice involved in private law settings. To illustrate, we can start with Stephen Smith's recent communicative account of corrective justice, as it offers a well-developed example of this perspective on what damages orders communicate.

Smith argues that compensatory damages are expressive, but the structure of his argument applies more broadly to nominal damages as well. On his view:

> What an award of compensatory damages (together with the trial that precedes it) does very clearly . . . is to communicate that the defendant has committed, and the claimant suffered, a wrong. And by making the defendant pay compensation to the claimant, the order makes clear that the defendant's wrong was a wrong done to the claimant.[41]

In Smith's understanding, court orders that require compensatory damages create new duties for defendants. Smith therefore suggests that corrective justice, in order to fit the way court orders are issued, will share a structural feature with penal orders in the criminal law setting—it will involve courts in the creation of duties that did not exist before the court's order.[42] He concludes that corrective justice plays a communicative role.

Again, we could adapt this view to explain the role of redressive justice in cases of nominal damages. From this perspective, a court's order of nominal damages would communicate that the defendant committed a wrong against the plaintiff. At this point, however, an immediate objection arises. Isn't

[41] Smith, 'Why Courts Make Orders' (n. 28) 85.

[42] *See* ibid. 81 (noting a structural similarity between damages orders and penal orders).

redressive justice an allocation back theory? If the expressive view is adopted, it might seem that we have moved far afield from an allocation back remedy. That is not necessarily so. What may actually be at stake is a different understanding of the transaction to be reversed: what may be at stake is an expressive transaction, subject to reversal by an expressive remedy. The defendant's tort will have wrongly communicated something about the defendant—for example, that the defendant is the kind of person against whom it is acceptable to trespass. Nominal damages will in turn communicate the falsity of this initial communication: the trespass is indeed a wrong. The expressive transaction that the trespass represents is, in this way, something that can be undone.

To see how such an argument would work, consider Jean Hampton's account of retribution as 'a form of compensation to the victim'.[43] Hampton adopts an expressive account of retribution, and suggests that it involves the undoing of an injurious message. As she argues:

> Whereas tort damages are supposed to be awarded to place the victim in the situation she would have been in had the tortfeasor not acted, retribution is supposed to be inflicted to nullify the wrongdoer's message of superiority over the victim, thus placing the victim in the position she would have been in had the wrongdoer not acted. Hence the real contrast between corrective justice and retributive justice is not that the former is compensatory whereas the latter is not, but rather that each compensates a different form of damage.[44]

Hampton has described the undoing of a transaction that is expressive in nature. If corrective justice is expressive, however, then corrective justice may be accomplishing the type of thing that Hampton suggests is accomplished by retribution.

Corrective justice may thus be undoing an expressive transaction, if corrective justice is understood to involve expression of the idea that the defendant committed a wrong against the plaintiff. Redressive justice could, in theory, operate in the same fashion. Accordingly, there is a way to describe nominal damages as an allocation back. Time cannot be reversed, but the symbolic message provided by nominal damages may at least partially undo a communicative misdeed. Naturally, the plaintiff cannot fully undo what the defendant did

[43] Jean Hampton, 'Correcting Harms Versus Righting Wrongs: The Goal of Retribution' (1992) 39 UCLA L Rev 1659, 1698.
[44] *See* ibid.

by wronging her. From an expressive point of view, the next best thing available to the plaintiff may be to force the payment of a symbolic sum.

An expressive account may well offer the best theory available to explain nominal damages. If we adopt that theory, moreover, it is conceptually possible to describe nominal damages in terms of an allocation back. Even so, we should pause before taking the nominal damages context as a template for other examples of allocation back in tort law, or in private law more generally. There is good cause to doubt that ordinary compensatory damages can be adequately explained in expressive terms, in part because this is in tension with the legal point of view.[45] The reversal of expressive transactions is not characteristic of private law reasoning outside of the nominal damages setting (assuming, *arguendo*, that nominal damages are best seen that way).[46]

As the above discussion suggests, there are ways to square nominal damages with an allocation back account, including the redressive justice approach. Yet these possibilities come with a decrease in plausibility, or else with a limited scope. Nominal damages may be described as an effort at reparative damages when repair cannot literally occur. Given that there are no losses to repair, nominal damages are a way that courts can still try to comply with their legal mandate. Such a view can be reconciled with the redressive justice picture, but at the cost of legal fiction. On the other hand, if we emphasize expressive transactions, there is a distinctive way to see nominal damages in terms of an allocation back. Expressing through damages that a wrong was committed can undo what was expressed by the original wrong, at least to a degree. Much of tort law, however, does not seem to be concerned with expressive transactions, and this potential switch in transaction types suggests a substantial variation in tort law's aims. Nominal damages are an area in which the standard allocation back picture is an awkward fit, even if it is a conceivable one.

C. Punitive damages

Even if nominal damages can be explained in redressive justice terms, this is not readily done for punitive damages. Punitive damages may allow a plaintiff

[45] These concerns are elaborated in detail in Andrew S Gold, 'Expressive Remedies in Private Law' in F Lichere & R Weaver, (eds), *Property and Remedies* (Presses Universitaires d'Aix-Marseille 2013). For an additional sceptical response to expressive accounts of private law remedies, see Ripstein, *Private Wrongs* (n. 19) 281–5.

[46] This is not to deny the possibility that all damages remedies have expressive effects. The relevant question is not whether damages remedies are expressive, but instead whether they are best conceptualized and explained in expressive terms.

to get even, or they may involve a form of private revenge.[47] They may be mechanisms for punishment, private or public. Alternatively, they may accomplish other aims, such as deterrence.[48] The accounts are various and they differ on a variety of fronts. I will not elaborate on their features here, as each of these theories is problematic for the redressive justice picture. Punitive damages do not seem to be aimed at undoing transactions in the way that allocation back is typically understood; instead, they offer revenge, or punish wrongful transactions in some sense, or play a role in shaping future conduct. Punitive damages do not amount to an allocation back if allocation back is given its standard meaning.[49] Corrective justice theorists are quick to recognize that punitive damages cannot be squared with their account,[50] and a redressive justice approach should face up to the same challenge.

The view that punitive damages are different is also a natural reading of the legal point of view. Courts act as if they are doing something distinctive when they award punitive damages and this point is especially evident in the individuation of remedies. Suppose, for example, that A maliciously destroys B's car, in an attempt to humiliate B. If B sues and successfully gets a compensatory make-whole remedy in the amount of the car's value, this will not be the only remedy available. B may also successfully seek punitive damages, and in a substantial amount. These punitive damages are *in addition to* the compensatory remedy. On the theory described in this book, the compensatory damages that the court awards are an example of an allocation back. The punitive damages award, by implication, must be something else: at the least, a qualitatively different kind of allocation back.

The redressive justice account developed here takes the same general perspective adopted by a variety of corrective justice theories: punitive damages are exceptional. That said, I agree with the civil recourse theorists that we cannot simply carve out punitive damages when we seek to theorize tort law.[51] One ought not to define the contours of the field to be explained so that it conveniently fits a proffered explanation. Punitive damages are a core feature of

47 For accounts that suggest an aim of punishment or revenge, see Benjamin C Zipursky, 'A Theory of Punitive Damages' (2005) 84 Tex L Rev 105 (finding a right to be punitive); Anthony J Sebok, 'Punitive Damages: From Myth to Theory' (2007) 92 Iowa L Rev 957 (finding a right to revenge).

48 *See* A Mitchell Polinksy & Steven Shavell, 'Punitive Damages: An Economic Analysis' (1998) 111 Harv L Rev 869, 896 (suggesting a deterrence rationale for punitive damages).

49 As with nominal damages, there is in theory an account of expressive transactions and their reversal that could fit here. Cf. Sebok, 'Punitive Damages' (n. 47) 1028 (analysing punitive damages in terms of Jean Hampton's expressive account of retribution).

50 *See*, e.g. Weinrib, *Corrective Justice* (n. 31) 97.

51 *See* Zipursky, 'Civil Recourse' (n. 7) 713 (suggesting that 'the corrective justice theorist who takes this route is voluntarily taking a loss in the battle among interpretive theories').

tort law practices—they are not simply an outlier that a theory of private law can afford to bracket. This suggests that, if redressive justice theory is correct as applied to other settings, we have multiple values at play in tort law. Whether this is a problem or not will depend on the type of theory we are developing and the scope of its explanatory ambitions. This brings us, then, to the next key question: the place for pluralism in private law.

IV. Towards Pluralism in Tort Theory

The above discussion shows the difficulty in addressing all of tort law's remedies in allocation back terms. Punitive damages are a difficult puzzle for a range of corrective justice accounts, and they are similarly problematic for a redressive justice theory of tort law. One responsive strategy is to say that punitive damages are simply not part of tort law. This book rejects this approach. Whether or not punitive damages are distinctive, they are an integral part of both tort law and private law, as they are presently constituted. Likewise, injunctive relief is a key feature of the tort law landscape, but it is not an ex ante example of redressive justice. Injunctive relief is a doubtful fit for ex post corrective justice theories, and it is similarly doubtful here. Nominal damages are, perhaps, open to an allocation back rubric, but it takes some explanatory effort to make the case. These are features for the tort theorist to explain, and they are not features that redressive justice explains well.

That said, it is not a realistic explanatory ambition to explain every component of tort law within a single theory. Each private law subject area has exceptional, outlier cases. Tort law, like other private law fields, has anomalous features. As a centuries old legal practice, with multiple judges, divergent legal and political perspectives, and a reasonably strong system of precedent, it would be astonishing if there were no inconsistent doctrines. With this in mind, one might say that a particular theory of justice or civil recourse is successful if it explains the standard features of private law. Accordingly, one might rise to the explanatory challenge not through a carving-up of tort law, but rather by scaling back the nature of one's explanatory claims, so that they only cover the run of the mill doctrine.

I will eschew this approach to punitive damages or injunctive relief, for it is questionable whether these remedies are anomalous outliers. There is, however, another possibility: theorists like Jules Coleman have attempted to describe the core features of tort law, while conceding that tort law does contain other features.[52] Even if they aren't anomalous, one might contend that remedies like punitive damages are not *core* features. This, too, seems questionable. Why shouldn't punitive damages be seen as a core feature? Given these concerns, I will not claim that redressive justice explains *the* core features—rather it explains *many* of the core features of private law. On the view developed here, there are multiple core features of private law that draw upon different values. Allocation back involves a different concern from getting satisfaction, which in turn involves a different concern from punishment.

Yet this latter approach raises a distinct methodological concern. Supposing that there are several core features of private law, each drawing on different values, this brings us to the problem of pluralism in private law theory. Coherence is a fundamental concern for private law theory, and the majority of private law theories adopt a coherence goal—indeed, coherence appears to motivate the unifying theories that are so prominent in this setting. It might be argued that if redressive justice only explains some of the core features of tort law—perhaps not even a majority—then it will run afoul of the coherence criterion that is at the foundation of these explanatory accounts. We face, then, two questions. If tort law incorporates multiple core features, does this mean that tort law is incoherent? Furthermore, if tort law turns out to be incoherent in some sense, does that mean something is lacking in our explanatory account?

On these questions, our answer will depend on what type of coherence we expect private law to have. Private law theorists characteristically seek coherence when they interpret private law fields, but there is more than one basis for this goal. For example, Ernest Weinrib contends that 'those who think about private law in its own terms must include the law's pervasive impulse toward coherence within their purview'.[53] Alternatively, a coherence criterion also fits the theorist's objective of rendering the social practice of private law intelligible. These are not identical concerns. Moreover, agreement breaks down once we focus on the type of coherence that private law theorists should seek.

How much coherence a successful theory should demonstrate is a matter of debate. Arguably, it is enough to expect that a legal theory will show the law to be non-contradictory.[54] This weak coherence criterion will allow for a

[52] Jules Coleman, *The Practice of Principle: In Defense of a Pragmatist Approach to Legal Theory* (OUP 2001) 36 ('It is not my view that all of tort law must be explained by corrective justice. What corrective justice purports to do is to explain the core of tort law.').

[53] *See* Weinrib, *Idea of Private Law* (n. 19) 13–14.

[54] *See* ibid. Even if we are thinking in terms of the morality of private law, it is arguable that a minimal level of coherence may be all that is required. Cf. John Gardner, 'What Is Tort Law For? Part 2. The Place of Distributive Justice' in John Oberdiek, (ed.), *Philosophical Foundations of the Law of Torts* (OUP 2014) 338 n. 11 ('Any justification has to be coherent in the thin sense of intelligible. But Weinribian

very broad range of successful theories, and it does not generally serve as a means to separate one leading account from another. There are, however, much more stringent approaches to the question of coherence. For example, the theorist might seek a theory that explains a legal field in terms of a single unifying principle.[55] This is a substantially more difficult standard to meet, and if we also require a fit between theory and legal doctrine, it may be impossible for any theory to attain this level of coherence.[56] Thankfully, there are also intermediate positions on coherence. For example, in his work in contract theory, Stephen Smith suggests a moderate coherence criterion. In his view, 'a good theory must show that most of the core elements of contract law can be traced to, or are closely related to, a single principle'.[57] This coherence criterion is plausible, at least as one factor to be weighed in the balance. As Smith points out, '[u]nless one assumes (as few people do) that all reasons for acting can, in the end, be reduced to a single master principle, it is accepted as perfectly intelligible, indeed appropriate, that people act for different reasons in different situations'.[58]

Nonetheless, I will offer a somewhat different approach from what Smith's moderate coherence criterion calls for. Redressive justice explains core elements of tort law—arguably the most important core elements of tort law—but it is unclear whether it explains the majority of core elements. Accordingly, some might object that a suitable coherence criterion is simply not met. My response to these concerns is to question the stringency of Smith's coherence criterion, as described above (and by extension, a stronger coherence criterion). Depending on the application of other interpretive criteria—such as morality, fit, and transparency—it could be that the proper role for a coherence criterion is more modest. At times, the better interpretive aim may be to coherently explain certain salient features of tort law rather than to provide a single principle that explains most core features of torts. In other words, an appropriate

unity (or Dworkinian integrity) is not, in my eyes, any kind of plus. Reality, including moral reality, is fragmentary.').

[55] *See* Stephen A Smith, *Contract Theory* (OUP 2004) 11 ('According to the more demanding version [of the coherence criterion], mere consistency is not enough. This version states that theories should also be evaluated according to the extent that they show contract law as a unified system.').

[56] For helpful analyses of fit criteria, see ibid. 7–11; William Lucy, 'Method and Fit: Two Problems for Contemporary Philosophies of Tort Law' (2007) 52 McGill LJ 605. In addition, appearances can be deceiving, since an abstract unifying principle may call for pluralism at the ground level of legal doctrine. *See*, e.g. Hanoch Dagan, 'Pluralism and Perfectionism in Private Law' (2012) 112 Colum L Rev 1409.

[57] *See* Smith, *Contract Theory* (n. 55) 13.

[58] *See* ibid. 12.

coherence criterion will look for local coherence rather than global coherence across a field.

To illustrate why this is a genuine possibility, suppose that a redressive justice account gives us a way to explain how most of the core elements of *private law* can be traced to, or are closely related to, a single principle. And suppose, hypothetically, that civil recourse theory—with recourse understood solely as a mechanism for a plaintiff to get satisfaction—gives us a way to explain how most of the core elements of *tort law* can be traced to, or are closely related to, a single principle. Let's also assume that redressive justice cannot explain the majority of principles in tort law, and that civil recourse (taken as a means to get satisfaction) cannot explain the majority of principles in private law. Either theory could then claim to meet a moderate coherence criterion, simply by shifting our focus between private law and tort law. Do we seek coherence across private law or coherence across tort law?

A coherence criterion on its own cannot tell us the answer, and the above hypothetical is not implausible. Moreover, pockets of tort law may draw on norms that exist in the non-tort areas of private law, even if they diverge from other features of tort law in doing so. For example, it may be that redressive justice explains the legal approach to conversion torts very well—thus showing common features that link contract law, unjust enrichment, and the law of conversion—even if redressive justice does not convincingly explain punitive damages. In my view, the private law landscape very much resembles this picture. Local coherence concerns suggest a reason to think of conversion in terms of redressive justice, even if redressive justice is not able to explain the majority of tort law under a single principle. Indeed, the scope of legal doctrine that potentially falls within such a picture could be quite broad, once we are willing to look outside the confines of tort. Contract, fiduciary, and unjust enrichment law all share a redressive justice principle in common with components of tort law. These doctrines are simply being unified in a way that cuts through private law subfields without incorporating those subfields in their entirety. A redressive justice theory has a strong claim to coherence when private law as a whole is our subject of study. This strength when we assess private law as a whole counterbalances its more limited explanatory scope in tort law settings.

A slightly different objection could also be made. Even if the reader concludes that unifying a majority of concepts under a single principle is not a requirement for a good account of tort law (or even private law), this reader might say nevertheless that such a theory is superior when available. All else equal, she might argue, a corrective justice or civil recourse approach is superior to the extent it can explain the majority of tort law in light of one guiding principle. The pluralism I am suggesting, on this view, is acceptable for lack of something better, but it is still second-best. The response to this objection is to point to the problem of fit. There simply is no tort theory consistent with the legal point of view that can adequately explain compensatory damages, punitive damages, and injunctive relief under the same principle.[59] And it is fair to conclude that each of these remedial features are core features. The objection, even if it is otherwise valid, will prove too much in this context. We can either downplay the importance of fitting the legal point of view—in which case a number of rival theories will work—or we can allow for tort theories that successfully explain portions of tort law rather than tort law as a whole.

There is also cause to anticipate this result in light of the structure of legal systems and the ways in which their resulting legal doctrines evolve. On such bases, we should anticipate local coherence in the law while rejecting global coherence. As Joseph Raz's work indicates, there are several reasons why. For example, we might start from a premise of value pluralism. From this perspective, Raz argues, 'we must recognize that the application of each of the distinct values ought to be consistently pursued, and this generates pockets of coherence which exist, or should exist, where the law should reflect one overriding moral or evaluative concern.'[60] In addition, Raz notes that social pluralism can be a significant additional consideration: 'the existence of a plurality of inconsistent views on moral, religious, social, and political issues in democratic (and in many other) societies, is likely to be reflected in a society's law'.[61] Furthermore, there may be choices legislatures and courts face that involve conflicts of values, with no particular solution to these conflicts holding superiority over the others.[62] Once made, adherence to a given choice can then readily result in local coherence.[63]

Does this mean we are describing a mish-mash of different private law values, jumbled together at the convenience of courts and advocates? Not necessarily.

[59] Certain theories come close in certain respects. An efficiency account might in the abstract be able to explain each of these, but adopted at the level of legal reasoning it would run into difficulty under a transparency criterion. A civil recourse account can explain each of these remedies, but only by adopting multiple principles of recourse or by rendering the account of recourse so abstract that it tells us little about the thing to be explained. *See* Andrew S Gold, 'The Taxonomy of Civil Recourse' (2011) 39 Fla St U L Rev 65.

[60] Joseph Raz, 'The Relevance of Coherence' in *Ethics in the Public Domain: Essays in the Morality of Law and Politics* (OUP 1994) 277, 315.

[61] *See* ibid. 316.

[62] *See* ibid. 317.

[63] *See* ibid. 318 ('Societies are faced with numerous discrete issues of conflict, and decide on solutions to them as they arise. Each solution gives rise to considerations of coherence within its scope, based on the need to secure co-ordination and rule of law values.').

John Goldberg has warned against what he calls a 'congenial pluralism' in tort theory.[64] I share his doubts. His cause for concern is valid, particularly if this means that courts are thought to balance distinct values on an ad hoc basis in deciding on a particular remedy.[65] For example, if a court measured the damages in a negligence case by intuitively weighing redressive justice, distributive justice, efficiency, and expressive benefits against each other, the resulting damages would be the product of a genuinely incoherent analysis. The balancing process, we can assume, would be ad hoc, and it would be surprising if this process is what the best theory found at work in tort law. In assessing a pluralist interpretation, a lot depends on which values are thought to comprise the grouping of values in private law, and on how they intersect, assuming they intersect at all. This need not be a congenial pluralism that calls for a frequent ad hoc balancing of diverse aims. For several reasons, the different principles embedded in private law can often avoid bumping into each other.

A key feature of private law is that a single component of private law can constitute an application of multiple norms. For example, suppose that courts consistently apply redressive justice norms when ordering compensatory damages in negligence cases. For each such dispute, it will simultaneously be the case that the court's order has expressed that the defendant committed a wrong against the plaintiff. There is no need to balance the value of redressive justice against the value of communicating that a wrong occurred, because satisfying the requirements of redressive justice will satisfy the requirements of communicating who wronged whom. Nominal damages may come into their own to the extent there is no genuine possibility of allocating back, but in the ordinary case where redressive justice applies, the import of communicating that a wrong occurred will fade into the background.

Another key feature is that multiple remedies can be layered one on top of the other, within the same case. Courts frequently provide both compensatory damages and punitive damages as separate remedies, in response to the same underlying tort. Neither remedy displaces the other, and in theory neither remedy will have a different content merely because of the availability of the other. If punitive damages were not treated as a separate remedy, it would be quite reasonable to wonder if courts sometimes blended

[64] *See* John CP Goldberg, 'Twentieth-Century Tort Theory' (2003) 91 Geo LJ 513, 579.

[65] *See* ibid. 580 ('The alternative, then, is to leave judges with the message that it is their job to exercise judgment by achieving an ineffable balance among diverse and sometimes antithetical considerations with respect to any given decision.'). At the legal theory level, our concerns may be alleviated if pluralist explanatory theories are sufficiently separable from pluralist adjudication. See Felipe Jimenez, 'Two Questions for Private Law Theory', available at: https://ssrn.com/abstract=3452909 (discussing this possibility).

punishment and compensation in an ad hoc fashion. But given the differentiation that exists in the typical case, these two distinctive modes of remediation are not brought into a single calculus. Indeed, plaintiffs have the ability to seek compensatory damages without seeking punitive damages—these remedies are separable from both legal and private perspectives. This approach to pluralism, which we might call a 'compartmentalization' strategy, allows courts or fact finders to avoid an ad hoc balancing between different justice-oriented goals.[66]

In addition, one type of justice may comfortably co-exist with another type because they are applied in different temporal settings. This possibility is evident when we turn to preventive and redressive justice. A case of ex ante injunctive relief does not implicate redressive justice precisely because it is ex ante, and a case of ex post damages does not implicate preventive justice precisely because it is ex post. The two types of justice occupy different spaces. More generally, we can see tort law as both concerned with the delineation of rights, ex ante, and with the undoing of wrongful transactions, ex post.[67] These two concerns are complementary, but not identical. It is, of course, possible for legal systems to decide to privilege ex ante relief over ex post relief, or vice versa. But, that said, at the level of judicial decision in individual cases, it will ordinarily not be necessary for courts to worry about an ad hoc balancing between the two categories of justice.

Distributive justice can also comfortably operate alongside redressive justice. It is true that courts would fall into an ad hoc pluralism if they weighed distributive justice against redressive justice when resolving individual tort law cases. Yet legal doctrines aimed at providing equal access to the courts implicate societal distributions of redressive justice itself.[68] Legal doctrine designed to ensure this equality of treatment is thus concerned with both distributive justice and redressive justice, but distributive justice does not generally enter into the judicial reasoning process regarding an individual plaintiff's claim. Furthermore, if we step outside of tort law, there are yet other ways that distributive justice can be incorporated into private law practices without ad hoc decision-making. There are private law cases in which local distributive justice calls for a particular remedy for a wrong, without implicating an allocation back. In fiduciary law, for example, a principal's recovery of illegitimate bribes

[66] I thank Noam Gur for suggesting the 'compartmentalization' terminology.

[67] For helpful analysis of the ex ante component, see Keating, 'The Priority of Respect over Repair' (n. 35) 293, 319.

[68] An analogous point has been developed in the corrective justice setting. *See* Gardner, 'The Place of Distributive Justice' (n. 54).

from her bribe-taking agent does not implicate a true allocation back.[69] The principal's remedy involves local distributive justice, and since allocation back is undesirable in this context (and also not sought) there is no need for multiple types of justice to be weighed against each other. The relation between such distributive allocations and redressive justice is analogous to the ex ante/ex post scenario described above: each type of justice covers a different type of legal dispute, and accordingly no ad hoc balancing is required.

***

Tort law demonstrates the explanatory strength of the redressive justice account—redressive justice provides explanations for tort remedies that characteristically take a make-whole form. Property-related torts are often a natural fit, but the scope of explanation extends much further. Indeed, in substantial subparts of tort law, redressive justice is a better match for legal doctrine than accountability-based civil recourse accounts. Redressive justice is a thread that runs through every private law field, tort law included. On the other hand, certain features of tort law are an important challenge for the redressive justice account, for tort law includes cases in which redress only incompletely repairs an injury. Tort law also presents us with cases like punitive damages, in which private law remedies do not fit the redressive justice picture. In these latter cases, the standard legal remedies do not appear to be allocations back, full stop.

Tort law thus offers several important insights. As noted, it indicates the breadth of the redressive justice account. Core aspects of tort law—ranging from conversion cases to personal injury cases—implicate a right holder's right to force an allocation back. Remedies for conversion are not about holding someone accountable, nor are they about getting satisfaction: conversions may be entirely innocent, and the standard tort law remedies are strikingly inflexible given that fact. A legally mandated return of property or its monetary equivalent is best explained in terms of what it appears to be: an undoing of a transaction in light of a property holder's enforceable right to the property at issue. Personal injury cases are more complex, but again they are broadly consistent with the redressive justice picture. A wrongdoer does not need to receive a gain in order for a wrongful transaction to merit reversal. Nor is it conceptually problematic if the wrong has produced injuries that are impossible to fully undo. Indeed, even woefully incomplete reversals of a transaction still qualify as allocations back.

[69] *See* Matthew Harding, 'Constructive Trusts and Distributive Justice' in Elise Bant & Michael Bryan, (eds), *Principles of Proprietary Remedies* (2013) 31–3.

Equally important, tort law suggests the need for pluralism. It is, however, a particular type of pluralism that tort law instantiates. Certain features of tort law, most notably punitive damages, are an awkward case for allocation back approaches to private law. They don't seem to fit. Ex ante injunctive relief is similarly challenging, and nominal damages are at best a debatable match. On the other hand, redressive justice is a sufficiently compelling explanation for conversion and for make-whole remedies that it would be a mistake to disregard its place in tort law. Where does this leave us? Effectively, tort law is a private law field that instantiates multiple independent remedial norms. The distinctive feature of the pluralism in tort law is that it frequently allows for local coherence. In the majority of cases, the norms that underpin punitive damages, compensatory damages, nominal damages, and injunctive relief do not have to be balanced against each other. Each is comprehensible within its appropriate sphere. In tort law, redressive justice is one of several categories of justice; redressive justice helps us to make sense of tort law, but it does this in combination with other norms of justice and other values.

6

The State as a Fiduciary

I. Introduction

It is one thing to explain private rights of action as a means to obtain redress; it is another to explain why the state is obliged (if it is) to provide for them. The idea that private rights of action are a legal entitlement is not especially controversial. The reasons given for this positive law feature, on the other hand, take different forms. In the interests of providing a more complete picture, this chapter will offer several interpretations of the state's role in providing private rights of action as a means for seeking redress.

This subject matter is importantly different from what we have discussed thus far. In part, this is because our focus is now primarily on the state's role. In addition, it is because the analysis is now (at least in part) focused on justifications for legal institutions writ large. Unlike some of the other topics we have considered, such institutional justifications need not share the same conceptual structure as the concepts internal to private law reasoning. For example, the concepts internal to contract law might make sense in deontological terms, while the justification for the state's establishment of contract law as an institution is consequentialist. If so, courts may rarely turn to the institutional justification for contract law in the course of deciding individual cases.[1] Multiple competing justifications for private law institutions can also be harmonized with ground-level private law concepts. It is quite possible for theorists to adopt a range of divergent theories regarding the justification for a private law field while still converging on the concepts courts use within that field.[2]

Figuring out whether and why the state owes its citizens private rights of action may also require a developed account of the state, its formation, its constitutional arrangement, and its interactions with its citizens. It is well beyond

[1] For helpful analysis of this point, see Liam Murphy, 'Purely Formal Wrongs' in Paul B Miller & John Oberdiek, (eds), *Civil Wrongs and the Justice in Private Law* (OUP 2020) (indicating that the internal normative order of private law may not express its purpose). See also Felipe Jimenez, 'Two Questions for Private Law Theory', available at: https://ssrn.com/abstract=3452909 (discussing the distinction between theories that focus on what private law is for and theories that focus on what is internal to private law).

[2] See Andrew S Gold & Henry E Smith, 'Sizing Up Private Law', forthcoming U Toronto L J.

The Right of Redress. Andrew S. Gold, Oxford University Press (2020). © Andrew S. Gold.
DOI: 10.1093/oso/9780198814405.001.0001

the scope of this book to provide such an account. A fully worked out theory of the state could require an additional book in its own right, and a fully developed constitutional law analysis could require several additional chapters, particularly if variances across jurisdictions are included. I will suggest reasons to think there is a state obligation to provide for private rights of action or their effective equivalent—or at least reasons for state actors to think so, which is important for interpretive purposes—but I will not try to demonstrate that such an obligation must exist.

Granting room for divergence at the level of institutional justifications, we should not assume that such justifications can be entirely bracketed from private law's conceptual structure. An account of private law with no concern for why the state provides for private law doctrine—with no concern for what the state owes to its citizens—can feel oddly detached from the broader legal system. And, on occasion, the institutional justifications that support private law bleed into legal doctrine and legal reasoning. In such instances, institutional justifications are part of private law's internal conceptual structure. With these possibilities in mind, this chapter will outline several theories of the state's role in providing private rights of action. These are by no means the only theories available, but they will show the plausibility of a state obligation to provide private rights of action (or, again, the reasonableness of such a belief by legal actors).

I will begin with the classic civil recourse approach. Civil recourse theorists have often adopted Lockean explanations of the state's responsibility to provide a means of recourse when its citizens are wronged. Private rights of action are taken to be a substitute for pre-legal rights to undo wrongs or hold tortfeasors accountable, and the proposed reason why the state owes this substitute draws on social contract theory.

John Goldberg and Benjamin Zipursky have recently questioned whether it makes sense to see rights of redress in terms of pre-legal, natural rights. As they note, an important alternative within the social contract tradition suggests a more reason-based, contractarian account. This approach is developed in Goldberg's and Zipursky's recent book, *Recognizing Wrongs*. They argue that there is a norm of civil recourse in political morality that meshes well with principles long regarded as central in a liberal democracy.[3] This picture, which has more in common with the work of Rawls and Scanlon, avoids some concerns posed by the Lockean account.

[3] See John CP Goldberg & Benjamin C Zipursky, *Recognizing Wrongs* (HUP 2020) 114.

This chapter will suggest a pathway that allows us to avoid reliance on a social contract. This alternative also helps to explain why the state should allow its citizens an expansive discretion regarding whether and how to bring suit. I will argue that the state is a fiduciary to its citizens, and that private rights of action are a way for it to meet its fiduciary obligations.

The state's fiduciary obligations include an obligation to advance our meaningful projects in life; projects which may be disrupted by both state intervention and private wrongs. There are multiple ways to pursue a goal of facilitating our projects in life, including through provisions for education or healthcare; one notable way of doing so, however, is for the state to facilitate spheres of private sovereignty. I will focus here on the private sovereignty case. The state may not be able to provide us directly with whatever we personally find meaningful—not only is that a highly particularized question, meaningfulness may require that we do things for ourselves—but the state can seek to provide conditions that allow us to pursue our projects in life. Significantly, the state can accomplish this through its provision of property, contract, tort, and other private law rules; private law institutions give us the means to advance a range of self-constituting projects.

But it is not just through provision of primary rights and duties that the state accomplishes this task. Private rights of action are a way to reinforce the benefits of these other private law institutions (such as the primary rights provided by a property regime). Indeed, private rights of action may make up for a specific expression of the state's power; the state to a large degree prohibits self-help forms of redress. So understood, private rights of action may be owed to individual citizens not because of a social contract, but because of the nature of the state's claim of authority over its citizens and the consequences of that claim on their options in life. By taking away rights of self-help (for the most part), the state takes on an obligation to provide adequate substitutes.[4]

I will suggest that the state owes a form of loyalty that respects and helps to advance the projects that give meaning to its citizens' lives. After developing the significance of this component of the state's loyalty obligations, I will then indicate how private law offers a means for the state to comply with this responsibility. Rights of redress are an integral component of this responsibility.

[4] This possibility may also suggest another interesting interaction between redressive justice and other types of justice. While I take redressive justice to be dynamic—i.e. courts *do* justice when they engage in redressive justice—it may well be that possessing rights of redress is a matter of constitutive justice. For discussion of these categories and their significance, see Benjamin C Zipursky, 'Integrity and The Incongruities of Justice: A Review of Daniel Markovits's A Modern Legal Ethics' (2010) 119 Yale LJ 1948, 1987.

II. Social Contract Approaches

To see how a Lockean perspective connects pre-legal rights of redress to private law, we can borrow a page from earlier work by civil recourse theorists.[5] Benjamin Zipursky has offered a detailed argument for the view that private rights of action implicate a wronged party's pre-legal right to act against the party who wronged her. The resulting theory is both sophisticated and compatible with the structure of private law litigation.

John Locke famously posits that in a state of nature individuals have a right to punish wrongdoings.[6] This right of punishment is given up when entering a civil society, and in return the state takes on that responsibility.[7] Yet Zipursky notes that Locke recognizes another natural right in a pre-legal world.[8] Locke contends that individuals have a natural right to redress injuries they have suffered.[9] And, Locke also argues that the individual's right of redress is given up upon entering a civil society; in return, the state provides for redress.[10] As Zipursky suggests, 'the obligation of the individual not to engage in private punishment is conditional on the state's having undertaken that role.'[11] Similarly, he adds, 'it seems likely that Locke held an analogous view as to the right to seek compensation for individual injuries. There is a natural right and power to seek compensation for an injury done to one.'[12]

Yet the picture is necessarily more complex, at least if we seek a fit with legal doctrine. There is a distinction between Locke's theory and private law doctrine, as a wronged party's private right of action involves both private action and state action. As William Blackstone notes, legal redress requires both the state and the plaintiff to play a role: 'where in the act of the parties and the act of law co-operate; the act of parties being necessary to set the law in motion, and the process of the law being in general the only instrument, by which parties are enabled to procure certain and adequate redress.'[13] This mixed regime

[5] While I will focus on the civil recourse example, there are now also corrective justice theorists who reference a Lockean standpoint. *See*, e.g. Linda Radzik, 'Tort Processes and Relational Repair' in John Oberdiek, (ed.), *Philosophical Foundations of the Law of Torts* (OUP 2014) 231, 247.

[6] *See* John Locke, 'The Second Treatise of Government' in David Wootton, (ed.), *Political Writings of John Locke* (Hackett Publishing 1993) 261, 264–5.

[7] *See* ibid. 304–5.

[8] *See* Benjamin Zipursky, 'Philosophy of Private Law' in Jules Coleman & Scott Shapiro, (eds), *The Oxford Handbook of Jurisprudence & Philosophy of Law* (OUP 2002) 623, 637 (hereinafter, *Private Law*).

[9] *See* Locke, *Political Writings of John Locke* (n. 9) 265–6.

[10] *See* ibid. 305.

[11] *See* Zipursky, *Private Law* (n. 8) 639.

[12] Ibid. 639.

[13] *See* William Blackstone, 3 *Commentaries on the Laws of England* (University of Chicago Press 2002) *22.

is in tension with a picture of the state taking on sole responsibility for ex post redress.

In response, Zipursky offers a compelling account of how Locke's social contract theory and Blackstone's description of the right of action can be brought together:

> The synthesis of Locke and Blackstone . . . is the view that the power to alter a defendant's legal status through having a judgment entered against him—the private right of action—is something a private party who has been wronged is entitled to from the state.[14]

On this broadly Lockean view, the individual's delegation to the state is a partial delegation. The state must enter judgment, but the plaintiff retains a role in the process.[15] As John Goldberg explains: 'Individuals do hand over completely their right to act as judge and executioner; but they do not give up their right of self-preservation or their related right to redress wrongs.'[16] In a sense, when plaintiffs initiate a suit by filing their complaint, they are still engaging in self-help.

Still, there is another distinction between the standard civil recourse theory and Locke's views. Arthur Ripstein contends that the civil recourse idea of acting against someone by holding them accountable is not a true match for Locke's understanding of pre-legal rights. As Ripstein notes of civil recourse theory:

> The account is broadly Lockean because it does not hew to Locke's own claim that the executive right is a right to enforce rights. [Goldberg and Zipursky] understand it as less of a right and more of an inclination or urge to get even with those against whom you suppose yourself to have a grievance. Having prohibited barbaric recourse, the state placates the aggrieved by providing civil recourse in its place.[17]

[14] Zipursky, *Private Law* (n. 8) at 642.

[15] As John Goldberg notes:

> With this transition from the state of nature to civil society, individuals delegate to government the task of defining wrongs and of responding to them. Locke, of course, argued that this delegation is revocable upon conduct by governors evidencing a breach of the trust placed in them. He also argued that it is incomplete.

See John CP Goldberg, 'The Constitutional Status of Tort Law: Due Process and the Right to a Law for the Redress of Wrongs' (2005) 115 Yale LJ 524, 543.

[16] *See* ibid.

[17] *See* Arthur Ripstein, 'Civil Recourse and Separation of Wrongs and Remedies' (2011) 39 Fla St U L Rev 163, 186.

Even with Blackstonian adjustments, Locke's account should call for private rights of action to enforce one's rights, rather than private rights of action to hold someone accountable or get satisfaction.

If Ripstein's reading is right, the redressive justice picture is a better fit for Locke's understanding. Redressive justice is precisely about the enforcement of rights; it concerns rights to enforce remedial rights in order to undo a transaction. As it happens, Ripstein is incorrect in suggesting a link between civil recourse and vengeance, but even as applied to accountability or 'getting satisfaction', this argument still has some purchase. Redressive justice is closer to the original Lockean template than the account developed by Goldberg and Zipursky in tort law contexts (although their views on contract law need not raise this concern). The redressive picture may also be more normatively plausible, given persistent doubts whether individuals act appropriately when they seek to get even with others, or even when they seek to get satisfaction from them. When wronged, many of us have experienced a strong subjective feeling that getting satisfaction is appropriate—and resentment of a wrong is often apt—but it is a harder task to argue for a natural right to get satisfaction than it is to argue for a natural right to enforce one's rights.

Civil recourse is not equivalent to revenge, or at least not necessarily. Civil recourse theorists have been critiqued for appearing to endorse a revenge-based picture of private rights of action. John Finnis, for example, has argued that: 'At its root recourse theory treats as worthy the emotional impulse of [the] victim of wrongdoing to "get even," by "act[ing] against"—having recourse against—the rights violator.'[18] Goldberg and Zipursky have made clear that their account is not actually an endorsement of revenge, and the notion of accountability they have in mind is not the same thing as vengeance.[19] Granting this perspective, it remains far from evident why there should be a natural right to get satisfaction.[20] Getting satisfaction is not the same thing as getting revenge, but it is, seemingly, in the same family. For those who doubt that getting satisfaction is a natural right, redressive justice can offer a more plausible pre-legal basis for the private right of action.

[18] *See* John Finnis, 'Natural Law: The Classical Tradition' in Jules Coleman & Scott Shapiro, (eds), *The Oxford Handbook of Jurisprudence and Philosophy of Law* (OUP 2002) 1, 57.

[19] *See* John CP Goldberg & Benjamin C Zipursky, 'Accidents of the Great Society' (2005) 64 Md L Rev 364, 406 (denying that the idea of civil recourse is a way of referring to vengeance).

[20] There are possible theories. For example, Locke ties together self-defense and the pre-legal right to punish; self-defense and a pre-legal right to obtain satisfaction could be similarly linked. Cf. A John Simmons, *The Lockean Theory of Rights* (Princeton University Press 1992) 133 ('Locke is not, then, committed to holding that considerations of self-defense justify my punishing just any criminal in a state of nature; such considerations do not, strictly speaking for Locke, justify punishment at all, but only the exacting of compensation.').

With appropriate adjustments, a social contract theory can then sensibly explain a great deal about civil recourse. This is especially so if we conclude that there are pre-legal enforcement rights covering many of the contract, tort law, or other private law scenarios recognized by the law today, for which self-help is no longer available. For some, it may be unsatisfying to use a social contract approach; Zipursky emphasizes that 'the Lockean social contract metaphor cannot take much pressure',[21] and instead it may be a placeholder for other arguments that provide reasons for the state to be bound. But with a sufficiently detailed analysis the contractarian case could be made with enough force to overcome a plausibility threshold.

Yet Goldberg and Zipursky have more recently stepped back from this picture of the social contract. They question whether there plausibly are pre-legal, natural rights to retaliate for which the state owes individuals a substitute. As they indicate: 'A raw liberty to inflict harm on others is not the sort of thing for which the state, once formed, is obligated to provide a substitute.'[22] Nor does it help to see pre-legal rights to retaliate as claim rights. A Lockean social contract does not carry much persuasive force if seen in such terms.

I am not sure this is the most charitable reading of the Lockean view. As the discussion of Ripstein's argument suggests above, a Lockean social contract approach does not require us to think in terms of retaliation, revenge, or even getting satisfaction. If rights of redress are taken instead to involve privileges and claim rights respecting the enforcement of remedial rights—the kind of redress elaborated on in this book—then the idea that there are pre-legal versions is more intuitively acceptable. Indeed, the view that there are state obligations to provide substitutes for such pre-legal rights (while still open to debate) is substantially more attractive.

Yet non-Lockean accounts also have significant strengths. In their new book, Goldberg and Zipursky draw a broad analogy between private rights of action and the right to vote.[23] In doing so, they adopt a reasons-based, contractualist framework, more akin to the contractualist frameworks developed by Rawls or Scanlon than the social contract argument elaborated by Locke.[24] As Goldberg and Zipursky argue:

> Part of what makes it reasonable to accept being subjected to laws and state control—and thus to be barred from doing many things one might wish to

[21] *See* Zipursky, *Private Law* (n. 8) 642.
[22] See Goldberg & Zipursky, *Recognizing Wrongs* (n. 3) 121.
[23] Ibid. 125.
[24] *See* ibid. 115, 122.

> do, as well as from responding in certain ways to problems that one faces—is the enjoyment of a right to participate, on fair terms, in decisions about who governs and what policies will be pursued. Another part of what makes it reasonable to accept governmental authority is being granted a certain degree of power to respond to problems generated by others.[25]

Goldberg and Zipursky build on several important values—equality, fairness, and independence—as reasons to think this way. These values, in combination with ideas about liberty and the efficacy of legal institutions, offer an appealing argument for legal structures that broadly track the present day forms of civil recourse.[26]

Which account should we prefer? Perhaps the need for a less Lockean account of the state's role in providing private rights of action is overstated. That, however, should not obscure the independent merits of a contractualist, reasons-based account like the one Goldberg and Zipursky have more recently offered. Quite possibly, both accounts are suitable for justifying or at least making sense of the state's positive law obligation to provide civil recourse through private rights of action. The next section of this chapter will turn to a third possibility: a fiduciary account.

III. The Fiduciary State

Is the state a fiduciary at all and, if so, what kind? Before proceeding, it may be helpful to discuss the contours of fiduciary relationships in general. Precisely what it takes to be a fiduciary is a matter of continuing debate, and there are several contending accounts that are reasonable. Although the arguments developed below can be adapted to more than one of these approaches, for simplicity's sake I will adopt the account developed by Paul Miller and extended in our joint work:

> A fiduciary relationship is one in which one person (the fiduciary) enjoys discretionary power to pursue an abstract other-regarding purpose or the significant practical interests of another person (an individual beneficiary or ascertained set of beneficiaries).[27]

[25] Ibid. 127.
[26] *See* ibid. 131.
[27] *See* Paul B Miller & Andrew S Gold, 'Fiduciary Governance' (2015) 57 Wm & Mary L Rev 513, 549. See also Paul B Miller, 'The Fiduciary Relationship' in Andrew S Gold & Paul B Miller, (eds), *Philosophical Foundations of Fiduciary Law* (OUP 2014) 63, 69.

With this definition, it is easy enough to see how the state falls within this category. The more difficult challenge is to determine what type of fiduciary relationship the state occupies.

Many seek to fit the state into a private law fiduciary category (e.g. agency law, trust law, guardianship); it is quite plausible to think, however, that the state is a *sui generis* fiduciary.[28] Analogies to specific fiduciary and private law relationships can help us to see the distinctive features of the relationship, but the relational origins of the state's responsibilities are not identical to those in private law settings, and the state's powers, rights, and obligations will not perfectly match fiduciary powers, rights, and obligations as developed in those smaller scale environments. Furthermore, such analogies may lead us off track if the state's fiduciary characteristics are sufficiently unique.

Voluntariness is often a sticking point. Private law fiduciary relationships are usually voluntary and, in cases like agency law, this may be a requirement.[29] Of those that are legitimate but not voluntary, the characteristics of the relationship are, to say the least, distinctive. When a doctor treats a patient in a coma, that treatment can involve a fiduciary relationship, at least in some jurisdictions. We should hope the state is not thought to be like that.[30] In some jurisdictions, parents are seen as fiduciaries to their children, but this is a highly controversial analogy in the government context. Evan Fox-Decent points to agents of necessity, yet these cases are distant from the state–citizen relation.[31] Trust law relationships are also distinguishable. The beneficiaries of a trust may not get to choose their trustees, but then again trustees don't ordinarily have the ability to command their beneficiaries. Locke suggests a trust relationship, but it is telling that the Lockean picture of legislative power as a fiduciary power is linked to the people's right to overthrow it.[32]

In all likelihood, the state is best seen as a *sui generis* fiduciary. That, at any rate, is the position I will adopt here for discussion purposes. If the state is

[28] *See* Paul B Miller, 'Principles of Public Fiduciary Administration' in Tsvi Kahana & Anat Scolnicov, (eds), *Boundaries of State, Boundaries of Rights: Human Rights, Private Actors, and Positive Obligations* (CUP 2016) 251, 256 (contending that 'public fiduciary authority can be juridically located only in the *sui generis* legal personality of the state and can be exercised only by officials personating the state').

[29] Note that commenters and jurisdictions may vary on the question whether agency relations must be voluntary.

[30] That said, some have drawn on this example for insights. *See* Evan Fox-Decent, *Sovereignty's Promise: The State as Fiduciary* (OUP 2011) 108.

[31] *See* ibid. 128–35.

[32] *See* John Locke, 'The Second Treatise of Government' in David Wootton, (ed.), *Political Writings of John Locke* (Penguin Books 1993) 337, §149 ('[T]he legislative being only a fiduciary power to act for certain ends, there remains still in the people a supreme power to remove or alter the legislative when they find the legislative act contrary to the trust reposed in them.'). For helpful discussion of this relationship, see A John Simmons, *On the Edge of Anarchy: Locke, Consent, and the Limits of Society* (Princeton University Press 1993) 70–2.

understood as a fiduciary, the next step is to consider how the state's fiduciary status can provide helpful guidance for understanding the state's obligations. This is a different concern and it challenges all efforts at public fiduciary theory. The next part will address this issue.

IV. What Kind of Loyalty Does the State Owe?

A. The conventional loyalty categories

Frequently, what people mean by fiduciary loyalty is compliance with proscriptive rules against conflicts of interest and conflicts of duty. Suppose, however, that we are concerned not merely with the traditional proscriptive rules, but also with potential prescriptive loyalty obligations. This type of state obligation (or group of obligations) poses a challenging set of puzzles. In some jurisdictions, fiduciaries may owe a fiduciary obligation to act in the best interests of their beneficiaries, but this is not the only type of obligation that will potentially apply. Certain fiduciaries, notably agents, must instead follow their beneficiaries' instructions, and the state may even owe obligations of both types. Some aspects of the state's obligations may also be customized: the terms of a written constitution may modify some of the state's fiduciary obligations.[33] Context will thus be significant in determining the precise contours of the state's loyalty obligations.

I will suggest an additional type of fiduciary loyalty governs the state. It is a common, if not dominant, view that the fiduciary state must act in the best interests of its citizens.[34] Often this is correct, but, if taken as an across-the-board implication of fiduciary principles, this is an error. In part, this is because the state may also owe its citizens consideration of their preferences (even deference to them) when properly expressed. Obedience to a principal's instructions represents an important type of fiduciary obligation and, in the agency setting, obedience to preferences does not equate to informed desires—the divergence between preferences and best interests is thus both frequent and substantial. Accordingly, even if the best interests perspective is correct as to some sovereigns, this is not a conclusion that is built into a fiduciary picture of

[33] For helpful discussion of some of the issues this possibility raises, see Seth Davis, 'The False Promise of Fiduciary Government' (2014) 89 Notre Dame L Rev 1145, 1168–9.

[34] For a strong version of this claim, see Fox-Decent, *Sovereignty's Promise* (n. 30) 36 ('The law cannot authorize the fiduciary to exercise discretionary control over the beneficiary's interests without requiring the fiduciary to act in what she reasonably regards as the beneficiary's best interests.').

state sovereignty. Agency law is just as fundamental a source of fiduciary principles as trust law and agency law is preference-based at its core. A fiduciary state is quite reasonably thought to owe some deference to the preferences of its citizens.

Of course, we could also be misled if we think that our only two options for the state are variations on agency-like obligations or trust-like obligations, in isolation. James Madison, for example, appears to have contemplated both categories co-existing. In 'Federalist No. 46', he argues: 'The federal and State governments are in fact but different agents and trustees of the people, constituted with different power and designed for different purposes.'[35] Combined theories also show up in modern political theory. Thomas Christiano describes an account of legislative obligations according to which legislators should leave choices regarding aims to the people, while exercising discretion regarding the means to achieve those aims.[36] This suggests the possibility of an agency relationship regarding a society's aims, and a trustee relationship regarding the means to get there.[37]

Without ruling out these possibilities in appropriate settings, I will elaborate here on a component of the state's fiduciary obligations that has not yet been developed, a category that the state owes given the expansive scope of its discretionary power. I will suggest that the fiduciary state bears an obligation to advance what its citizens find to be meaningful.

B. Meaning, well-being, and loyalty

The state's involvement in our lives is often desirable—and sometimes necessary—but it is nonetheless also widespread and continuous, and its decisions inevitably have all sorts of effects not only on our particular decisions, but also on the direction of our lives. That is not an ordinary type of discretionary power. Granted, if the relationship between state and citizen is genuinely consensual, the state may owe whatever obligations stem from that consent. These might involve best interests-centred loyalty, or perhaps a hybrid loyalty obligation that incorporates other features such as agency principles. In the absence

[35] *See* James Madison, 'Federalist No. 46' in Isaac Kramnick, (ed.), *The Federalist Papers* (Penguin Books 1987) 297.

[36] *See* Thomas Christiano, *The Rule of The Many: Fundamental Issues in Democratic Theory* (Westview Press 1996) 215–19. I am grateful to Tim Scanlon for noting this combined possibility.

[37] In some cases, it might also be the case that the fiduciary state is responsible for advancing abstract purposes. *See* Miller & Gold, 'Fiduciary Governance' (n. 27).

of such consent, the state owes us substantial freedom in the making of our large-scale life choices.

Not every preference deserves the same weight, even if citizens' preference satisfaction is understood as a primary consideration. On the view suggested here, the state as a fiduciary should be especially concerned with our comprehensive goals in life,[38] and with those ground projects that are fundamental to our self-understanding. Over time, we often adopt ground projects that give our lives meaning.[39] As Bernard Williams notes, a person may be 'identified with his actions as flowing from projects and attitudes which in some cases he takes seriously at the deepest level, as what his life is about'.[40] These are, in certain instances, projects that people are willing to die for.[41]

Comprehensive goals and ground projects add an additional dimension to the problem of advancing well-being, for they suggest something beyond happiness or ordinary preferences will matter. Such goals and projects are integral to what we find meaningful in life, and this should give them a special import for the fiduciary state that cares about our well-being. Indeed, Susan Wolf suggests that meaningfulness is a non-derivative component of well-being: 'its goodness does not result from its making us happy or its satisfying the preferences of the person whose life it is'.[42] Whether derivative or non-derivative, however, it is clearly a feature of well-being that merits our attention.[43] When people find something meaningful, it affects their lives in a way that is qualitatively different from their other pursuits.

There is a further complication. In light of the linkage between meaningfulness and well-being, one might therefore think that with suitable adjustments, a fiduciary state that focuses on advancing the best interests of its citizens would, by extension, be a state that is concerned with advancing its citizens' interest in what is meaningful. That seems right. Yet a state that takes its citizens' best

[38] Cf. Joseph Raz, *The Morality of Freedom* (OUP 1986) 293 (describing such goals and their importance) 293; TM Scanlon, *What We Owe to Each Other* (HUP 1998) 122 ('Success in these more comprehensive goals has a larger effect on a person's life than success in more limited aims, and consequently . . . makes a greater contribution to well-being.').

[39] For seminal accounts of ground projects and their role, see JJC Smart & Bernard Williams, *Utilitarianism: For & Against* (1983) 116–17; Bernard Williams, 'Persons, Character and Morality', in *Moral Luck* (OUP 1981) 1, 13–14.

[40] Smart &Williams, *Utilitarianism: For & Against* (n. 39) 116.

[41] *See* Williams, 'Persons, Character and Morality' (n. 39) 13.

[42] *See* Susan Wolf, 'Happiness and Meaning: Two Aspects of the Good Life', in *The Variety of Values: Essays on Morality, Meaning, and Love* (OUP 2015) 108–9. For further development of Wolf's account of meaningfulness, see generally Susan Wolf, *Meaning in Life and Why It Matters* (Princeton University Press 2010).

[43] Wolf contends that a concern with advancing well-being in light of what is meaningful does not reduce to a concern for preferences, while recognizing the overlap with preferences in most cases. *See* Wolf, 'Happiness and Meaning' (n. 42) 122.

interests as its goal could fail, at least some of the time, to give our ground projects their proper place. This is because, to the extent our projects happen to cut against our best interests, the state that just seeks to advance our best interests would apparently be free to disregard those projects or even act to impede them. If what we find meaningful is sufficiently important from a fiduciary state's perspective, then our best interests may sometimes need to be traded off against this concern. This possibility suggests that the fiduciary state may owe us more than just advancement of our best interests, and perhaps sometimes that what we find meaningful should be its primary consideration.

C. The aggregation problem

Allowing for the above possibilities, the fiduciary state's goals might seem aspirational at best, for this perspective raises an intractable practical challenge. We can see the nature of this challenge if we focus more closely on the identity of the state's beneficiaries. For some public fiduciary theorists, the beneficiary is 'the people' as a unit.[44] Yet, while there may be specific contexts in which states owe fiduciary duties to citizens as a 'people', in the ordinary case fiduciary principles support state duties of loyalty that are owed to individuals. The structure of the relation between the state and its individual citizens (and in some cases non-citizens) supports imposition of fiduciary obligations toward each individual subjected to the state's power. The comprehensive and often quite overwhelming discretionary authority of the state vis-à-vis its citizens is experienced not only by those citizens as a group, but also quite evidently in their lives as individuals.

Unsurprisingly, a range of theorists have recognized that the fiduciary state owes its loyalty duties to individual citizens. From an entrustment perspective, a prominent example is the co-authored work of Evan Criddle and Evan Fox-Decent.[45] From a principal-agent perspective, Oren Bar-Gill and Cass Sunstein draw the same conclusion.[46] Given the broad discretion possessed by the fiduciary state, and the corresponding vulnerability that individuals necessarily

[44] *See* Evan J Criddle & Evan Fox-Decent, *Fiduciaries of Humanity: How International Law Constitutes Authority* (OUP 2016) 30 (citing as an example of this view Hugo Grotius, *The Law of War and Peace*, bk 2, ch. 25, §§1–3).

[45] *See* ibid. ('Under international law today, a state must respect the legal and practical interests of each of its subjects individually; it may not treat any of its subjects as mere instruments for advancing the "greater good." '). *See also* Fox-Decent, *Sovereignty's Promise* (n. 30) 36–7.

[46] *See* Oren Bar-Gill & Cass Sunstein, 'Regulation as Delegation' (2015) 7 J Legal Analysis 1 ('It is common to talk about government as the agent of the People in a democratic society. Our focus is not on the People, but rather on an individual person.') (citation omitted).

face *as individuals*, it is appropriate to think at an individual level when we assess the fiduciary state's obligations. I will follow that approach here. Each of these theories also faces challenging problems in figuring out how to implement fiduciary loyalty across a diverse and often disputatious group of citizens, and the challenge is at least as great (if not greater) for the theory offered in this chapter; that is, a theory that calls on the state to advance its citizens' comprehensive goals and ground projects, or whatever its citizens find to be meaningful.

What is meaningful to us is characteristically dependent on our own personal idiosyncrasies. It is in part a product of our life experiences, and in part a product of our choices. While there are contexts in which it makes sense to focus on someone's informed desires, such notions do not translate well to the realm of the meaningful. In addition, we cannot easily determine what would be meaningful if someone were sufficiently well-informed, and especially not when we are operating at the state level.[47] In other words, to the extent the state may wish to assist us in advancing what is meaningful in our lives, it cannot readily do so by determining what we ought to consider meaningful if we were acting in an ideal fashion, or even by attempting to approximate what the typical person might find meaningful. The state would need to know which comprehensive life goals, which ground projects, an individual has selected (or even just fallen into) in her life.[48] That which is meaningful is highly particularized even where there are common patterns.

I do not see any perfect solutions to this challenge from an institutional design perspective. There are, however, ways that the state can provide an indirect form of support for its citizens' pursuit of comprehensive goals and ground projects—in short, what they find meaningful. Some of these mechanisms track the kind of benefits that welfare states generally seek to provide. Making certain that citizens have ready access to food, education, transportation, and guaranteeing that they have various capabilities, are ways of providing for a wide range of existing and potential ground projects. Many of the benefits discussed in the positive rights literature can be understood in this way.[49] Other mechanisms are designed to give individuals or groups space to develop their

[47] In other words, part of the difficulty is a problem we see more generally with private law principles—a challenge in moving from the micro level to the macro level. For further discussion of this challenge, see Gold & Smith, 'Sizing Up Private Law' (n. 2).

[48] Cf. Scanlon, *What We Owe* (n. 38) 140 ('Another consequence of the fact that what advances a person's well-being depends on what aims he or she has adopted is that the content of well-being itself depends on decisions that are plausibly seen as the responsibility of the person in question.').

[49] On that topic more generally, see Laura S Underkuffler, 'Fiduciary Theory: The Missing Piece for Positive Rights' in Evan J Criddle, et al., (eds), *Fiduciary Government* (CUP 2018).

own preferences, goals, and self-conceptions. I will focus here on a specific mechanism of the latter type: private law.

Private law gives individuals room for a variety of largely unfettered choices, irrespective of the effects those choices will have on their overall well-being. In the process, it opens up space for what individuals find meaningful on an individual basis. Facilitating spheres of private sovereignty is thus a core means by which the fiduciary state can meet its loyalty obligations. Private law is not alone in this concern: public law also shows an important concern for what the state's citizens will find meaningful. Jack Balkin has noted that the First Amendment protection of free speech can be justified in light of how people constitute themselves.[50] Rights to privacy may offer similar benefits.[51] Yet private law has received less attention from a public fiduciary perspective, and the next part will centre on the private law component.[52]

V. Spheres of Private Sovereignty

There is a nested quality to this argument. Private law fiduciary principles in effect govern a public law institution—the state—in the determination of its obligations. But, as a consequence of these obligations, the state owes us a certain kind of private law: the state owes us a private law that gives us significant spheres of private sovereignty. Private law is thus a means for individuals to develop comprehensive goals, to develop ground projects—it is a means to advance what they find meaningful. Fiduciary principles also offer us interpretive insights that can help us to understand existing law: to a significant degree, what the state owes its citizens is the kind of private law that a number of modern legal systems already possess. Substantial spheres of private sovereignty are recognizable in our property ownership, in our contractual freedom, and in our fiduciary relationships themselves.

First, consider property law. Property ownership can be seen to occupy a central place in our self-constitution, and it certainly enables pursuit of deeply valued ground projects. Nor is this just a product of the freedoms that land

[50] *See* Jack Balkin, 'Cultural Democracy and the First Amendment' (2015) 110 Nw U L Rev 1053, 1061 ('In a free society . . . people should have the right to participate in the forms of meaning-making that shape who they are and that help constitute them as individuals.').

[51] Cf. Timothy Macklem, *Independence of Mind* (OUP 2006) 50 ('As those who would identify privacy and liberty rightly recognize, and as Woolf emphasized, private space is crucial to the development of individual voice.').

[52] An exception is Margaret Jane Radin, 'The Fiduciary State and Private Ordering' in Paul B Miller & Andrew S Gold, (eds), *Contract, Status, and Fiduciary Law* (OUP 2016) 315.

ownership provides; personal property can likewise be central to our self-understanding.[53] The state not only ought to facilitate property ownership, it ought to provide for a property law that gives owners space to use their property as they see fit, thus providing room for meaningful pursuits. This is also what property ownership generally accomplishes in common law systems. Not only does property law provide for a broad set of rights and powers, it allows for their exercise based on a largely unfettered set of motivations.[54] Property law even includes a right to destroy what one owns, a feature that suggests the truly wide breadth of owner discretion.[55]

Contract law follows a similar pattern. While there are clear limits, contract law allows for a very wide range of choices regarding substantive terms, and it likewise takes a largely hands-off approach to contractual purposes. Indeed, Curtis Bridgeman has developed a planning-based theory of contracts that illuminates the central features.[56] As he notes: 'Although the contracts as plans view is an instrumental theory in that it sees contract law as a solution to a practical problem, it is neutral as to exactly what good is to be achieved by solving the coordination problem.'[57] Although contract law is justified by more than just its link to plans, there is a key insight here: common law jurisdictions often adopt a detached, content-neutral perspective on contractual authority. There is a very wide swath of contracting discretion over which the state takes an effectively hands-off perspective.

And there is also another way that private law advances the projects that a state's citizens find meaningful. Most contractual relationships are not constitutive of comprehensive goals or ground projects, although they can be.[58] Contracts involve a type of relationship, but it is a relatively thin one. By way of contrast, fiduciary law often involves thicker relationships, and this has bearing on their significance. The reasons for the law's support of these thicker fiduciary relationships can vary. This support can be a product of societal views that certain relationships are socially valuable—think of marriage, or the parent–child

[53] *See* Margaret J Radin, 'Property and Personhood' (1982) 34 Stan L Rev 957, 959 ('Most people possess certain objects they feel are almost part of themselves. These objects are closely bound up with personhood because they are part of the way we constitute ourselves as continuing personal entities in the world.').

[54] On some accounts, the discretion may be especially broad. For example, James Penner contends that 'clearly, one can exclude others from things for any reason at all, or for no reason whatsoever'. James E Penner, *The Idea of Property in Law* (OUP 1997) 70.

[55] For discussion of this right, see Lior J Strahilevitz, 'The Right to Destroy' (2005) 114 Yale LJ 781.

[56] *See* Curtis Bridgeman, 'Contracts as Plans' [2009] U Ill L Rev 341.

[57] *See* ibid. 378.

[58] Relational contracts suggest the import of the relationship itself. There are also contract theories that emphasize the value of contractual relationships in general. *See*, e.g. Stephen A Smith, *Contract Theory* (OUP 2004) 74–8; Daniel Markovits, *Contract as Collaboration*, 113 Yale LJ 1417 (2004).

relationship—but not always. The relationships themselves are seen as intrinsically valuable whether or not they advance social interests, and this brings us to another mechanism through which private law can advance what citizens find meaningful.

Various interpersonal relationships assist us in pursuing ground projects in settings beyond the relationships themselves. Contract law can serve this purpose, and so can a number of more instrumental fiduciary relationships, such as the relationship between a client and financial advisor or a client and lawyer. Yet the legal relationship itself can also be meaningful, for its own sake. Indeed, as Susan Wolf has recognized, the phrase 'ground projects' may be imprecise.[59] There are cases where what we really have in mind when we talk about ground projects are in fact relationships.[60] For some fiduciary relationships, the relationships themselves may constitute a ground project or be inextricably tied to our meaningful pursuits.[61]

Each of the above examples dovetails with a picture in which the state bears an obligation to advance our meaningful goals and ground projects. As a fiduciary, the state owes us some room to pursue relationships (and to adopt concurrent obligations) that are part of our identity. It likewise owes us the space that property provides for various projects and pursuits as we ourselves understand them, from our own perspective. And it owes us the ability to reach agreements with others so that we can advance those projects in whichever direction moves us.

VI. The State, the Private Right of Action, and Rights of Redress

What then of the private right of action? A partial answer is already hinted at in Chapter 3: redress can indirectly advance the value in authorship provided by primary rights. Restoring someone's means through a private right of action or other form of legally sanctioned redress is a way to enable that person to pursue the various meaningful projects and goals that the primary rights of property, the primary obligations of tort law, and the various power-conferring rules of

[59] *See* Susan Wolf, 'The Meanings of Lives' in *The Variety of Values: Essays on Morality, Meaning, & Love* (OUP 2015) 89, 94 ('[T]he use of the word "project" is not ideal: It is too suggestive of a finite, determinate task, something one takes on and, if all goes well, completes.').

[60] *See* ibid. ('Relationships, in particular, seem at best awkwardly described as projects.').

[61] Cf. Daniel Markovits, 'Sharing *Ex Ante* and Sharing *Ex Post*: The Non-Contractual Basis of Fiduciary Relations' in Andrew S Gold & Paul B Miller, (eds), *Philosophical Foundations of Fiduciary Law* (OUP 2014) 209, 223 (describing the attorney–client relationship as intrinsically valuable).

contract law all facilitate. A state that seeks to advance what its citizens find meaningful will have reason not only to set in place various core private law institutions, but also private rights of action or the equivalent so that its citizens can restore what is lost when the rules of those institutions are broken by other individuals.

There is likewise another way in which private rights of action contribute to citizens' meaningful projects and comprehensive goals—the act of redress itself may be meaningful. This is implicit in arguments that private rights of action are the 'best of both worlds' in light of what private rights of action express about the state's support for its citizens and what they do for a citizen's sense of self-reliance. Quite possibly, a right holder will only care to a limited extent about her primary rights, yet she may derive substantial meaning from sticking up for herself when she has been wronged. While litigation of a claim is very rarely a plaintiff's life's work, it may well be closely tied to her comprehensive goals in life, and this may hold true irrespective of whether the underlying private law institutions (property, tort, or contract) serve in that capacity. And, if the process of litigation itself allows people to hold further attachments to the state and its legal system, rights of redress may likewise assist individuals in pursuing what they find meaningful by this means.[62]

Finally, note that the state has other fiduciary duties in light of its status, beyond those concerned with meaningfulness. States have fiduciary obligations to advance their citizens' well-being, understood in terms of citizen preferences and also in terms of their best interests.[63] These obligations are very much in play when we consider private rights of action and other mechanisms that permit wronged parties to undo a wrong to the extent possible, and they may be in play even if the preferences or interests advanced are not especially meaningful to the state's beneficiaries. Rights of redress may contribute to other valuable aspects of citizens' lives (whether or not meaningful), much as provision of education or voting rights do.[64] Even when states are focused

[62] Cf. Daniel Markovits, *A Modern Legal Ethics: Adversary Democracy for a Democratic Age* (Princeton University Press 2008) 187 (noting the 'affective consequences of engagement with the legal process—the transformations wrought by the process').

[63] A full account of well-being would require an extensive discussion, but I note here that several leading theories of well-being are plausibly advanced by private rights of action or their equivalents. Note also that the arguments in this section may support state efforts to facilitate access to justice, and not merely state provision of private rights of action on their own. I thank Sinead Agnew for emphasizing this point.

[64] For an illuminating comparison between civil recourse and voting rights, see Goldberg & Zipursky, *Recognizing Wrongs* (n. 3).

on these more conventional features of the state's role, the state may take on a responsibility to provide private rights of action or their equivalent in order to ensure the general welfare of its citizenry.[65]

One might ask whether there is also another implication of the fiduciary account. It might seem that, unlike the Lockean social contract, a fiduciary account of the state's role in providing for private rights of action is an account that removes the idea of pre-legal, natural rights of redress. Because the fiduciary account need not build on the state's prohibition of self-help, such an account could fit an understanding according to which there are no such pre-legal rights. Still, it will not automatically have this implication. The state's relationship to its citizens is dependent on the particular type of fiduciary relationship at issue (and in this respect, it may also be dependent on one's theory of natural rights). The state may very well owe fiduciary obligations that require substitutes for self-help remedies—much as in the Lockean account.[66] Alternatively, the state may owe its citizens a private right of action irrespective of the existence of pre-legal rights of redress. These are features that a political theory of the state's role must fill in, and a fiduciary account in the abstract does not entail one view or the other. Moreover, a given legal system can adopt any of the above views on political morality—or none of them—without having a direct impact on most private law concepts at the ground level of legal reasoning. As noted at the outset of this chapter, developing an account at the level of institutional justifications need not require private law doctrine that directly reflects such justifications.

Social contract accounts and fiduciary accounts of the state can help us make sense of private rights of action, but they can also support private rights of action that redress widely varied wrongs and give expression to widely divergent values. This chapter hopefully shades in some of the possibilities, but it by no means locks in particular conceptions of redress as they relate to particular views on natural law or pre-legal rights. Likewise, it by no means locks in particular conceptions of redress at the level of legal reasoning, where private rights of action must be assessed in the setting of specific legal disputes.

[65] Note also that goals that are often set to one side by private law theorists—such as deterrence of future wrongdoing—can contribute to this analysis. Even where deterrence is not part of legal reasoning at the ground level, it can help to justify the existence of legal institutions within private law, and help in determining what the state's fiduciary obligations entail.

[66] For elaboration of such a view, see Andrew S Gold, 'The State as a Wrongful Fiduciary' in Evan J Criddle, et al., (eds), *Fiduciary Government* (CUP 2018).

And yet we shouldn't think that the availability of institutional justifications is irrelevant. If the state has reason to provide for private rights of action—or even an obligation to provide for them—from the perspective of political morality, this has bearing on what it should take to overcome the conventional choice to provide for private rights of action. A New Zealand-style approach that avoids private rights of action is by no means illegitimate, but proponents of such an approach may shoulder the burden of proof in showing the merits of that path. Institutional justifications may have interpretive implications as well, depending on the legal doctrine at issue. For example, if equitable doctrines impede private rights of action (a topic that will be discussed further in Chapter 8), it is fair to ask why the state provides for such doctrines within its private law institutions.

***

The state's legal obligation to provide for private rights of action implicates questions of political morality. One leading way to explain and even justify the state's role in this setting is to turn to a Lockean social contract. That approach has proven controversial. Another, more recent approach is to build on a reasons-based, contractualist analysis. This chapter suggests a third approach, grounded in public fiduciary theory. As developed here, a fiduciary account ties private rights of action—and the state's role in providing for private rights of action—to individuals' efforts to pursue their ground projects and comprehensive goals.

On this view, private law offers a means for the state to make space for, and indeed facilitate, the individualized projects that each of its citizens find meaningful. Recognizing this also helps to justify many existing private law institutions. Property owners can often exclude non-owners for any reason they wish, and within legal constraints they can use their property for whatever aim that they fancy. Contracting parties have the ability to adopt contracts for a wide range of goals, many of which are quite personal to the parties. Fiduciary relationships offer a broad menu of options, and while there are unquestionably well-worn channels, the end result is a capacity to enter into multiple distinctive relationships, with a variety of different loyalty types. Notably for our purposes, private rights of action can reinforce these institutions and advance citizens' projects in their own right.

In short, private rights of action and other forms of redress can be justified by the state's public fiduciary obligations. It is up to individual citizens to find meaning for themselves, but the fiduciary state can help give us the tools to do so. In this way, we need not look for a social contract to justify the state's obligation to support rights of redress or appropriate equivalents. It does matter that self-help is largely prohibited, but that is just part of a larger picture. The state owes its citizens fiduciary loyalty in light of the state's own assertion of authority. Indeed, the state owes fiduciary obligations that incorporate many things. Not least among these is a certain kind of private law, with rights of redress occupying a central place.

7
The Meaning of Self-help

I. Introduction

If the state offers private rights of action as a substitute for legally prohibited acts of self-help, a natural question is where the *permissible* acts of self-help fit in. After all, modern legal systems do permit people to chase down a thief and recover their stolen goods, and self-help lingers in isolated pockets throughout private law. Indeed, self-help is the very example this book started with. Such cases clearly are examples of redress; in fact they are the most basic illustration. And if the state deems it wise to leave residual practices of self-help in place, a theory of private law should take them into account.

Self-help is worth thinking about not only because it helps complete our picture of redress and its legal role. Self-help remedies also pose difficulties for some alternative theories of private law, notably Kantian theories. The central concern for such theories is that ex post self-help appears to involve a private party unilaterally enforcing her rights against another, or, as it is sometimes put, being 'in charge of' another. On the Kantian view, such conduct is prohibited by private law, and also by norms of justice. As Arthur Ripstein suggests: 'Private enforcement is not merely inconvenient: it is inconsistent with justice because it is ultimately the rule of the stronger.'[1] If self-help involves this very thing, then this suggests the Kantian interpretation of private law will not fit real-world private law practices.

On the other hand, if the Kantian view on the morality of private enforcement is correct, it may suggest a problem with thinking about private law in terms of redressive justice, at least to the extent that redress allows one private party to act against another through unilateral enforcement of her remedial rights. The problem is not merely moral; it is interpretive. One might think that the redress-centred account offered in this book is implausible if it calls for us to interpret private law in a way that is morally dubious. I will suggest below that the Kantian account has sufficient fit problems and counterintuitive implications that it is

[1] *See* Arthur Ripstein, 'Private Order and Public Justice: Kant and Rawls' (2006) 92 Va L Rev 1391, 1418.

The Right of Redress. Andrew S. Gold, Oxford University Press (2020). © Andrew S. Gold.
DOI: 10.1093/oso/9780198814405.001.0001

not a convincing alternative to the account offered here. Of equal importance, I will suggest that an interpretation of private law that allows for unilateral, private enforcement can be a reasonable interpretation. We should not think that a redress-centred account of private law is an unlikely one, simply on the basis that it allows for private enforcement and builds on moral principles that accept such enforcement. This chapter will begin with the challenges posed by self-help remedies and then turn to more general questions of interpretation.

***

Consider first a classic case of redress through self-help. Suppose Jane falls asleep on the beach, and she forgets to take off her watch. She stirs from a restful sleep to see that someone is in the process of unclasping her watch and stealing it. As she awakens, Jane sees that the watch is no longer on her wrist, it is hanging in the air just above her arm and the thief is about to abscond with it. She reaches up and pries the watch out of the thief's hands, calling for help as she does so. Friends arrive quickly and the thief flees the scene.

Let's call this the *Watch* example. This case involves a tort doctrine known as 'recaption of chattels',[2] and the conduct in taking the watch back can be perfectly legal. But it is not self-defence and it is not even ex ante conduct. Taking the watch back is an ex post undoing of a wrong, rather than a prevention of a wrong that might occur. It is also a case in which one private person gets to coerce another, indeed, to be in charge of another. Accordingly, to the extent that tort law relies on a principle that one person does not get to be in charge of another, it does so inconsistently. Particularly in cases of hot pursuit, private parties do get to enforce their rights, undoing the wrongs they have suffered.

In developing these points, I will begin with an overview of Arthur Ripstein's recent book, *Private Wrongs*.[3] That account, together with Ripstein's earlier work, offers once of the most influential expositions of the Kantian view, and it allows us to assess where the weaknesses in that view lie. In the course of this analysis, it should also become clearer just how accounts that draw on moral enforcement rights can assist in explaining core features of private law doctrine.[4]

[2] *See Restatement (2d) of the Law of Torts* (1965) §100 (recognizing the defence of recaption of chattels). A classic example of recaption is found in the English case of *Blades v. Higgs*, 142 E.R. 634 (Court of Common Pleas, 1861) (addressing the retaking of rabbits that were caught on the defendant's land). For helpful discussion of that case, see Zoë Sinel, 'De-Ciphering Self-Help' (2017) 67 U Toronto LJ 31.

[3] *See* Arthur Ripstein, *Private Wrongs* (HUP 2016).

[4] While this chapter will focus on ex post cases of redress, it bears emphasis that private law also allows for ex ante forms of private enforcement. Think of self-help in cases involving abatement of a nuisance. I thank John Goldberg for noting the example.

II. The Account in *Private Wrongs*

Ripstein's interpretive account is broadly Kantian, although not developed as such in *Private Wrongs*: common law judges rarely refer to Kant, and the argument is not meant to show otherwise.[5] Rather, he argues that the correct understanding of tort law matches a Kantian vision of private law even if courts don't consciously intend it to. Ripstein's argument in support 'begin[s] with the moral idea that no person is in charge of another'.[6] With the exception of defamation, each category of tort is a private wrong involving the use of another's means. In turn, legal remedies are justified by this same structure: even after a wrong has been committed, no person gets to be in charge of another. Remedies are a way of enforcing the plaintiff's right, a right that survives whatever wrong has occurred.

A central concern is with the right holder's means. On this account, your 'means' are 'just those things about which you are entitled to decide the ends for which they will be used'.[7] Tort law is concerned with these means in three respects:

> First, [tort law] protects the means that each person has for setting and pursuing purposes. Second, it restricts the means that each person can use by precluding one person from using means that belong to another without that person's authorization. Third, it restricts the ways in which each person can use his or her own means, to those ways that are consistent with everyone else being able to do the same.[8]

Individuals may use their property or body for whatever ends they wish, so long as they do not use another's property or body without that person's permission, and so long as their conduct does not have effects that interfere with the entitlements of others.

III. The Problem of Self-help

Yet there is a key doctrinal challenge: tort law is apparently quite open to the idea of one person being in charge of another. To see where the problem lies, it

[5] *See* ibid. xi–xii (recognizing that 'common law judges of earlier centuries did not read Kant').
[6] *See* ibid. 6.
[7] *See* ibid. 9.
[8] Ibid.

may help to think further about what it means for one party to be in charge of another. We might think, after all, that whenever a court orders the payment of damages, one person is in charge of another: either the judge is in charge of the defendant, or, perhaps, the plaintiff is in charge of the defendant. These understandings are prima facie reasonable, but Ripstein's account is very different. On his account, courts emerge as a central requirement if we are to *avoid* having one person be in charge of another.

Ripstein contends that '[w]ithout courts, one person's say-so or enforcement of tort law's requirements would just be a different way of being in charge of others'.[9] Or, in another formulation, 'If the plaintiff is not in charge of the defendant, then the plaintiff's allegation that the defendant has violated some right of the plaintiff's is just that—an allegation—until a third party with authority over both the plaintiff and the defendant has resolved the dispute on its merits.'[10] On this view, we need courts precisely because they are 'institutions that can claim to be speaking (that is, exercising judgment) and acting (that is, ordering people to do things, backed by the possibility of enforcement) on behalf of everyone.'[11] Ripstein's concern with unilateral coercion by private individuals thus seems to mandate decisions by third parties with authority over both the plaintiff and defendant: courts are not examples of one individual being in charge of another, but instead alternatives to that scenario. If matters were different—if there were no such third party involved—then plaintiffs would be in charge of defendants.

At first glance, self-help looks like a glaring counter-example to the Kantian picture. It is counterintuitive to think that when someone acts in self-defence, she is doing anything other than acting on her own behalf, at least in the ordinary case. And the same is true ex post in the *Watch* example, when Jane seeks to grab her watch back from the thief. She is seemingly a private party unilaterally enforcing her rights, acting on her own behalf; the average bystander would not think of Jane's acts in any other capacity, and it would be surprising if Jane herself thought differently. Unless a legal system has determined otherwise, the natural understanding of this fact pattern is that Jane is a private party who gets to be in charge of another.

We may even see the legitimacy of self-help as a basis for questioning Ripstein's approach on normative grounds.[12] Why shouldn't a private party

[9] *See* ibid. 13.

[10] *See* ibid. 273.

[11] *See* ibid.

[12] This may depend on both the type of self-help involved and the theory of self-help at issue. Recent work addresses a broad range of contexts and perspectives. *See*, e.g. Sinel, 'De-Ciphering' (n. 2); Adam B Badawi, 'Self-Help and the Rules of Engagement' (2012) 29 Yale J Reg 1; Jason Solomon,

sometimes be able to make a determination—correctly, let's assume[13]—that his right has survived a wrong, and then within appropriate limits enforce that right through a private remedy? In recaption of chattels cases, this understanding will strike many as perfectly reasonable. Especially in exigent circumstances, it is not obvious what is problematic about private parties enforcing their rights in the absence of a judicial determination. Given that tort law seems to allow for such conduct in appropriate contexts, we may accordingly think that a good explanatory theory ought to explain why tort law sometimes permits one party to be in charge of another.

Here is a potential response. In describing how public authorities are entitled to decide on behalf of everyone, Ripstein notes that '[t]his structure manifests itself even in cases in which the law permits self-help; the question of whether the circumstances warrant it is subject to review, even in cases of self-defense'.[14] In a footnote to this same sentence he then cites to Malcolm Thorburn's work, which analyses self-defence in the criminal law setting.[15] In combination, these points suggest an account that is, at least in the abstract, capable of addressing the above concerns with self-help.

Arguably, ex post self-help is simply the exercise of a power or privilege by a party acting on behalf of the state. The private party is, in effect, a proxy for a public actor when he engages in self-help. On Thorburn's view (developed in the criminal law setting), there is something unusual about the cases in which self-defence is permissible. Urgency occupies a central place in the legal analysis:

> That is, we are entitled to decide that it is justified to kill in self-defense, that it is justified to violate a prohibition to avoid a greater harm, or that it is justified to use force to perform a citizen's arrest only when it is essential to make that decision promptly and there are no properly qualified public officials available to consult.[16]

'Judging Plaintiffs' (2007) 60 Vand L Rev 1749; Mark P Gergen, 'A Theory of Self-Help Remedies in Contract' (2009) 89 BU L Rev 1397; Henry E Smith, 'Self-Help and the Nature of Property' (2005) 1 J L Econ & Pol'y 69.

[13] It is a different question whether a private party should be able to define the contours of his or her rights, such that her judgment on their scope becomes binding. For present purposes, I am solely considering the possibility that a private party can enforce pre-existing rights, consistent with their boundaries as they already exist.

[14] *See* Ripstein, *Private Wrongs* (n. 3) 274.

[15] *See* ibid. (citing Malcolm Thorburn, 'Justifications, Powers, and Authority' (2008) 117 Yale LJ 1070.

[16] *See* ibid. 1126.

On Thorburn's understanding, private citizens are 'exercising these powers only as stand-ins for public officials who have the power to make these decisions'.[17] As he concludes: 'Private citizens do not have the authority to make such decisions in their own right.'[18]

Even if we are sympathetic to this account in criminal law settings, it is less clear that it fits private law. The ex post self-help available in private law settings is not always a response to extremely exigent circumstances, in which public authorities are of necessity unavailable.[19] Moreover, while the wrongs at issue in criminal law are public wrongs, the wrongs at issue in private law are private wrongs.[20] Perhaps only a public actor has the proper standing to undo a public wrong—particularly if one is drawn to expressive accounts of legal remedies—but private wrongs are more plausibly fixable by the specific victims of those wrongs.

But there is another, more striking feature of Thorburn's account. For Thorburn, the party engaging in self-defence is a stand-in for a public official; she is a public official *pro tempore*. This view could readily have an analogue in private law and, if so, it could help rescue the idea that self-help is consistent with a tort law in which no private party gets to be in charge of another. Intuitively, this reading is an awkward fit for reception of chattels, but it does fit well with a citizen's arrest case. Parties engaging in self-help might be understood as stand-ins for public officials, and if viewed in their public capacity they would then (in theory) represent an omnilateral will instead of exemplifying the unilateral coercion that troubles Ripstein. This is a conceptual possibility—nothing precludes the idea that private parties can be stand-ins for public officials when they engage in self-help. This is not, on the other hand, a very convincing interpretation of private law in the United States, at least not in all cases.

Bear in mind that the question whether private parties are stand-ins for public officials when they engage in self-help is not something to be resolved as a matter of political theory, as it is ultimately a matter of positive law. Some historical sources support the Thorburn view on self-defence,[21] while other

[17] *See* ibid.

[18] *See* ibid.

[19] This appears to be true in reception contexts—a setting where we might anticipate a limitation to more exigent circumstances. *See* Badawi, 'Self-Help and the Rules' (n. 12) 32 (noting 'the rather odd result that, through continual pursuit of a stolen chattel, it can be retaken with force even if a significant amount of time has elapsed and even if the victim of the theft does not know the identity of the person who stole the good').

[20] This is not to deny that the wrongs that matter for tort law may also implicate criminal law. In the ordinary case, however, the wrongs that concern courts in applying private law doctrine are of concern to those courts qua private wrongs.

[21] *See* Thorburn, 'Justifications' (n. 15) 1127.

sources do not. John Gardner contends that Thorburn's analysis is inconsistent with the understanding of the English common law.[22] Yet even taking the supportive historical sources into account, the ultimate question still concerns the current legal point of view within a given legal system. As Gardner notes with respect to self-defence:

> [T]he historical sources of the law, the causal antecedents of interest to historians, are not the sources of the law that matter to lawyers. The law of self-defence has its legal source, its legal derivation, in whatever case law and statute law is currently authoritative in the legal system under scrutiny.[23]

Indeed, current law is exactly where we need to be looking if our aim is to take tort law, and private law more generally, at face value.

Even if it is counterintuitive to see private parties as stand-ins for public officials when they engage in self-defence or recaption of chattels, that view could still be the legal point of view. Does the legal point of view support this perspective? On self-help, the current legal landscape looks uncertain at best for that picture: when it comes to the law in the United States, case law on the private-ness of self-help is a shaky foundation for the views of both Thorburn and Ripstein.[24]

On the other hand, the law in this area is not exactly pellucid. In addition, in some areas of the law on self-help there is sparse precedent to draw upon. As others have noted, there is limited case law on recaption or necessity doctrines.[25] The view that self-help generally involves private parties acting as stand-ins for public officials might not always be intuitively obvious, yet it may have some life in it. Moreover, there are two interpretive criteria that arguably point in Ripstein's favour. A supporter of the Kantian interpretation of tort law might claim that interpretive theories should conform to a morality criterion, and, arguably, this criterion could lend support to Ripstein's reading. Alternatively, a supporter might adopt a justice criterion, to similar effect. Neither argument succeeds, and the reasons why are worth developing.

22 For Gardner's basis of disagreement with Thorburn's account, see John Gardner, 'Justification Under Authority' (2010) 23 Canadian J L & Juris 71; John Gardner, 'Criminals in Uniform' in RA Duff, et al., (eds), *The Constitution of the Criminal Law* (OUP 2013) 97. For Gardner's discussion of the English common law, see Gardner, 'Justification' 95–6.

23 *See* ibid. 95.

24 *See* Andrew S Gold, 'Private Rights and Private Wrongs' (2017) 115 Mich L Rev 1071, 1077–80.

25 *See* Sinel, 'De-Ciphering' (n. 12) 36 (referencing the *Blades v. Higgs* case as one of the 'few self-help cases on the books'); Gideon Parchomovsky & Alex Stein, 'Reconceptualizing Trespass' (2009) 103 Nw U L Rev 1823, 1851 (noting that necessity cases 'are rather rare').

IV. The Morality Criterion

It is natural to interpret self-help as a way that one private individual gets to be in charge of another, and, while not definitive, some decisions reinforce this reading. Still, one might object that appearances can be deceiving, and that the natural reading of self-help is problematic under standard criteria for explanatory theories. Interpretive accounts are often assessed for their consistency with interpersonal morality, and it might be argued that Ripstein's account does better under this criterion than alternative readings. From this perspective, when private parties engage in self-help they should be seen as stand-ins for public officials so as to provide tort law with an apparent moral legitimacy that it would otherwise lack. This is not necessarily because the law must be moral; instead, it is more likely that an interpretation accurately captures the law's self-understanding if it adopts concepts that legal actors could consider moral (whether or not they are in fact moral).[26]

In order to assess this kind of argument, we need to think carefully about our approach to interpretive methodology. The manner in which interpersonal morality figures in interpretation varies from one private law theorist to another. Superficial resemblances in language mask very different ideas on interpretation, and reliance on prior work in the field can lead us astray if we don't first figure out what methodology a theorist is adopting. I will assume that our aim is to understand tort law in terms of its self-understanding, or, as it is sometimes expressed, in terms of the internal point of view.

With this starting point, one might adopt an interpretive theory of law like Ronald Dworkin's.[27] In that case, a good interpretive theory may need to show how tort law actually *is* justified. Many private law theorists eschew Dworkin's mode of interpretation, and I think this is right. It seems too much to ask if we insist that a theory of tort law must show that the principles of tort law or other private law fields are in fact morally justified. As Stephen Smith aptly notes, part of the law's self-understanding is that the law can be mistaken.[28] The legal point of view makes room for error, and by extension a theory of tort law that tracks law's self-understanding should not be called into doubt if it happens to describe conceptual features that are regrettable.

[26] For discussion of this point and its place in private law theory, see Andrew S Gold, 'Internal and External Perspectives' in Andrew S Gold, et al., (eds), *The Oxford Handbook of New Private Law* (OUP forthcoming).

[27] *See* Ronald Dworkin, *Law's Empire* (HUP 1986) 285 (contending that a 'successful interpretation must not only fit but also justify the practice it interprets').

[28] *See* Stephen A Smith, *Contract Theory* (OUP 2004) 17–18.

There are, however, more moderate versions of a morality criterion, and these moderate versions allow for legal error. Smith offers one of the leading examples in his account of interpretive criteria. As he indicates, private law theorists are characteristically concerned with figuring out the law's self-understanding; they want to explain the law from the internal point of view.[29] And, as Smith argues: 'there has been general agreement that a central feature, if not *the* central feature, of that self-understanding is law's claim to authority—the claim or belief that law is morally justified'.[30] From this standpoint, a good explanation of a private law field should show how a legal field *could be thought to be* morally justified, whether or not it actually is morally justified.[31]

In some cases a weaker morality criterion might have merit, particularly if our interpretive criteria are grounded on a theory of what law claims. Notably, the law apparently claims to be morally binding, rather than morally correct.[32] Thus, very little purchase on private law interpretation can be gained by relying on law's claim to authority, if any. A moderate morality criterion is more realistically grounded in suppositions about the way legal actors are likely to think, as a matter of psychological and sociological factors.[33]

With these limits recognized, let's start from the premise that a moderate morality criterion is appropriate here. In that case, an explanatory account of tort law should indicate how tort law doctrine could be thought to be morally justified, whether or not it actually is. Would this rule out a theory of tort law that allows one private party to unilaterally coerce another? Ripstein's theory of tort law is effectively an extension of Kant's theory of private law, and the answer to this question depends on how morally compelling courts would find the Kantian theory. If courts would inevitably agree with Kant on the core moral issues, then a moderate morality criterion offers support for Ripstein's theory. If reasonable minds could differ, then self-help becomes a more difficult hurdle for the Kantian approach.

Before proceeding, it may be helpful to provide a brief overview of some key Kantian premises.[34] Ripstein contends that on Kant's account there are three

[29] *See* ibid. 15 ('Since at least the publication of H.L.A. Hart's *The Concept of Law*, there has been broad, if not quite universal, agreement amongst legal theorists that law's self-understanding (an aspect of what Hart called "the internal perspective on law") is a feature of law that legal theories must take into account.').

[30] *See* ibid.

[31] *See* ibid. 18–19.

[32] *See* John Gardner, 'How Law Claims, What Law Claims' in *Law as a Leap of Faith* (OUP 2012) 125, 139–44. I discuss some of the interpretive implications in Andrew S Gold, 'Interpreting Fiduciary Law' in D Gordon Smith & Andrew S Gold, (eds), *Research Handbook on Fiduciary Law* (Elgar Press 2018).

[33] *See* Gold, 'Private Rights' (n. 24).

[34] Much of the key discussion is set forth in Immanuel Kant, *The Metaphysics of Morals* (Mary J Gregor trans. 1797) (CUP 1991). As my aim is to assess Ripstein's account, I will respond to his interpretation of Kant's theory of private law.

defects in the state of nature: a) it is impossible to acquire a right to anything (beyond a provisional right) because doing so would allow individuals to make a unilateral choice regarding the entitlements of others; b) acquired rights cannot be enforced due to a lack of assurance regarding the conduct of other individuals; and c) the application of private rights to particulars can only be determined 'in accordance with standards that are not unilateral exercises of judgment of one of the parties to a dispute', yet objective standards cannot be established in a state of nature.[35] On this view, private enforcement of rights raises a problem of unilateral choice, a problem of assurance, and a problem of indeterminacy.

For Kantians, self-defence is a special case: self-defence involves innate rights, and the rights involved are considered to be enforceable.[36] But once we depart from self-defence, a unilateral enforcement of private rights is wrongful. This understanding also means that remedial rights cannot be enforced by private parties: '[t]he absence of enforceable rights to external objects of choice . . . means that you can have no remedial right if someone commits a wrong against your person'.[37] Thus, on the Kantian view, the only way that such private rights can be legitimately enforced is by means of public institutions acting on behalf of everyone; the state is needed because it can enforce these remedial rights through an omnilateral will.

As Ripstein notes, Kant 'needs to explain how institutions can act omnilaterally'.[38] The answer is through the use of public roles, by which officers of the state act on behalf of everyone rather than on behalf of private actors. State actors occupy a status relationship, and the state's relation to its citizens can be analogized to the relation between a parent and his or her children.[39] And the consequence of this official capacity is that unilateral choices are avoided: 'So long as everyone acts in his or her official capacity, the result is authorized by law, and so is not arbitrary from the standpoint of others.'[40] On this view, 'a rightful condition can give authority to laws

[35] *See* Arthur Ripstein, *Force and Freedom: Kant's Legal and Political Philosophy* (HUP 2009) 145–81. For the quoted language, see ibid. 146.

[36] *See* ibid. 161 ('Your entitlement to use force to exclude others from your own person is consistent with your obligation to refrain from interfering with the person of another, because your right to self-defense is purely protective.'); ibid. 179 ('Your right to repel those who invade the space occupied by your body does not require an omnilateral authorization.').

[37] *See* ibid. 180.

[38] *See* ibid. 183.

[39] *See* ibid. 194 ('The parent guides a child to make it into its own master; the state creates a rightful condition in which each person can be his or her own master.'). That said, I doubt that the parent–child relation is a helpful starting point for theorizing state authority. *See* Andrew S Gold, 'Reflections on the State as Fiduciary' (2013) 63 U Toronto LJ 655.

[40] *See* Ripstein, 'Force and Freedom' (n. 35) 197.

rather than human beings, so that the actions of particular human beings in making, enforcing, and applying laws can be exercises of public rather than private power, and so are instances of an omnilateral will.'[41] The required omnilateral will is something deemed by law; it is not the product of an affirmative act.[42]

The Kantian account of private rights faces challenges in several areas: one objection has been powerfully elaborated by Victor Tadros.[43] From the Kantian perspective, private enforcement of property rights is wrongful conduct to the extent it means that one person gets to be in charge of another. Yet, as Tadros indicates, there are cases in which it is quite counterintuitive to deny private parties the authority to enforce their rights against others in a state of nature. Tadros's core example involves Jews who have had their food taken away by a Nazi sympathizer during the Nazi rule of Germany, an act done with the knowledge that this will lead to their deaths. The Nazi regime is illegitimate, and its illegitimacy is such that these individuals are effectively in a state of nature.[44] Do the Nazi sympathizer's victims have enforceable rights to the food taken from them, such that they personally can take it away from the thief? Do they have such rights even if this requires physical interference with the individual who took the food from them? Tadros suggests the answer is yes, and I agree. This conclusion, however, is hard to square with the Kantian view Ripstein describes.[45]

There is also an additional concern: the attraction of the Kantian approach to private law presupposes a Kantian political philosophy. Even if Kant is right that no private party should get to be in charge of another, it need not follow that he is also right in thinking that the state and its institutions are a realistic solution to that problem. The Kantian approach solves the problem of one party being in charge of another by viewing the state's enforcement of private rights in terms of an omnilateral will.[46] Yet, in order for an omnilateral

[41] *See* ibid. 191.

[42] *See* ibid. 196.

[43] *See* Victor Tadros, 'Independence Without Interests?' (2011) 31 Oxford JL Stud 193, 202–6.

[44] *See* ibid. 200 ('[P]eople living under Nazi rule in Germany were not in a rightful condition by Ripstein's own lights: those governed by a law that has slavery or genocide at its foundation are in a barbaric condition.').

[45] It is not impossible to reconcile these views, but, for reasons Tadros develops, the potential responses to this problem are not very convincing. *See* ibid. 203 (discussing potential responses).

[46] *See* Ripstein, *Private Wrongs* (n. 3) 13 (describing the importance of institutions 'that can claim to be speaking (that is, exercising judgment) and acting (that is, ordering people to do things, backed by the possibility of enforcement) on behalf of everyone', and concluding that '[w]ithout courts, one person's say-so or enforcement of tort law's requirements would just be a different way of being in charge of others').

will to be something more than a tempting legal fiction, we need a basis for thinking that individuals participate in that will, and it is extraordinarily unlikely that every citizen has consented—tacitly or otherwise—to share in this omnilateral will.[47]

If Kant is right about the morality of unilateral rights enforcement and is wrong in thinking that a purported omnilateral will is a plausible solution, then the enforcement of private rights may involve a tragic circumstance—a sad but inevitable wrongfulness in the way we treat each other—rather than something that can properly be addressed by courts deciding private law cases. Judges could easily reach this conclusion if confronted with the issue. They might not think that a private law under which private parties are legally seen as stand-ins for public officials is morally better if they do not also think that having private parties act in this capacity will offer a truly omnilateral will. Interpreting tort law or private law more generally to incorporate an omnilateral will does not make the law more obviously consistent with the ideas on morality that judges hold, even if we are convinced that judges are concerned with the legitimacy of unilateral rights enforcement.

Of course, whatever doubts we may harbour about Kantian views on private rights and/or political philosophy, a Kantian understanding of tort law might still prevail as an interpretive matter if we had nowhere else to turn. One might think that there is no alternative account that adequately fits the structure of tort law while still appearing morally plausible. And some, at least, are drawn to the view that it takes a theory to beat a theory (although I do not share that view). Regardless, there are appealing alternatives to a Kantian analysis that fit the structure of private law adjudication, not to mention the concepts of right, duty, wrong, and remedy that are immanent in that structure. A leading example is the Lockean account developed by John Goldberg and Benjamin Zipursky.

Recall that Goldberg and Zipursky have suggested in the past that private rights of action implicate a wronged party's pre-legal right to act against the party who wronged her. As developed in that work, Locke's views on natural rights are quite capable of grounding private rights of action.[48] Private rights of

[47] Cf. Tadros, 'Independence' (n. 43) 206 ('Ripstein's answer is that the law provides the answer for the law, in a rightful condition, is identified with all of our wills. This, I should say, will strike many people as an unsatisfactory answer—it is not clear how governance by law under a rightful condition is equivalent to the law acting through my will.').

[48] *See*, e.g. Benjamin C Zipursky, 'Civil Recourse, Not Corrective Justice' (2003) 91 Geo LJ 695; John CP Goldberg, 'The Constitutional Status of Tort Law: Due Process and the Right to a Law for the Redress of Wrongs' (2005) 115 Yale LJ 524.

action are a mechanism for the exercise of individuals' natural right of redress, provided by the state as a substitute for self-help. With suitable adjustments, that account also suggests a picture of private law in which self-help can be legitimate even if private parties are not stand-ins for public officials. If private rights of action are needed substitutes for the self-help that we could otherwise legitimately engage in in a state of nature, it is a short step to the idea that some unilateral acts of self-help remain legitimate when legally permitted.

This same point applies if we adopt the fiduciary account developed in Chapter 6. Whether the reason for the state's provision of private rights of action is that this meets the terms of a Lockean social contract, or whether the reason instead is that this follows under the state's fiduciary obligations to its citizens, in either event it is reasonable to understand self-help as a form of residual private power. Even if the state has a responsibility to provide substitutes for self-help in appropriate cases, it need not follow that self-help is illegitimate where not specifically prohibited.

Ripstein notes that the legal processes that civil recourse theorists emphasize are just as explicable from a Kantian point of view, and he is right.[49] But this type of argument cuts both ways: what can be explained in Kantian terms can frequently also be explained in Lockean terms or in fiduciary terms. Insofar as we may need an alternative to Ripstein's view—especially given the intuitive force of the idea that self-help often involves private parties acting on their own behalf—there is no lack of reasonable alternatives. Various distinctive accounts are available, and each of them is capable of explaining tort law duties, defences, standing doctrines, and remedies in a credible way while also allowing for private enforcement.[50] These theories have the additional advantage that they are capable of explaining why one private party sometimes gets to unilaterally (or multilaterally) coerce another in the recaption context.

Courts could be drawn to the idea that private enforcement is acceptable under appropriate conditions, particularly in cases where the state is not well positioned to provide an adequate alternative remedy. Furthermore, our interpretive inquiry does not depend on whether Kant or Locke (or another theorist) is actually correct on the underlying moral questions, for what matters is simply whether courts could think private enforcement of rights is morally

[49] *See* Ripstein, *Private Wrongs* (n. 3) 287 ('All of the facts about legal processes to which defenders of civil recourse draw attention are just what tort law would look like if remedies turned on the axis of rights.').

[50] Examples include not only the Lockean account originally developed by Goldberg and Zipursky, but also the fiduciary account in Chapter 6, and another Lockean account offered by Linda Radzik. *See* Linda Radzik, 'Tort Processes and Relational Repair' in John Oberdiek, (ed.), *Philosophical Foundations of the Law of Torts* (OUP 2014) 231, 247.

appropriate. Even if a perspective that allows for private enforcement were mistaken, as long as such views might be thought to be correct, that is enough to conform to a moderate morality criterion. Such perspectives are well within the mainstream, attracting legal theorists of various sympathies and building on ideas that judges could readily accept.

V. The Justice Criterion

Perhaps, however, the interpretive problem is not precisely a concern with the morality of private law, so much as a concern with its justice. Private law theorists typically espouse a morality criterion rather than a justice criterion, yet there are good arguments for adding a justice criterion to the mix.[51] Even if law as such does not claim to be just, legal actors characteristically act as if they are engaged in bringing about justice—and particularly so in the setting of adjudication.[52] The resolution of private law disputes is described in legal opinions as if it involves justice, and private law is filled with concepts and conceptual inferences that concern just results.

We may need to assess a theory of private law to see whether it properly reflects these features of adjudication. If a theory of private law presents private law doctrine as something flagrantly inconsistent with principles of justice, or even just blissfully indifferent to such principles, we might wonder if the subject has been accurately understood. Barring some doctrinal reason to think otherwise, the clash between the internal point of view on justice and the proposed theory of private law would be too severe for the theory to pass the threshold of plausibility.

Agreeing on this point still leaves important questions open. Like a morality criterion, a justice criterion could also take various forms, with differing levels of strength. For example, one might think that the only acceptable explanations of tort law are explanations that show tort law to actually be just. As with principles of morality, courts can be mistaken about what is just, and the

[51] Cf. Andrew S Gold, 'A Theory of Redressive Justice' (2014) 64 U Toronto LJ 159, 204 (suggesting that connecting private law concepts and norms of justice can make an explanatory theory more cogent). It is important to distinguish accounts that seek to square private law concepts and norms with a broader, systemic understanding of justice (such as those concerned with having a just society). Cf. Benjamin C Zipursky, 'Civil Recourse' in Andrew S Gold, et al., (eds), *The Oxford Handbook of New Private Law* (OUP forthcoming). The kind of justice that courts have in mind is justice as between the litigating parties.

[52] On the link between adjudication and justice, see John Gardner, 'The Virtue of Justice and the Character of Law' in *Law as a Leap of Faith* (OUP 2012) 238. For the view that law does not claim to be just, see Gardner, 'How Law Claims' (n. 32) 141.

legal point of view allows for this. I will adopt a moderate justice criterion: all else equal, if a theory of tort law presents tort law such that legal actors could not plausibly think it is just, we have cause to doubt whether that theory has accurately captured tort law.

On a leading view, justice governs questions of allocation—questions of who gets how much of what.[53] Not all moral problems are problems about how to allocate, and so from this perspective justice has its own sphere of operation. If we recognize this distinction between the just and the moral, it might not be clear how unilateral enforcement of rights involves a question of justice. One might object to unilateral enforcement on purely moral grounds, without implicating justice, if one's objection is not premised on allocative concerns. And, potentially, this is the concern when unilateral enforcement is challenged on the view that one person should not impose their will on another. What is the allocative objection to unilateral enforcement of private rights?

We can see a tighter connection to justice and its allocative concerns if we turn to another critique of unilateral enforcement. Drawing on Thomas Hobbes, Evan Fox-Decent has argued that the key problem with a unilateral enforcement of rights is that it means an individual gets to be a judge in his own cause.[54] Fox-Decent notes that 'Hobbes insists that it is a law of nature "that they that are at controversy, submit their right to the judgment of an arbitrator", and that it is a further such law that "no man is a fit arbitrator in his own cause." '[55]

This understanding bears some similarities to Ripstein's Kantian account, but the arguments are not identical. For Fox-Decent, the core problem is a problem of asymmetry between the parties to a dispute. As he argues:

> It is important to underscore, however, that the fundamental wrongfulness of unilateralism lies not in the possibility of unresolved disputes, nor even the prospect of disputes decided by the will of the stronger. While these concerns are serious, they are not fundamental. . . . These instances of unilateralism are wrongful because they implicitly deny the equality of the parties to a dispute by giving to one, but not the other, adjudicative and executive authority.[56]

[53] For views that tie justice to allocative questions, *see*, e.g. HLA Hart, 'Prolegomenon to the Principles of Punishment' in *Punishment and Responsibility* (OUP 1968) 21; John Gardner, 'What Is Tort Law For? Part 1: The Place of Corrective Justice' (2011) 30 Law & Phil 1, 6.

[54] *See* Evan Fox-Decent, 'Unseating Unilateralism' in Lisa Austin & Dennis Klimchuk, (eds), *Private Law and the Rule of Law* (OUP 2014) 116.

[55] Ibid. 127 (quoting Thomas Hobbes, *Leviathan with Selected Variants from the Latin Edition of 1668* (first published 1651), (ed. Edwin Curley) (Hackett Publishing 1994) 98 (ch. xv par. 30 and ch. xv par. 31)).

[56] *See* ibid. 128–9.

On this view, one party is getting the advantage, illegitimately, of an authority that the other party does not get to share in.[57]

This is an allocative concern and, as this discussion suggests, the key norm of justice at issue is the principle of *nemo iudex in sua causa*—no one should be a judge in his own cause. This is a well-known norm of procedural justice and the objection is a justice-based objection. Fox-Decent's argument also sets up a very interesting legal theory problem, for there is a potential tension between conformity to the *nemo iudex* principle and other norms of justice. It might well be the case that a victim of a tort will miss out on another type of justice if *nemo iudex* is satisfied. For example, if we return again to the *Watch* case, imagine that Jane does not grab the watch back. The thief will predictably run away, never to be seen again. The justice involved in a right holder's undoing a wrong by allocating back what was taken from her—redressive justice—is no longer an option if the thief disappears. Attempted conformity with *nemo iudex* means that redress will be unavailable.

The relationship between norms of justice is complex, however. Possibly, there was never an opportunity for legitimate redressive justice in the *Watch* example, because redressive justice can only be legitimate when it meets the terms of procedural justice. On one reading, procedural justice may be a necessary condition for another type of justice to operate. For example, *nemo iudex* could relate to redressive justice in a constitutive way, with procedural justice as a condition on the exercise of redressive justice. If so, this would rule out unilateral exercises of redressive justice.

Yet there is also another way to think about the interplay between procedural justice and other norms of justice. Gardner offers the following suggestion about a hypothetical allocation:

> Perhaps the fact that the doctrines of *audi alterem partem* and *nemo iudex in parte sua* were observed not only made it more likely that a just settlement of a dispute would be arrived at, but also made whatever settlement of the dispute was arrived at *more just* than it would have been had it been arrived at by other means.[58]

[57] Fox-Decent also builds on another norm of procedural justice—the maxim that 'justice should not only be done, but should also be seen to be done.' *See* ibid. 130. The argument developed below is as much a response to this norm of procedural justice as it is to the *nemo iudex* principle.

[58] *See* ibid. (emphasis added). *Audi alterem partem*—'hear the other side'—is a norm of procedural justice concerned with both sides getting to have their case heard. *Nemo iudex in parte sua* is a variant of the *nemo iudex* principle discussed elsewhere in this book.

In other words, procedural justice may not be a prerequisite for other norms of justice to be met. There may be a sliding scale, with conformity to procedural justice impacting the degree to which other norms of justice are met. From this point of view, procedural justice may enhance redressive justice—with the right procedures in place, an outcome may be *more* just—even though redressive justice can be achieved in the absence of procedural justice.

To the extent there is an interplay between these norms of justice, the latter reading is the better one, and I will offer some examples to show why. First, consider the way that *nemo iudex* plays out in public law. Adrian Vermeule has recently argued in *The Constitution of Risk* that public law institutions regularly violate the *nemo iudex* principle.[59] Moreover, he contends that they ought to do so. His reasons are compelling, and they merit consideration for anyone who adopts the *nemo iudex* principle as a *sine qua non* for justice of other types.

As Vermeule notes, 'in some cases there is no impartial official or institution in the picture, so that wherever decision-making authority is lodged, someone or other will have to be the judge in his own case'.[60] A leading example is the case of judges adjudicating their own salaries: 'When federal judges sit to decide cases concerning judicial salaries—cases brought by judge-plaintiffs to determine the salaries of the whole group of sitting judges, including the judges who will decide the case itself—there is no attenuated conflict of interest, but rather a direct violation.'[61] Such cases are clearly permissible under United States law, and given the need for adjudication, this seems desirable.[62] It seems a stretch to say that the outcomes in this sphere are incapable of being just.

A response might be that these examples are public law illustrations and that, accordingly, they do not implicate the concerns Fox-Decent has in mind. Perhaps each public law institution is properly understood to be representing the state's citizens as a whole, and this form of representation might (arguably) differentiate such public law settings from private law settings. Granted, it seems naïve to think that when judges adjudicate their own salaries this is just a matter of judges acting on behalf of everyone. Even so, let's assume that public law institutions are somehow distinguishable from their private law counterparts when it comes to *nemo iudex*. What then of self-defence?

Imagine a case of self-defence within a legal system that permits self-defence, yet without viewing the defending party as a stand-in for a public

[59] *See* Adrian Vermeule, *The Constitution of Risk* (CUP 2014) 107–40.
[60] *See* ibid. at 110.
[61] Ibid. 114.
[62] As Vermeule adds, 'The Court . . . allows such suits to proceed under the common-law rule of necessity, which holds that if all judges would be disqualified, none are.' Ibid. 123.

official.[63] Such self-defence involves the very asymmetry that purportedly violates *nemo iudex*. On the other hand, conventional morality supports the defender's right to defend himself, as do conventional views on preventive justice. On a common understanding, an attacked party quite appropriately gets to unilaterally enforce his rights whether or not the attacker agrees on the scope of those rights: he gets to be a judge in his own cause.[64] And the victim of an attack had better have the ability to enforce his rights in this way, because if he waits for a neutral adjudication or a public office holder to assist, it will often be too late. The damage will already have been done. If he is not a stand-in for a public official—a genuine possibility, depending on the legal system—are we ready to say that he can't legitimately engage in unilateral preventive justice, given the *nemo iudex* principle? Isn't it more plausible to say that he can legitimately engage in preventive justice, but that it would be even better (and more preventively just) if he were able to obtain a neutral third party's determination *ex ante*?[65]

Kantians are not troubled by self-defence as a unilateral enforcement of rights, since for them self-defence is a special case. But Fox-Decent's asymmetry argument does not readily incorporate the idea that self-defence is anomalous, as his argument is premised on a problem with unequal treatment. The legitimacy of self-defence is thus a very real challenge for the asymmetry argument. And, once we allow for self-defence as a permissible exception to *nemo iudex*, we can easily make room for exceptions that cover other forms of self-help. The same point that applies to self-defence—that there are cases in which violations of the *nemo iudex* principle can't be helped—is available in other self-help settings. Notably, this point applies to recaption of chattels.

It might be argued that there is a problem if complying with one norm of justice means that you are consequently not complying with another norm of justice. One might think that if a sound norm of justice is applicable to a given fact pattern and it is not complied with, something has gone wrong. Not

[63] Note that being a public official is not the same as being an institutional actor. *See* John Gardner, *From Personal Life to Private Law* (OUP 2018) 215. Nothing in my argument turns on whether the defender occupies the latter role.

[64] There is some ambiguity when people refer to being a judge in one's own cause in these settings. I have in mind here the fact that the potential victim gets to decide whether to defend himself, thereby enforcing his rights on his own behalf. The possibility that he could also authoritatively determine the scope of his rights involves a different type of decision making, and I am not claiming that self-defence involves that type of decision making. For helpful discussion, see Gardner, 'Justification' (n. 22) 84–5.

[65] Or, perhaps, that *nemo iudex* has no bearing on whether his conduct is preventively just. We should be open to the idea that *nemo iudex* does not play a constitutive role at all in this setting. I thank Victor Tadros for emphasizing this point.

necessarily. It is a feature of norms of justice, and their interrelation, that the application of one type of justice will sometimes displace the application of another. While perhaps regrettable, this is not always a sign that the ultimate result is undesirable all things considered: it just means that a particular type of justice was foregone. These are cases of justice trade-offs, and they arise in legal contexts more often than one might expect. In such settings, there is a lost opportunity to obtain a particular type of justice because another type of justice has been opted for instead.

Choices among norms of justice can be difficult, particularly if the norms of justice at issue are supported by incommensurable values. In such cases a legal system might need to adopt second-order norms of justice that govern trade-offs between other norms of justice.[66] These second-order norms of justice—justice-allocating norms of justice—may be relevant to private law in multiple settings. The interplay between the justice of law and the justice of equity sometimes calls for such a norm, as we will see in Chapter 8. Similar norms may govern the interplay between procedural justice and corrective justice, or between procedural justice and redressive justice. Whatever the best approach in justice trade-off settings, it is doubtful that conformity to the *nemo iudex* principle is always required in order for courts to do justice. More importantly, courts could believe that they are advancing the cause of justice when they allow for self-defence or recaption of chattels by private parties, acting on their own behalf.

Once we see that the principle of *nemo iudex* is not necessarily a precondition for other types of justice to legitimately apply, and also that courts readily select one norm of justice to advance over another, it is difficult to rule out interpretations of the law of self-help according to which it involves unilateral, private enforcement. Recall that under a moderate justice criterion, an interpretive theory need not show tort law to actually be consistent with justice, so long as legal actors could plausibly think that it is consistent. It is reasonable (whether or not correct) to adopt a picture of preventive justice, corrective justice, or redressive justice that is not preconditioned on conformity with *nemo iudex*. With this in mind, it is also reasonable to interpret self-help as a legal means of unilateral rights enforcement.

[66] For analysis of how one norm of justice may govern the allocation of another norm of justice, see John Gardner, 'What is Tort Law For? Part 2: The Place of Distributive Justice' in John Oberdiek, (ed.), *Philosophical Foundations of the Law of Torts* (OUP 2014) 335, 340–1 (describing how distributive justice may govern allocations of institutional support for corrective justice).

VI. Variations on the Theme

There is, however, another reason to consider the moral merits of self-help as a source of redress. We may discover that this form of redress is not only legitimate under the right conditions; we may also learn something valuable about private law more generally by assessing what those conditions are. Significantly, some modes of undoing a wrong through self-help bear a greater resemblance to private rights of action than others.

Victor Tadros has suggested the following adjustment to the example offered at the beginning of Chapter 1.[67] Assume that a thief has run off with your bag, as described earlier. Now assume also that it is not possible to catch up to the thief in order to grab the bag back. Instead, you are only able to grab some money which is hanging out of the thief's back pocket. Should you have the right to take the money instead? For some of us, the intuitive answer will simply be, 'no'; but for others, we will need to know more information. Can we tell how much money is in the thief's back pocket? Is it roughly similar in amount to the value of the bag that the thief stole?

Simply grabbing the money risks taking a mistaken quantity. And, to the extent the thief is in possession of a pile of cash that substantially exceeds the value of the stolen bag, there are at least two difficulties. First, there is the proportionality constraint discussed in Chapter 3. Not everything that will help a wronged party to undo a wrong is a legitimate example of redress; if the right holder will visit disproportionate harm on the wrongdoer in the process, redress may not be a morally viable option. Second, there is the concern that taking too much money from the thief will not actually provide the right measure for a genuine act of redress. Redressive justice calls for undoing a wrong, and no more than that. If taking more money from the thief is a matter of justice, perhaps some other norm of justice is in play. For example, a larger quantity of money may implicate retribution rather than redress.

Still, let us assume that epistemic and proportionality concerns regarding the amount of money are set to one side. Suppose that you can see the thief has a single twenty dollar bill in his back pocket, and that the value of the bag he stole from you is precisely twenty dollars. The reader may now anticipate the significance of this modified example of redress through self-help. While private rights of action are a far cry from recaption of chattels—private

[67] I am grateful to Victor Tadros for raising this hypothetical at a conference at King's College London. Note that the subsequent analysis of this hypothetical is my own, and it may not reflect Tadros's views.

rights of action are channelled through courts and they implicate the state as both arbiter and enforcer—the fact remains that in each case a right holder may have to accept a monetary substitute for recovering a stolen object, enforcing a contractual performance, or restoring an injured limb. Whatever makes it morally acceptable (if in fact it is) to grab the money from a fleeing thief may also help us make sense of private rights of action for monetary damages. In other words, there may be a substantial degree of continuity between private rights of action and at least some recaption of chattels cases, notwithstanding the differences in venue, adjudicative process, and available remedies.

***

Part of what makes civil recourse 'civil' is that it occurs by means of a private right of action—through a judicially provided venue rather than through self-help. It is worth recalling that some of private law works differently. We need a theory of redress in these unilateral contexts as well, and civil recourse theories do not directly address such questions because they centre on adjudicative venues. A redress-centred account does more than fill this gap, however, as it also suggests that cases of ex post self-help may be illuminating examples for private law theory to study. And this is not only because self-help cases are integral parts of private law (rather than outliers). The moral plausibility of self-help can enable us to better understand what is going on in contexts where courts play a more active role.

Self-authored acts of private redress show how an account that recognizes pre-legal rights of redress offers more than just an alternative to the Kantian picture. An account that builds on their moral features has explanatory force not only at the level of doctrines like the consideration doctrine in contract law (as we saw in Chapter 4), but also for purposes of explaining a range of private law remedies that do not require direct intervention by public office holders. Self-help is also something to be explained rather than bracketed, and understandings that allow for private enforcement allow self-help to fit within private law practices more generally. In this respect, such accounts offer an explanatory advance over rival theories.

In the case of self-help cases like recaption of chattels, it makes sense to think the behaviour at issue is properly attributed to the right holder herself. As we have seen, questions of authorship also have an important bearing on the value of rights of redress. It will now be worth considering another form of authorship in private law, the authorship of the courts themselves. The state's potential involvement in authoring private law remedies bears on the availability of those legal remedies. Complicity is a genuine concern when the state assists someone in enforcing her rights. Courts should not always have to assist private parties in enforcing their rights because sometimes those parties are acting wrongfully in standing on their rights—even where the rights themselves are legitimate. Such concerns will be the subject of Chapter 8.

8

Choice, Equity, and Redress

I. Introduction

Sometimes the interesting features of redress turn on right holder choices. To return to our theme, imagine that Jack has stolen Jill's bag and attempted to run away with it. Jill chases after him in hot pursuit and eventually wrestles the bag back. That is our classic example of recaption of chattels. Now suppose instead that Jill decides not to chase after the bag, even though she knows she has the capability of getting it back. Suppose, further, that Jill knows who Jack is and could readily sue him for damages. She may choose not to sue. In this latter case, does this mean that Jane has done something wrong because she did not pursue justice in redress? Most people would say that this is Jill's prerogative—she gets to decide whether to seek redress.

Right holders do not have an obligation to obtain redressive justice; it is up to them. This raises a question about whether we truly are looking at norms of justice when we consider redressive justice. Isn't it a standard feature of justice that it is something we have a duty to seek? And, if redressive justice is not really a type of justice, the justice criterion discussed earlier is now in play. All else equal, a theory of private law that can show how private law concepts are understandable in justice-related terms will be more plausible than a theory that fails to do so.

I will argue that norms of redressive justice are genuine norms of justice even if right holders can choose not to pursue them, for some kinds of justice are optional from a right holder's perspective. But this argument only addresses one concern, for we might also approach the morality of the right holder's choices from other angles. Chapter 2 noted that there are proportionality and other constraints on sound exercises of redressive justice. The problem discussed now will be slightly different. When constraints on legitimate redress are met, there may still be individual cases in which the optionality of redress means that right holders will fail to act when they ought to, or else will choose to act when they ought not to.

What if plaintiffs do not bring suit when they should? Nothing in the present account indicates that the state has an obligation to seek allocation back

The Right of Redress. Andrew S. Gold, Oxford University Press (2020). © Andrew S. Gold.
DOI: 10.1093/oso/9780198814405.001.0001

in all such cases. It is important to recognize that sometimes people truly ought to bring suit, even if they choose not to—this could reflect the right holder's individual circumstances, or it could be for reasons that concern the legal system or society as a whole. Such challenges are not easily solved in a way that shows respect for a right holder's autonomy, but we should not overlook their importance when assessing redress's operation within a legal system.

There is also a mirror image set of questions. What if people bring suit when they ought not to? Surely that will happen in some cases. Can one commit a wrong in the course of pursuing justice? Even if no wronging is involved, can there be immoral yet just actions? Here, the conceptual challenges are more significant. I will argue that it is possible to commit a wrong while still acting justly, and, more relevantly for purposes of private law, it is possible to have morally wrongful justice—that is, justice that it is wrongful to seek, even if no one's rights are violated in the process. Sometimes, redressive justice is legitimate, yet nonetheless it ought not to be pursued by a right holder. In these latter cases, a court that provides a remedy to a plaintiff may be acting justly while nevertheless assisting someone in immoral behaviour.

Moving past these conceptual challenges, there are also interesting normative questions. For example, how do cases of wrongful redress bear on the state's responsibilities? Morally wrongful redress could make the state complicit in harsh and otherwise undesirable behaviours by overzealous plaintiffs. Is it problematic for the state to assist when a private right of action will result in disproportionate hardship, or when a claim is brought by individuals who lack the moral standing to complain about the wrong they suffered? Here, we face a complex picture. The state may owe its support to individuals who bring suit when they ought not to sue; yet, when the case is egregious enough, the state may also have a responsibility to step aside.

This chapter will suggest that various equitable doctrines limit the problem of morally wrongful redress (though they do not eliminate the concern). Such equitable doctrines provide multiple ways in which the state can avoid participating in morally dubious acts of redress. Likewise, settlements allow plaintiffs themselves to act more equitably in cases where they accept less than they are legally due. Redress does implicate a moral right to do moral wrong, and at times redress will be both legitimate and wrongful. Yet, legal systems can provide support in some of these cases without having to provide support in all of them. Moreover, redressive justice may be rendered equitable under the right circumstances, even if that is not its default condition.

II. Optional Justice and Justice Forsaken

A claimant's choice not to enforce her rights poses several concerns. First, we might think that people have obligations to act justly, or that they have reasons to do so. From this perspective, we might think that if redressive justice is a genuine norm of justice it should not simply be a matter of unfettered right holder choice whether to seek an allocation back. Optional justice may seem counterintuitive as a category of justice, and this right holder discretion may appear too lax. Second, we might think that there are cases in which right holders (or those acting on their behalf) have a moral responsibility to allocate back, whether or not that responsibility is grounded in a norm of justice. On a case-by-case basis, it may seem problematic that some wrongs are uncorrected because potential plaintiffs decide not to sue. I will suggest that the first challenge need not trouble us, while the second challenge merits further attention.

A. Consistency with criteria for norms of justice

An initial concern might be that justice is a source of duties or obligations. Norms of justice, it might be argued, impose duties to seek the just outcome, and norms of justice that allow right holders to choose whether such justice should occur are inconsistent with this picture. This view is overly strong. Preventive justice—the type of justice involved in self-defence—does not usually impose duties on potential victims to defend themselves. Barring special circumstances, we do not say that the victim of an attack was in the wrong if she didn't fight back. A similar point applies for redressive justice, if a tort victim chooses to forego compensation. Barring special circumstances, right holders have no duties to bring about these types of justice if they would prefer not to, yet it remains plausible to think that it would be just if they should choose to enforce their rights.[1]

On the other hand, justice arguably is linked to reasons for action. This suggests a different formulation of the challenge: optional justice may seem to ignore the ways in which norms of justice ground reasons for action. For example, consider Gardner's claim that norms of justice provide grounds for

[1] This isn't to say that these norms of justice never ground duties. To the extent such norms of justice ground duties, however, they characteristically ground duties of non-interference by third parties or by the wrongdoer himself (or, in some cases, they ground duties of assistance by the state).

allocations. As he argues: 'Norms of justice, to put the lesson concisely and more generally, answer questions about who is to get how much of what *and why* (i.e., on what grounds).'[2] At another point he elaborates:

> A norm of justice is one that mentions a *ground* for allocating whatever it is that it allocates. A ground for allocating is a condition of allocation that is also a reason for that allocation. That I am a wrongdoer, most people think, is not just a condition but a reason for punishing me. I should be punished only if *and because* I am a wrongdoer.[3]

Perhaps norms of justice must mean that there are reasons for certain allocations to occur.

The concern then is the following: if redressive justice norms operate at the whim of right holders, it may appear that these norms are not truly norms of justice at all. And there is cause to think that redressive justice does operate in a way that leaves the choice to the right holder. Consider again the *Watch* example from Chapter 7. While a property holder may sometimes legitimately grab back a watch that was wrongfully taken from her, we do not ordinarily believe she has a duty to grab back the watch. Unless she has some special reason why she must get that watch—perhaps she promised it to someone else—she has no duty to seek redress.

Jeff McMahan's work on preventive justice suggests one possible answer to this puzzle. As he contends:

> The deontological version [of justice] is compatible with the idea that self-defense is optional; for deontological ethics holds that self-sacrifice, even for the sake of those who are culpable, can be meritorious and cannot be opposed by impersonal considerations of justice, provided, of course, that no one other than the beneficiary is involved.[4]

As McMahan continues:

> According to this version, when a person voluntarily forgoes the option of self-defense, the reason she has to sacrifice herself does not eliminate the

[2] *See* John Gardner, 'What Is Tort Law For? Part 1: The Place of Corrective Justice' (2011) 30 Law & Phil 1, 8.

[3] *See* ibid. 7.

[4] *See* Jeff McMahan, 'Self-Defense and the Problem of the Innocent Attacker' (1994) 104 Ethics 252, 261.

> injustice of the [Culpable Attacker's] action, but it does, if she chooses freely, cancel the reason she would otherwise have to prevent the injustice.[5]

Accordingly, we might think that preventive justice grounds reasons for right holders to defend themselves, but that those reasons are subject to cancellation. A similar theory could apply for redressive justice, as it might provide reasons for redress that are subject to right holder cancellation.

Another possibility is to conclude that there generally are reasons for right holders to engage in redressive justice, and that these reasons continue in existence even when right holders choose not to enforce their rights.[6] It would not follow that there is an obligation to enforce or even a reason that outweighs any countervailing reasons. We might have a continuing reason to fix a wrong committed against us even if we appropriately decide that the better choice, all things considered, is to leave that wrong uncorrected. In other words, when right holders choose whether or not to engage in redress, they might legitimately conclude that the best decision is not to enforce their rights. All of this could be true without the right holder having a *duty* to engage in redress. Those who choose not to engage in self-defence or not to undo a wrong committed against them might fail to conform to certain reasons, while nonetheless acting consistently with their overall moral duties or obligations.

As these possibilities suggest, there are interesting questions raised by categories of justice that allow for right holder choice. That said, the optionality of redressive justice need not disqualify it as a category of justice. Whether we think that right holders have reasons to engage in redress that are cancelled out if they choose not to enforce their rights—or alternatively, that those reasons continue to exist but the choice still belongs to the right holder—the norms of redressive justice are understandable as norms that govern questions of allocation and, furthermore, as norms that provide grounds for allocation.

B. Optional justice and justice forsaken

It is a separate question how individuals and legal systems should respond to these features of redressive justice. Plaintiffs may choose to ignore a wrong committed against them, despite the fact that it would be just to undo that wrong.

[5] *See* ibid.

[6] One might also query whether the reasons that govern right-holders in these cases are will-dependent reasons. *See* Joseph Raz, 'Reasons in Conflict' in *From Normativity to Responsibility* (OUP 2011) 173, 183–4 (discussing will-dependent reasons and their significance).

Plaintiffs often don't sue, or else sue for less than they might. Alternatively, plaintiffs may settle their cases, agreeing with the defendant on a compromise outcome. At least some of the time, it would be better if they sued and did not settle, yet the state is usually indifferent. Is this legal arrangement a desirable state of affairs? How should the state react to these possibilities?

One reason a plaintiff might choose not to sue even if he is convinced that his claim has legal merit is that this would show mercy. The plaintiff might think that we are all flawed, and in some cases it might be better to accommodate the errors of others and show tolerance towards wrongful defendants.[7] Or, perhaps what the defendant did to the victim was sufficiently awful that the potential plaintiff would prefer to never confront her again.[8] In that case, it is not mercy but rather an understandable disgust that could motivate the right holder's choice.

And yet there are cases in which a plaintiff ought to sue, but chooses not to. Perhaps the plaintiff has made a mistake in her assessment of the merits of her claim, given a lack of expertise about the law. Or perhaps instead she does not take her own rights seriously enough. Some people are overly diffident, and the victim of a tort who has low self-esteem could blame herself when she ought to realize that a third-party wrongdoer was truly at fault. It is even argued that we can have a moral duty to insist on our rights.[9] While there is room to debate exactly which cases qualify, it is reasonable to think that certain cases are not brought when they ought to be (either because it would be the better choice to bring suit, or because there is a moral duty to bring suit).

More broad-based, systemic concerns are also relevant. In some contexts, the state might conclude that it has substantial reason to intervene on behalf of right holders given the overall effects of a class of case. Imagine a state whose populace is frightened of the mob and therefore rarely asserts its legal claims; or a state that lacks an adequate precedent pool because people infrequently

[7] *See* Seana Valentine Shiffrin, *Speech Matters: On Lying, Morality, and the Law* (2014) 165 ('Sometimes a victim forbears on the grounds that she understands the mistake of the wrongdoer and sees that she might have made a similar mistake herself.'). *See also* John CP Goldberg, 'What Are We Reforming? Tort Theory's Place in Debates Over Malpractice Reform' (2006) 59 Vand L Rev 1075, 1078 (noting the possibility that tort victims may 'sincerely take the view that mistakes happen').

[8] Cf. Linda Radzik, 'Tort Processes and Relational Repair' in John Oberdiek, (ed.), *Philosophical Foundations of the Law of Torts* (OUP 2014) 231, 244 ('The victim's duty not to prevent wrongdoers from attempting amends would be trumped, of course, if further contact with the wrongdoer posed an unreasonable risk of harm to the victim.').

[9] *See* Dennis Klimchuk, 'Equity and the Rule of Law' in Lisa M Austin & Dennis Klimchuk, (eds), *Private Law and the Rule of Law* (OUP 2014) 247, 260 ('Sometimes, one might argue, one ought to be a stickler for one's rights. "Do not let others tread with impunity on your rights", says Kant, in a list of injunctions issuing from the duty to treat oneself with respect.') (quoting Immanuel Kant, *The Metaphysics of Morals* 188 (6:436) (M Gregor, trans.) (CUP 1996)).

bring suit. Maybe a state considers its citizens to be too forgiving in light of the wrongs they suffer. Or, for those that focus on efficiency, failures to bring suit might result in inadequate deterrence of wrongdoing.

Indeed, Anita Bernstein has suggested that women can be unequally impacted by tort law doctrine—especially in light of the way that it requires individuals to bring and pursue claims against each other.[10] Her critique suggests that failures to bring meritorious claims may not be evenly dispersed across populations, and the reasons why may be part of the problem. In such cases, the state might recognize systemic reasons to desire more rectification of wrongs in certain contexts. Even so, it is characteristic in common law jurisdictions that private actions are exclusively up to the choice of the right holder.

To the extent the state refuses to intervene absent such plaintiffs filing a complaint, there may be times when serious wrongs go uncorrected. Should we feel that the non-suing tort victim falls short from a justice perspective? Perhaps not, if we think that the right holder's choice not to bring suit cancels out reasons for the right holder. But even if this is true for the right holder, we might wonder if that cancellation applies to third parties as well. That is, if the right holder does not wish to undo a wrongful transaction that she suffered, does this mean that a third party no longer has a duty (or at least a reason) to undo the transaction on her behalf?

Some corrective justice theorists emphasize the role of third parties for bringing about corrective justice. John Gardner argues that corrective justice is an agent-neutral concern: 'be it corrective or be it distributive, an injustice perpetrated by anyone is in principle everyone's business, and anyone at all has reason to help in securing its avoidance (whether by the agent himself or by another person acting on his behalf.'[11] Linda Radzik likewise notes the important role of third parties. In her view: 'Third party contributions to corrective justice are *possible*; in some cases, they are also *necessary*.'[12] Corrective justice need not be a concern solely for those people who committed a wrong.

It may thus seem puzzling that the state generally leaves the choice to initiate litigation to private parties, and usually only a subset of them: those who were wronged. A potential answer is to recognize that the state's role in redressive justice cases is to act *on behalf of* the right holder.[13] Under a right-focused,

[10] *See* Anita Bernstein, 'Feminist Perspectives: Private Law as Unjust Enrichment' in Andrew S Gold, et al., (eds), *The Oxford Handbook of New Private Law* (OUP forthcoming).

[11] *See* Gardner, 'What Is Tort Law For?' (n. 2) 11.

[12] *See* Radzik, 'Tort Processes' (n. 8) 243.

[13] Cf. Arthur Ripstein, 'Civil Recourse and Separation of Wrongs and Remedies' (2011) 39 Fla St U L Rev 163, 200–201 ('A right constrains the conduct of others, but the bearer of the right determines whether to exercise it. In this, a remedial right is no different from the primary right. It follows from this

redressive justice account, the norms of justice allow for third parties to bring about just outcomes by acting on behalf of another party. We might think that this relationship resolves any questions about when suit should be brought in favour of the right holder's preferences, if 'on behalf of' means according to her wishes. If the right holder doesn't wish to assert her rights, there may not be a role for someone acting on her behalf to assert those rights.

Yet there is a lurking ambiguity here. There is more than one way that a party can act on behalf of another, and the distinctions are significant. Under an agency model, the agent should act pursuant to her principal's instructions or known preferences.[14] Under a trustee model, there is room for paternalistic behaviour on behalf of a beneficiary. If we understand courts and other state actors to be like agents when they act on behalf of right holders in enforcing their rights, then a right holder's choice not to pursue an allocation back should end the matter. On the other hand, if some room for paternalism is permitted, then it is conceivable that courts and other state actors should sometimes undo transactions that would-be plaintiffs have no desire to see undone. And indeed there are some settings in which paternalism on behalf of right holders is (comparatively) uncontroversial: think of guardians who sue on behalf of incompetent wards.[15] We need to know more about the relationship pursuant to which state actors are acting on behalf of right holders before we can fully assess the state's allowing right holders to choose when a private right of action should be pursued.

Whether we look to corrective justice or redressive justice, the norms at issue may be sufficiently open-ended that they don't answer the question. At least as redressive justice is defined here—in terms of allocation back by a right holder, or someone acting on their behalf—it is unclear whether there is space for some paternalism. Whether the state should act as an agent rather than a trustee is not built into the above account of these norms of justice, and this means that the reasons for the state's deference to a wronged party's choices requires a further justification. Perhaps paternalism should generally be rejected

analysis that a tort suit must be initiated by plaintiff, simply because plaintiff, or someone authorized to act on plaintiff's behalf, is the only one with standing to exercise any right that she has.').

[14] For further discussion of this distinction in fiduciary law, see Andrew S Gold, 'Accommodating Loyalty' in Paul B Miller & Andrew S Gold, (eds), *Contract, Status, and Fiduciary Law* (OUP 2016) 185, 205. Versions of this distinction have also been noted in political theory. *See*, e.g. Jeremy Waldron, *Political Political Theory* (HUP 2016) 169 (distinguishing between agent accountability and trust accountability, and noting in the trust accountability setting that '[t]he beneficiary is mostly passive').

[15] Other contexts worth considering may include class actions (see Chapter 9), and also derivative litigation on behalf of corporations that do not sue thanks to a conflicted board of directors. I thank Ted Janger for suggesting the latter example.

in this setting (I am inclined to think so), but the reasons why require further exploration of the state–citizen relationship.

This volume is not the place for a fully worked out account of how states should respond when citizens choose not to sue, but an interest in private law's adoption of redressive justice norms should invite an inquiry into that subject. The answers may hinge not only on the nature of the state's obligations to its citizens, but also on the primary and secondary rights at issue in specific private law contexts, as well as on the status of a potential claimant (such as in guardian–ward cases). If paternalism is ruled out, non-suits where suits are desirable may simply be a tragic cost of a system that builds on rights of redress.

III. Justice that Wrongs and Justice that is Wrongful

A different concern is that plaintiffs will opt for redress when they shouldn't. There are several forms that this concern might take. It might be argued that one cannot act justly if one's acts require the commission of a wrong against someone else. That view has its adherents,[16] but under the right circumstances seems mistaken. Justice that requires a wrong is not a commonplace occurrence in the law, thankfully. Another challenge is that redress may be just, yet morally wrongful, all things considered. This concern is valid, and it arises more frequently. Bringing about justice can involve us in morally wrongful conduct, and this is a reason for legal systems (and individuals) to care about which claims private plaintiffs choose to pursue.

Before proceeding, it may be helpful to start with some clarification of terminology. As David Owens indicates, it is possible to divide up 'wrong' behaviour in multiple ways.[17] When used as a noun, 'a wrong' tends to 'render blame apt'.[18] Yet people can engage in various forms of conduct that are unwise without meriting blame—to use Owens' example, one may make the wrong move in a chess game.[19] In addition, we can also distinguish among types of blameworthy conduct depending on whether that conduct violates rights, or instead is simply immoral. For our purposes, a 'wrong' (or a 'wronging' in

[16] Cf. Jules Coleman, *Risks and Wrongs* (OUP 1992) 308–9 (raising the possibility).

[17] *See* David Owens, *Shaping the Normative Landscape* (OUP 2012) 45. Owens' particular approach is not the only way to divide up the relevant concepts and terminology. Cf. Coleman, *Risks and Wrongs* (n. 16) 329–2 (distinguishing 'wrongdoing' from 'wrong'). For Coleman, wrongs are actions contrary to rights. *See* ibid. 332. It appears that Owens' notion of a 'wronging' corresponds to Coleman's notion of a 'wrong'.

[18] *See* Owens, *Shaping the Normative Landscape* (n. 17) 45.

[19] *See* ibid.

Owens' terminology) will refer to cases in which conduct violates someone's rights (moral or legal).[20]

A. Justice that wrongs

Suppose we start with the question of whether norms of justice allow for conduct to be just even if it involves the commission of a wrong. One might think people cannot commit wrongs as a way to bring about justice.[21] Under the right circumstances, however, it is reasonable to think that interpersonal justice can be done even if it requires a wrong to bring this justice about. Consider the following case:

Amy obtains tickets to a concert by her favourite band, and she promises the tickets to her friend Brian. She also obtains tickets for a second concert by the same band, for a concert one week later. She promises these tickets to her friend Chris. A family emergency comes up, and Amy (quite reasonably) chooses to address the emergency and cannot keep her promise to Brian. As a result, she can't give Brian the tickets in time for his concert; she has broken her word. Assume that any additional tickets will now be impossible to get. Brian realizes the second concert may be his last chance to see this band (it is rumoured they will break up), and as a devoted fan he is desperate to have the tickets. Chris, on the other hand, wouldn't mind going, but he doesn't care that much about the concert, and he would happily see another show with a different band.

What should Amy do? If Amy gives Brian the tickets that were intended for Chris, she will allocate back precisely as corrective justice would require, by giving him the 'next best thing'. She will be doing what she can to meet the terms of her first promise and arguably doing what she morally ought to do, all things considered. While promises have been made to both Brian and Chris, the promise to Chris allows for an easy substitute performance.[22] On the other

[20] While I will adopt this view for present purposes, it should be noted that there is an alternative view according to which wrongs do not require violations of rights. *See* Nicolas Cornell, 'Wrongs, Rights, and Third Parties' (2015) 43 Phil & Pub Aff 109.

[21] Cf. Coleman, *Risks and Wrongs* (n. 16) 306 (hypothesizing that '[a]ny mode of rectification that does not create wrongful gains and losses is compatible with corrective justice; and any mode of rectification that creates wrongful losses violates corrective justice'). Coleman's definition of wrongful conduct includes the commission of wrongs in Owens' sense, which suggests that his hypothesized view would incorporate a no-wrong principle. *See* ibid. 332 (indicating that 'wrongful losses' can result from 'wrongs').

[22] Cf. Neil MacCormick, 'The Obligation of Reparation' in *Legal Right and Social Democracy: Essays in Legal and Political Philosophy* (OUP 1982) 212, 213 ('This indeed ought to be a material consideration to be borne in mind when duties conflict—can either, and, if so, which, of the conflicting duties be more or less made good by some substitute performance offered later?'). I am grateful to John Gardner for helpful discussion of this point.

hand, she will wrong Chris if he refuses to release her from her promise. I see no good reason to deny that Amy does corrective justice when she fixes the wrong suffered by Brian by giving him the tickets to the second concert—even though this means she inevitably wrongs someone else in the process. She would, of course, still owe Chris the next best thing to compliance with her promise to him.

Now it may also turn out that the commission of some wrongs is inconsistent with the possibility of doing justice. Suppose we modify the above example so that the only way for Amy to get the concert tickets to Brian is if she breaks into Chris's car and steals the tickets.[23] This might no longer be corrective justice, or at least not under sound norms of corrective justice. My suggestion is not that wronging someone is always irrelevant to our criteria for justice. Rather, the context matters; it may sometimes be possible to act justly even though a wronging is required as a precondition for that justice. To the extent redressive justice is sometimes conditioned on a wrong, it could still count as a type of justice.[24]

B. Justice that is morally wrongful

There may be cases in which a plaintiff's choice to sue involves a moral wrong against the defendant in some respect. This could be problematic, but it need not mean that the plaintiff's claim is inconsistent with justice (or, more precisely, that it is inconsistent with the norms of justice that govern acts of redress).[25] We would have to know more about the wrong at issue before reaching a conclusion on that question. Still, even if we think that it is sometimes acceptable to commit wrongs in the course of doing justice, there may be an additional concern related to plaintiff choice. The problem is not that bringing suit wrongs someone, but that it is the wrong thing to do. This may be the more significant concern for the morality of redress, and it is a much more common outcome in the law.

Sometimes, plaintiffs bring suit when it is morally questionable for them to do so. The difficulty is not necessarily that they are wronging someone in bringing suit—they may not be acting contrary to anyone else's moral or

[23] I thank Diego Papayannis for suggesting the theft example.

[24] This possibility could be relevant if the reader thinks that non-compliance with the *nemo iudex* principle involves wronging the other party to a dispute. On that possibility, compare Chapter 7.

[25] This is not to deny that committing wrongs could sometimes be inconsistent with legitimate acts of redressive justice. That is one of the implications in Chapter 2 concerning disproportionate harm.

legal rights when they file their complaint. The difficulty, rather, is that they are acting badly in bringing suit. We are concerned now with another type of blameworthy conduct: the plaintiff's conduct is morally wrongful, but it need not involve a wronging of anyone in particular. We are concerned with conduct that ought not to occur, all things considered.

A good example appears in fiduciary law settings, where it is possible for beneficiaries to seek a powerful disgorgement remedy against fiduciaries who were acting in the beneficiaries' best interests, where those fiduciaries had good intentions, and where they did not harm the beneficiaries by their conduct.[26] It is often enough for liability if the fiduciary had a conflict of interest.[27] While plaintiffs have legitimate claims in these cases, the fact remains that sometimes they ought to show mercy. Defendants do not have standing to demand mercy, but plaintiffs should sometimes show mercy nonetheless. In other words, the beneficiary's claim to recourse is valid, but it ought not to be pursued.

Although fiduciary law provides classic illustrations, it is not the only area in which plaintiffs might, morally speaking, behave better if they chose not to sue (or chose to accept a weaker remedy). For example, there are instances in which a tort defendant is just careless enough to qualify as negligent, but barely. If the potential liability is huge, and if the defendant is poor and apologetic (and the plaintiff rich), it may be that the tort plaintiff ought to settle the case for less than it is worth.[28] Outside the context of litigation, a similar point may apply even in cases of self-defence.[29] On occasion, we ought to permit an infringement of our rights.

In contexts where the plaintiff is nonetheless a stickler for his rights, is the plaintiff's conduct still just?[30] Quite possibly, yes. Conduct that is just is ordinarily consistent with what ought to be done, but justice will not always converge

[26] For a justification of these features, see Paul B Miller, 'Justifying Fiduciary Remedies' (2013) 63 U Toronto LJ 570.

[27] A classic case in this genre is *In re Will of Gleeson*, 124 N.E.2d 624 (Ill. App. Ct. 1955). For further discussion, see Andrew S Gold, 'Justice, Redress, and the Right to Do Wrong' in Simone Degeling & Jason Varuhas, (eds), *Equitable Compensation and Disgorgement of Profit* (Hart 2017) 41, 42–3.

[28] For discussion of negligence cases involving massive losses, see Jeremy Waldron, 'Moments of Carelessness and Massive Loss' in David G Owen, (ed.), *Philosophical Foundations of Tort Law* (OUP 1995) 387.

[29] For a helpful example, see John CP Goldberg, 'Inexcusable Wrongs' (2015) 103 Cal L Rev 467, 472 n. 14.

[30] To add to the growing tradition of *Curb Your Enthusiasm* examples used in private law theory, I should note that the problem of undesirable stickling is likewise addressed in that television show. For example, see the character Larry David's comment in Season 9, Episode 5: 'Do you think that's a good quality, stickling? Don't stickle.' For a more extensive illustration from *Curb Your Enthusiasm*, see John Gardner, *From Personal Life to Private Law* (OUP 2018) 102–7, 217–18. Gardner's illustration also involves a form of stickling, but interestingly the behaviour is coming from the wrongdoer who wants to correct his wrong.

with what is morally best—in some cases, doing justice is unfortunate from a moral perspective. As others have indicated, the just and the moral are not always identical.[31] Being just and being charitable at the same time, or being just and being merciful at the same time, can pose a challenge. Focusing solely on being just may be in tension with the pursuit of a different virtue.[32] This opens up the possibility of wrongful justice, and the types of justice that help explain private law pose such concerns quite starkly.

When we confront redressive justice (much like preventive justice), we are dealing with a category of justice that a right holder does not have a duty to bring about. This is a type of justice that is centrally concerned with the question whether a right holder's acts are legitimate, and not with whether they are desirable. It is thus entirely possible for a right holder to permissibly enforce her rights even in cases where it would be a morally better choice for her not to enforce her rights. When that happens, her conduct can still be just. In other words, redressive justice can implicate moral rights to do moral wrong.[33]

It is a separate question whether legal systems ought to support such conduct, even if it qualifies as a type of justice. This question presents the mirror image of a problem discussed earlier in this chapter at II.B. As noted above, there may be cases in which the state should be interested in the reversal of transactions even if plaintiffs do not wish to enforce their rights. In other cases, the state might understandably be reluctant to assist plaintiffs in cases where those plaintiffs nonetheless hold legitimate rights to redress.[34] This latter possibility is our concern now.

Note also that this challenge is an acute one, given the adjudicative role. Courts are usually tasked with doing justice, first and foremost. To the extent one thinks that adjudication must be concerned primarily with questions of justice, it might seem that redressive justice should be facilitated even if it is

[31] *See* John Gardner, 'How Law Claims, What Law Claims' in *Law as a Leap of Faith* (OUP 2012) 140 ('It is possible for something to be morally correct yet unjust, or *vice versa*. This is because, although all considerations of justice are moral considerations, not all moral considerations are considerations of justice.').

[32] *See* John Gardner, 'The Virtue of Justice and the Character of Law' in *Law as a Leap of Faith* (OUP 2012) 244–5 (describing the possibility of divergence between the views of the just person and the humane person).

[33] For further discussion of this point, see Gold, 'Justice, Redress' (n. 27). On the topic more generally, see Jeremy Waldron, 'The Right to Do Wrong' in *Liberal Rights: Collected Papers 1981–1991* (CUP 1993); Ori J Herstein, 'Defending the Right to Do Wrong (2011) 31 Law & Phil 343. *See also* David Enoch, 'A Right to Violate One's Duty' (2002) 21 Law & Phil 355, 379–80 ('A right to violate one's duty is not merely . . . a conceptual possibility. A moral theory that fails to justify such rights fails to take autonomy seriously.').

[34] For helpful analysis of when the State has a moral responsibility to assist right holders in contract law settings, see Seana V Shiffrin, 'Paternalism, Unconscionability Doctrine, and Accommodation' (2000) 29 Phil & Pub Aff 205, 221–4.

sometimes exercised wrongfully. On this view, courts should help such plaintiffs, period. On the other hand, courts can also do justice even when they refuse to assist a morally wrongful plaintiff. There are other types of justice that legal systems should concern themselves with aside from redressive justice, and pursuit of such types can occasionally soften the harshness of redressive justice. For example, equity provides a distinctive type of justice, and, on an Aristotelian account, equity may call for right holders to accept less than their due.[35]

The morality of redress is not always co-extensive with the justice in redress, and accordingly moral agents should not only be concerned with the legitimacy of their legal claims—they should also be concerned with the desirability of pursuing those claims. But the state should also be concerned with the morality of redress, and this added complexity has important bearing on how private law treats rights of redress. The discussion below will consider how private law can handle morally wrongful cases of redress while still appropriately pursuing justice between the parties. A key concern is to recognize the legitimacy of a plaintiff's rights without having the state be complicit in egregious exercises of such rights.

IV. The Self-Regarding Account of Equity

A. Introducing the self-regarding account

How can courts take seriously a claimant's right of redress without becoming complicit in wrongful acts of redressive justice? There is an answer, and Seana Shiffrin's analysis of unconscionability doctrine points us in the right direction. Shiffrin claims that unconscionability doctrine need not rely on a paternalist grounding; instead, she suggests that the doctrine may be 'self-regarding'. In other words, her account sees unconscionability doctrine from the perspective of judicial morality. A court's moral obligations will not always require assistance to a right holder even where the rights at issue appear to decide a case in her favour.

[35] For Aristotle's account of equity, see Aristotle, 'Nicomachean Ethics' in Jonathan Barnes, (ed.), *The Complete Works of Aristotle*, vol. 2, bk V (Princeton University Press 1984) 1795–6. On accepting less than one's due, see ibid. 1796 ('It is also evident from this who the equitable man is; the man who chooses and does such acts, and is no stickler for justice in a bad sense but tends to take less than his share though he has the law on his side. . . .'). For an extension of an Aristotelian account to modern legal systems, see Dennis Klimchuk, 'Equity and the Rule of Law' in Lisa Austin & Dennis Klimchuk, (eds), *Private Law and the Rule of Law* (OUP 2014) 247.

As Shiffrin notes in the contract setting, 'unless we assume that one must ensure that others' obligations are met, the promisor's genuine responsibility does not entail that unaffected parties or the community at large must take it upon themselves to enforce promises'.[36] On her view, 'refusal to enforce would . . . make sense when the content and outcome of the contract were morally objectionable in such a way as to implicate the judge's and the state's moral stature'.[37]

Equity is a mechanism for the state to avoid assisting citizens in immoral behaviour, and even a way that the state seeks to undermine such behaviour: the motivation can be a concern for the morality of the state's conduct. Adopting Shiffrin's terminology, I will refer to this as a 'self-regarding' account of equity's role. The justification for this equitable approach, if we extend the argument, is that the state has a permission, or sometimes a deontological commitment, not to help out a party who insists on her rights when it is sufficiently wrong for her to do so. The state may even have a permission or a deontological commitment to interfere with a right of redress in the more extreme cases.

From this perspective, the moral concerns of private law extend beyond what the plaintiff and defendant may owe to each other, although that concern is relevant. There are also important questions regarding the proper responsibilities of additional parties—in particular the state and its judges—with respect to the interactions of the plaintiff and defendant. Some cases in which courts refuse to assist (or to assist in the most effective way) may simply reflect attention to judicial economy, or perhaps epistemic challenges that courts wish to avoid. A classic reason why expectation damages are readily provided—but not specific performance—is that specific performance can be costly to monitor.[38] But other considerations sound more directly in interpersonal morality, and these will be the focus here.

For example, equity's sensitivity to cases of extreme hardship is well recognized.[39] As Henry Smith notes, building encroachments are a good illustration.[40]

[36] *See* Shiffrin, 'Paternalism' (n. 34) 222.

[37] See ibid. 231. As Shiffrin indicates, her argument is analogous to the argument made in the constitutional case of *Shelley v. Kraemer*, 334 U.S. 1 (1948) (in which the court refused to enforce a racially discriminatory restrictive covenant). See Shiffrin (n. 34) 233.

[38] *See* Emily L Sherwin, 'Law and Equity in Contract Enforcement' (1991) 50 Md L Rev 253, 254 (noting that equitable defences to specific performance include both the practical difficulties of administration as well as moral standards).

[39] See, e.g. Henry E Smith, 'Equity as Second Order Law: The Problem of Opportunism', available at: https://ssrn.com/abstract=2617413, at 9 ('[E]quity courts got at opportunism by employing proxies and presumptions that typically sounded in disproportionate hardship or other dramatic harmful surprises, bad intention, and vulnerability of the victim.'). See also ibid. 49 (discussing the equitable maxim that 'equity abhors a forfeiture').

[40] See ibid.17–18.

Courts won't automatically require a building to be torn down when it is one inch over a boundary line, assuming the encroachment occurred in good faith. A similar idea is at work in contract law, in cases like *Jacob and Youngs v. Kent*.[41] In such cases, the consequences of the remedy are sufficiently extreme that plaintiffs ordinarily ought not to insist on their rights to the fullest extent. Courts will also quite reasonably hesitate before assisting the right holder if she does insist on her rights. If assisting another person will do sufficient damage to a third party, we often should be reluctant to assist, even if we would otherwise have a duty to help them out.

Undue hardships are not the only considerations at work in this type of analysis. Other doctrines impede right holder claims by focusing on the prior history between the parties. A whole set of equitable maxims addresses the history of a right holder's past behaviour, and for these purposes the degree of hardship that the other party will suffer is potentially less significant. For example, consider equitable maxims such as: equity will not allow someone to profit from her own wrong; she who seeks equity must do equity; one who comes into equity must do so with clean hands. Estoppel is an equitable approach that emphasizes prior conduct as well, and laches is sensitive to a plaintiff's prior failure to act.[42]

These doctrines often reflect opportunism concerns and, even where opportunism is not clearly demonstrated, the applicable doctrines may still serve as proxies. Nonetheless, equity's maxims and applications also correspond to moral factors that go well beyond opportunism. Someone might seek to profit from their own wrong, for example, without ever having shown any ex ante awareness that the wrong at issue would enable the subsequent profit. A laches fact pattern may not involve advantage-taking, yet the context can still undercut a right holder's claim to help from the state. Likewise, we don't need to believe that opportunism has occurred or even is likely in order to find estoppel appropriate.[43]

[41] 129 N.E. 889 (N.Y. 1921). Smith notes the similarity in Henry E Smith, 'The Equitable Dimension of Contract' (2012) 45 Suffolk L Rev 897, 910. For additional analysis of such remedies, see Samuel L Bray, 'The System of Equitable Remedies' (2016) 63 UCLA L Rev 530, 577–8 (discussing the potential asymmetric effects of equitable remedies).

[42] While the overarching concern with the morality of state assistance is a common factor, note that the moral principles implicated by these doctrines may be different from those operating in a disproportionate hardship case. In cases involving unclean hands, for example, we may confront a question of moral standing. For analysis of unclean hands in standing terms, see Nicolas Cornell, 'A Complainant-Oriented Approach to Unconscionability and Contract Law' (2016) 164 U Pa L Rev 1131, 1161–3; Ori J Herstein, 'A Normative Theory of The Clean Hands Defense' (2011) 17 Legal Theory 171.

[43] We might, however, think that allowing people to take inconsistent positions is an invitation to opportunism. That is surely a valid concern. But if estoppel covers situations where that risk is unlikely (compare classic agency by estoppel fact patterns), or if estoppel would be independently justifiable even if we doubted the opportunism risk, these features are worth our attention. Estoppel may

From this perspective, we can see a stickler as the genus and the opportunist as a species.[44]

In each case, these doctrines are sensitive to what courts and the state owe to their citizens. The state is justified in not providing a remedy (or the most effective form of remedy), even if it ordinarily owes it to its citizens to assist them in enforcing their rights. The state should not have to be complicit in some behaviour.

B. Explaining the law's allowance for sticklers

A self-regarding account of equity explains why courts would interfere with some sticklers, or at least refuse to assist them despite the validity of their rights. We still need insight into those cases in which courts facilitate a right holder's behaviour when it is morally wrongful for the right holder to pursue her claims. Yet a self-regarding account is consistent with—indeed supportive of—enforcement of rights on behalf of such sticklers as long as there are sufficiently compelling moral reasons to provide this assistance.

With appropriate adjustments, civil recourse theory offers justifications of the state's obligation to help right holders in a way that occasionally includes sticklers who ought not to pursue their rights. In modern societies, the state has largely scaled back individuals' ability to engage in self-help, and this has moral consequences. In the state of nature it is quite plausible to think that people not only have a range of moral rights, but also legitimate mechanisms of private enforcement.[45] On this view, individuals could originally engage in self-help to protect themselves, and they could likewise engage in self-help to seek redress. By curtailing these self-help remedies, the state takes on a responsibility to fill the gap with alternative mechanisms for seeking redress. Civil

ultimately have more than one ground, or serve more than one function. I thank Henry Smith for emphasizing that estoppel fact patterns may involve an invitation to opportunism.

[44] I thank Dennis Klimchuk for this formulation. Klimchuk's own account offers a powerful extension of Aristotelian views on equity to address the problem of sticklers. *See* Dennis Klimchuk, 'Equity and the Rule of Law' in Lisa M Austin & Dennis Klimchuk, (eds), *Private Law and the Rule of Law* (OUP 2014) 247. While our accounts differ in some respects, I have been influenced by Klimchuk's general approach.

[45] *See* John Locke, 'The Second Treatise of Government' in David Wootton, (ed.), *Political Writings of John Locke* (1993) 261, 265–6. An important exposition of this idea is in Benjamin Zipursky, 'Philosophy of Private Law' in Jules Coleman & Scott Shapiro, (eds), *The Oxford Handbook of Jurisprudence & Philosophy of Law* (OUP 2002) 623, 637. For further development in connection with the United States legal system, see John CP Goldberg, 'The Constitutional Status of Tort Law: Due Process and the Right to a Law for the Redress of Wrongs' (2005) 115 Yale LJ 524.

recourse theorists have shown that the private right of action can then be explained in light of this understanding (and a similar explanation is available if our theory instead works from a fiduciary starting point). Such approaches, however, also have the resources to make sense of the state's responsibility to assist sticklers, including sticklers who ought to show mercy.

We can see why if we modify the conventional civil recourse account slightly. In some contexts, individuals may have more than a pre-legal right to self-help; they may have a moral right to do moral wrong by means of that self-help. In the pre-legal setting, then, such right holders would have the option to be sticklers in a bad way. Yet, as noted, the state in most contexts precludes exercises of self-help (for both sticklers and non-sticklers). If individuals' pre-legal rights allow them not only to enforce their rights, but also to be sticklers in doing so, the state may presumptively owe these individuals a venue in which to insist on their rights.[46]

C. Equity and justice

What we have described above is a hybrid regime—one in which courts sometimes help provide redress and other times don't help, or even impede redress. And that type of regime may be quite reasonable, given the competing demands on the state and its courts. Courts do sometimes owe assistance to parties who wrongfully insist on their rights of redress, and at times courts may instead pursue equity to reach a different result. To be clear, equity can also generate rights of redress.[47] Equity nonetheless often acts as an impediment to redress, and this raises an additional puzzle about institutional roles. Aren't courts supposed to be doing justice between the parties? And isn't equity in particular thought to do justice?

There is an answer to this puzzle that respects both the judicial role and the common perception that equitable conduct brings about a type of justice. The source of difficulty is that more than one type of justice is involved when courts address private rights of action, and equity involves its own distinctive type.

[46] Again, one way of understanding this relationship might draw on a social contract metaphor. Cf. Zipursky, 'Philosophy of Private Law' (n. 45) 642 (offering a social contract analysis of civil recourse). As noted in Chapter 6, one could also adopt a picture of the state's obligations grounded in fiduciary principles. For a version that takes those obligations to be remedial, see Andrew S Gold, 'The State as a Wrongful Fiduciary' in Evan J Criddle, et al., (eds), *Fiduciary Government* (CUP 2018).

[47] I thank Sinead Agnew for emphasizing equity's role in this regard. For further analysis of equity's other roles, see Paul B Miller, 'Equity as Supplemental Law' in Dennis Klimchuk, Irit Samet, & Henry Smith, (eds), *Philosophical Foundations of the Law of Equity* (OUP 2020).

Pursuing equity is potentially a means to do justice between the parties (equitable justice), but in a way that is only sometimes consistent with pursuing redressive justice to the fullest extent. Aristotle's view was that equity is concerned with sticklers for justice in a bad sense. But note also that Aristotle nevertheless indicated there was an equitable form of justice: this equitable form is its own category.

Building on this Aristotelian perspective, we can discern a distinctive type of justice that governs the doctrine of unclean hands, estoppel, laches, and various other mechanisms by which courts refuse to assist a right holder in pursuing redress or even impede her efforts. Equitable justice can mean many things, but in this setting I would argue that it is the category of justice that determines allocations based on how a right holder *ought to exercise* his rights.[48] Understood in these terms, the question of how we ought to exercise our rights is thus a matter of justice and not solely a matter of morality. In some cases, the moral concern that bears on how we ought to exercise our rights is that we have wronged the party against whom we would exercise them. Courts that take such moral wrongs into account in deciding whether to enforce an unconscionable contract or whether to recognize an unclean hands argument are plausibly concerned with a distinctive, equitable form of justice. In other cases, the moral concern at issue may be the extreme harshness imposed by insisting on our rights, combined perhaps with opportunistic conduct. Courts that take that moral concern into account in deciding how (or whether) to assist a right holder are likewise plausibly concerned with a distinctive, equitable form of justice.

Yet this view also poses an additional set of questions which ultimately bear on how we should interpret the relation between private law rights and equity. Aristotle thought that equitable justice could be superior to the legal kind.[49] If we adopt the above definition of equitable justice, is equitable justice better than legal justice? More importantly, is equitable justice better than redressive justice? We might think that if the answer is yes, it will suggest that private law should be much more equitable than it actually is. The answer to these questions is that it depends. Authorship matters for the relationship between law and equity, much as it matters for other private law concerns. Aristotle speaks of the 'equitable man' as someone who 'is no stickler for justice in a bad sense'.[50] Someone who is equitable demonstrates a kind of justice when he accepts less

[48] For further discussion of this idea and its implications, see Andrew S Gold, 'The Relevance of Wrongs' in Paul Miller & John Oberdiek, (eds), *Civil Wrongs and Justice in Private Law* (OUP 2020).
[49] *See* Aristotle, 'Nicomachean Ethics' (n. 35) 1795.
[50] *See* ibid. 1796.

than his due—he 'tends to take less than his share though he has the law on his side'.[51] But the equitable judge is a different author from the person who voluntarily accepts less than his due, and the distinction is significant.

An equitable plaintiff who accepts less than what his legal rights allow is being just in a way that (ordinarily) is consistent with the moral obligations he owes to others. It's up to him if he wants to settle for less than he has a right to. The equitable judge, on the other hand, could very well be violating a moral obligation owed to all of the state's citizens if she gives the plaintiff less than his legal rights require, or simply fails to assist. In such a case, it could be morally appropriate for the plaintiff to accept less than his legal due (perhaps by settling the case),[52] yet morally inappropriate for the judge to give him less than his due. The equitable right holder acts as he ought, while the equitable judge, potentially, does not. When this divide will occur is a contingent matter, but it is not difficult to imagine cases of divergence.

Equitable plaintiffs are ordinarily engaging in a better kind of justice when they choose to act equitably. Whether equitable *judges* are engaging in a type of justice that is better than legal justice is dependent on context. Sometimes the imposition of equitable justice is merited, while at other times it is not. This can be the case, moreover, even if a voluntary equitable act by a right holder would be the ideal outcome. Equally important, if rights to do wrong are robust enough, or if reasons to accommodate the plaintiff's foibles are sufficiently compelling, the cases in which courts ought to apply equitable reasoning should be exceptional. Whatever the correct balance may turn out to be, neither equitable justice nor redressive justice can claim priority without a factual context for drawing the comparison.[53]

On the other hand, perhaps the challenge needs refinement. It may not be that courts are failing to do justice when they do equity, as initially suggested. The problem instead may be that they aren't doing justice in the way that private law is supposed to do justice—by allocating back to the extent possible when one party has wronged another. Whether we adopt a corrective justice theory or a redressive justice theory, aren't courts supposed to undo wrongs to

51 See ibid.

52 Cf. Aristotle, 'Rhetoric' in Jonathan Barnes, (ed.), *The Complete Works of Aristotle*, vol. 2 (bk 1.13 1374b) (Princeton 1984) 2189 (indicating that equity 'bids us . . . to be patient when we are wronged; to settle a dispute by negotiation and not by force').

53 Note that this account provides a response to what John Goldberg and Benjamin Zipursky describe as the 'overreaching plaintiff' problem. Cf. John CP Goldberg & Benjamin C Zipursky, *Recognizing Wrongs* (HUP 2020) 356. Courts that assist overreaching plaintiffs can still be doing justice between the parties and, in my view, that is the most plausible understanding of the legal perspective given the longstanding legal claim that courts' role is to do such justice.

the extent possible? Isn't that the point of the allocation back picture? Equitable justice, even if it is seen as a type of justice, often impedes that outcome.

The existence of cases in which courts limit the effectiveness of redress or impede it altogether suggests another kind of pluralism in private law. Courts do not always seek to allocate back to the fullest extent possible, and if that is because they are pursuing equitable justice we should recognize this fact. As noted, different types of justice may coincide with each other in private law, existing comfortably together without any major conceptual tensions. At times, one type of justice and another type of justice won't interact in any direct fashion (compare compensatory and punitive damages). At other times, a given type of justice may supplant an alternative type of justice (compare corrective and redressive justice). In cases involving equitable justice, redressive justice may be available in some form—but the two types of justice can genuinely be in tension. Equity sometimes requires a less complete allocation back than redressive justice would countenance. Whether this produces an ad hoc balancing or instead plays out in a more ordered fashion is contingent on how courts engage in equitable reasoning.

V. Redress and the Justice in Settlements

The discussion of authorship above suggests another way that redress can be obtained: through settlement. When Aristotle speaks of the equitable person who accepts less than his due, Aristotle is discussing a virtue. People who accept less than their due show a certain character trait, and they are generally understood to be acting voluntarily. When equitable justice is brought about by doctrines like estoppel or laches, an individual gets less than her rights allow—but the equitable outcome is not by the right holder's choice. Settlement is different, for in this context a right holder will get less than her due because she has agreed to do so.

One might question whether this is redressive justice since the right holder is getting less than a full allocation back. As noted in Chapter 5, however, partial redressive justice is still redressive justice. If A negligently injures B such that B incurs $100,000 in medical bills, a settlement for $80,000 is still a means to of undoing the wrongful transaction to a degree. Note also that equitable justice and redressive justice may be interlaced. Perhaps the $80,000 number reflects the hardship that the defendant B would suffer if he paid the full amount, as well as the plaintiff's sense that B is truly apologetic and that his negligence was minor. The outcome is both redress and equity at once.

There may be a considerable benefit in such cases. The settlement provides a form of justice that has a different moral valence from redress in its harshest form: it is not just a case of legitimate redress, but also a case of non-wrongful redress. In cases where insistence on full allocation back would be morally wrongful, settlements offer a morally preferable outcome. Thus, if we turn to settlements, there are new angles to consider. The legal option of settlement can potentially provide for a more valuable type of redress, in light of what redress in some settings will mean about the right holder's moral choices.

What makes settlement a borderline case is that the plaintiff is only a part author of the equitable outcome, and in a unique respect. Redress through settlement may reflect not only what the right holder ought to do, it may also reflect her own personal views on what that redress should look like. She has a type of authorship. But the duty bearer also plays a role. Settlement may even provide a form of corrective justice as a consequence; this is because the end result is a product of a joint effort by both right holder and duty bearer. What makes settlement a distinctive source of redress (if we accept that it is) is the right holder's exercise of influence over how that ought to occur. She is not only an author of the result through her initiation of the lawsuit, she has helped customize the manner and extent of allocation back. That latter authorship has its own value. This fact should not undercut the reality that the duty bearer is also an author (and perhaps that co-authorship has an important value here as well).

Note also that a plaintiff seeking redress through a private right of action may ultimately encourage corrective acts by the defendant by bringing her claim. This is especially likely through the availability of settlement and its negotiation process. To the extent we consider corrective justice a superior outcome in some cases—for example, due to the wrongdoer's choice to rectify her wrongdoing to the extent possible—the prospect of redressive justice may turn out to be an important precursor because of the way it incentivizes voluntary rectification by a wrongdoer. Settlement is a way for that rectification to transpire. Of course, if an equitable settlement represents an opportunity for the wrongdoer to act well, it is also an opportunity for the right holder to act well.

***

The optionality of redress is important in several ways. The right holder's choice suggests that there will be cases in which redress is forsaken despite its desirability, and also cases in which redress is sought despite the moral difficulties posed by enforcing one's rights. Both of these challenges matter. The former challenge (involving cases of forsaken justice) is difficult for private law institutions to solve in a way that gives sufficient respect to a right holder's autonomy. The latter challenge is alleviated (though not eliminated) by equitable doctrines, and also by the availability of settlement.

If equity is provided in limited quantities—in small doses, as it were—it can co-exist comfortably with redress in a private law system centred on norms of redressive justice. Indeed, the possibility of equitable interventions can help to justify the state's role in providing redress, as it makes it less likely that the state will need to be complicit in particularly egregious instances of allocation back. Equity is a safety valve in more than one way, and one respect in which it serves as a safety valve is by limiting the more harsh or opportunistic cases of redress.

Notice, however, that the authorship of an equitable outcome also matters. It may be an act of virtue for a right holder to accept less than her due in some cases; it could still be a case of overreaching or a failure of the court system for the state to force equitable results. On the other hand, since equity itself provides a type of justice, it is quite possible for courts to meet the obligations of their institutional role when they provide for equitable outcomes—even though rights of redress may be curtailed in the process. Since redressive justice is capable of existing even in cases of incomplete allocation back, it is also possible that at least some equitable results that impinge on redress will allow for redressive justice in practice.

As indicated, the authorship of an equitable outcome makes a difference, and the authorship in cases of settlement is significant. The above discussion only scratches the surface on questions of authorship and their relation to redress. As we will see in the next chapter, authorship matters for private law in multiple respects, sometimes directly implicating redressive justice and other times touching on it indirectly. We will turn to that topic now.

9
Modern Variations on the Theme

I. Introduction

We have seen that rights of redress are effectuated in more than one way. Sometimes, equity intervenes; at other times, right holders must rely on self-help. Yet, while we have now observed multiple pathways to redress, in contemporary legal systems the possibilities open up considerably. In the process, contemporary legal systems also pose new puzzles for private law theory. For example, suppose a lawsuit arises between two corporations instead of two human beings. Should we be as concerned about redress when a corporation is wronged? What of class actions, where a plaintiff may participate in a lawsuit without even realizing he is a member of the class? Or arbitration, which limits the state's role in resolving disputes? Or damages caps, which can prevent a plaintiff from receiving a full make-whole remedy?

These are not challenges to the viability of a redress-based interpretation, but they require us to see redress from novel directions. In certain cases, the values that justify redress support legal reform. For example, damages caps may mean that redressive justice is not being advanced adequately, given an aspiration to do justice to the fullest feasible extent. In other cases, modern legal features may call for celebration, or at least acceptance as second-best measures. This chapter will consider several contemporary versions of redress, with an eye towards the insights they can provide about the place of redress within a modern legal system. While the chosen examples cover disparate topics, in combination they tell us something about how redress can proceed through multiple paths within private law.

Several themes will emerge. The first theme concerns partial redress. Not every modern approach is designed to provide full redress (let alone capable of providing it). The second theme concerns plaintiffs who, in one way or another, are not the kind of plaintiffs we ordinarily associate with a right to redress. This issue arises not only in corporate settings, but also in litigation finance or subrogation settings. The third theme concerns a right holder's degree of control over acts of redress taken on her behalf. In some cases, such control is effectively limited; class actions are a prime example. The fourth and final theme

The Right of Redress. Andrew S. Gold, Oxford University Press (2020). © Andrew S. Gold.
DOI: 10.1093/oso/9780198814405.001.0001

concerns variations in the law. Redress today takes many forms, and a full appreciation of its role in private law requires us not only to see how individual acts of redress can advance multiple values, but also how the varied types of redress matter.

In particular, the value of authorship depends on how redress is exercised. The manner of exercise is a central concern for arbitration, and in a different way for class actions, but in truth it is an issue for every variation. Indeed, we are now in a position to see that redress is understandable across several dimensions. From more private versions (recaption, arbitration) to more public (private rights of action, parens patriae suits). From more plaintiff control (conventional private rights of action) to more third-party control (class actions; derivative actions; guardian-initiated suits). From unilateral decision making (recaption) to third-party dispute resolution (arbitration; private rights of action). From an aspiration to fully make whole to institutions designed for producing partial redress (equity; damages caps). And for many of these examples, the degree to which authorship is shared or isolated to a right holder can vary considerably. Each point on these continuums is potentially valuable or costly, depending on our goals.

I will begin with cases of partial redress and then turn to other modern variations on redress. Once we have a feel for what makes these variations distinctive, this chapter will consider what makes them worthwhile—at least in some contexts. Bear in mind that redress can be harmful, as we have seen. That said, the overall picture developed here is one in which rights of redress can be exercised in more than one way, with reasons for each type's existence. All of these types are also interlaced with the fields of private law itself, which likewise have their own import. Redress is a common thread that links private law institutions. In each instance, while rights of redress are a way of doing justice, we will also see that they play an enabling role.

II. Partial Redress and Damages Caps

In the United States, tort reform is a prominent feature of modern tort law and it sometimes requires a dramatic shift in legal doctrine. Tort reform is also controversial, and analysis of its strengths and weaknesses exceeds the scope of this book. Yet it is a development that legal theory cannot afford to ignore. A corrective justice or civil recourse perspective can help us to see why tort reform matters, but a focus on rights of redress offers insights as well, and the discussion below will consider several of these.

To begin, note that tort reform takes many shapes. Some instances pose significant challenges to effective redress within a tort law system (others, such as a limit on punitive damages, concern non-redressive remedies). Consider a statute that precludes liability for certain forms of negligence.[1] This reform removes a right to redress altogether for a set of claims. With other reforms, redress is still available; it is just that it is an incomplete version. A good example of the latter category is when legislation imposes damages caps that limit the extent to which plaintiffs can hope to undo a wrong they suffered. I will focus on damages caps here.

Damages caps are generally creatures of statute and they are not flexible in a way that takes into account the merits of an individual plaintiff's claim. That these caps are controversial should be unsurprising.[2] Even if a plaintiff is acting in good faith and genuinely was harmed by a wrong in excess of the damages cap, she will not be able to seek the full level of damages that would make her whole. Indeed, a damages cap may add insult to injury, if the wrong at issue is severe enough that even the full level of damages would be a poor substitute for her pre-wrong state. Courts apply these rules regardless.

Part of the judicial role is to follow the terms of valid statutes, and so the difficulty here is not that judges are failing to adjudicate properly. But viewed more broadly, in terms of what the state owes its citizens, we might think a system that chooses to provide only partial redress is not meeting its responsibilities. Where self-help is unavailable, and the private right of action only gives an incomplete form of justice, isn't this a significant failure? True, states could offer something else instead of redress—such as a New Zealand-style fund—but we still might think that the state should attempt to make a tort victim whole to the extent feasible. Damages caps do not represent an effort to make a tort victim whole to the extent feasible.

Then again, damages caps are not an avulsive change when compared with prior practices. Looking back to Chapter 8, we might even think that limits on full redress are well-established in common law adjudication. Courts acting equitably already provide incomplete allocations back, choosing not to assist in a plaintiff's exercise of her remedial rights when equity requires it. Can't this be acceptable, even desirable, when the state confronts an opportunistic or overly

[1] As John Goldberg has emphasized, private rights of action implicate due process concerns, and a case can be made that citizens in the United States have a constitutional right to recourse when they have been wronged. See John CP Goldberg, 'The Constitutional Status of Tort Law: Due Process and the Right to a Law for the Redress of Wrongs' (2005) 115 Yale LJ 524. Tort reform in some cases may thus raise constitutional concerns.

[2] For further analysis of the controversy from a civil recourse perspective, see John CP Goldberg & Benjamin C Zipursky, *Recognizing Wrongs* (HUP 2020) ch. 5.

harsh attempt at redress? Damages caps are not connected to the moral wrongfulness of a plaintiff's claims, but once we allow for cases of partial redress for equitable reasons, there are presumably other reasons why a state might reasonably decide that partial redress is best. If the aim of securing redress is so easily defeasible, perhaps damages caps should not raise any eyebrows.

Yet there is an important difference in the equity case. When equity intervenes, we are dealing with partial redress as a way of doing a different type of justice between the parties. Equity's limitations on otherwise viable remedies are not imposed because the court is doing incomplete justice in pursuit of some other, non-justice-related goal. Rather, the court when it acts equitably is providing *equitable justice* between the parties by allocating back less completely, and partial redress may amount to full-fledged equity.

Equity's role does not displace the ordinary judicial aspiration of doing justice between the parties. Courts doing justice in a case involving redress usually have (and should have) a characteristic aspiration: allocation back to the fullest extent possible.[3] When concerns like cost or other extrinsic considerations don't intervene, legal remedies that follow norms of redressive justice are intended to make a wrong 'as if it had never happened'.[4] Equitable justice *can* mean that a remedy is supposed to fall short of a complete allocation back. But this is a special case involving an independent norm of justice, and the common law default is that full allocation back should be the goal.

This relationship between legal outcomes and norms of justice no longer holds in the case of damages caps. Damages caps do not generally mean that a norm of justice is more successfully pursued than it would be otherwise.[5] There are potential justifications for damages caps, but these aren't based on the idea that a damages cap will provide more complete justice in any particular case. Damages caps are a response to perceived tendencies of tort damages to exceed their proper measure, or perhaps they are a way to protect an important industry, such as the medical industry. This predictably results in individual

[3] This view is implicit in John Gardner, 'What Is Tort Law For? Part 1: The Place of Corrective Justice' (2011) 30 Law & Phil 1, 33 (indicating that the reasons that support primary obligations prior to a wrong 'call for next-best satisfaction, the closest to full satisfaction that is still available'). See also John Gardner, *From Personal Life to Private Law* (OUP 2018) 121 (describing a picture of justice where losses stemming from a wrong should be reversed 'so far as possible'). To the extent courts adopt a 'next best thing' view of corrective justice, they will seek to get as close to full allocation back as they can, all else equal.

[4] The phrase is best known from an account of corrective justice that differs from the account here. *See* Arthur Ripstein, 'As If It Had Never Happened' (2007) 48 Wm & Mary L Rev 1957. The general idea carries over into this analysis with appropriate adjustments.

[5] Except arguably in one context: where the consequence of a damages cap is to cause the amount of allocation back to more closely approximate the correct amount, given an otherwise erroneous allocation back that would have occurred in its absence.

cases where courts are not in a position to allocate back fully based on what justice requires as between a specific set of litigants.

When damages caps intervene, partial redress is not due to infeasibility (as with certain severe injuries), nor a result of equity (as with estoppel or related doctrines). Suppose that A is injured in the amount of $200,000, but that due to a damages cap she receives only $180,000 in damages. In such a case, redressive justice is still done—partial redress is a kind of redress—but it is done in a way that comports less fully with norms of justice than the legal system is capable of achieving. The judicial responsibility to allocate back to the fullest extent is not limited here by either facts on the ground or by complicity concerns; and failure to meet that responsibility means the court is fulfilling its role less completely.

That outcome is not per se unacceptable, as external policy concerns do sometimes justify institutions that increase the likelihood that plaintiffs will only receive partial redress. For example, legal systems adopt evidentiary and procedural rules with an eye to administrative costs, and that can limit accuracy in a way that impacts rights of redress. Such losses in accuracy may produce partial redress in some instances, and thus an incomplete form of justice. But it is a different thing where legal actors impose a partial allocation back, without at least the aspiration of fully undoing a wrong. Damages caps may be justifiable in the right circumstances, but doing full justice between the parties is no small thing, and this suggests that such measures should be closely scrutinized.

In the end, part of the problem may also be empirical. It might turn out that, on average, courts more closely achieve the standard allocation back goal—full allocation back but not more than full—as a consequence of imposing damages caps. If so, that would allow for a redress-based justification of the practice. Still, this result comes at the cost of providing a less than full allocation back in a wide run of cases. Whether this is acceptable may then depend on how far the deviations caused by such caps happen to fall from a make-whole remedy, how frequently this occurs, and also on our understanding of the proper judicial role. And, if damages caps do not on average approximate a full allocation back, then their justification should be more difficult under a redress-based approach to private law.[6]

[6] Note that a related set of concerns could arise if settlements tend to push outcomes toward 'flat' damages rather than 'finely tuned' damages. *See* Nathaniel Donahue & John Fabian Witt, 'Tort as Private Administration' (forthcoming) Cornell L Rev 1, 35 (available at: https://ssrn.com/abstract=3349858). Here, however, the possibility that the outcome is consensual as between the parties is a major difference. A key question will be how repeat-player attorneys represent their clients in such settings.

III. The Problem of Plaintiff Identity

A. Litigation finance and claim alienation

Other cases involve claims pursued by parties who are either not the original parties that suffered a wrong, or else parties who do not suffer wrongs in the same way that human beings suffer wrongs (as with corporations). This chapter will focus on litigation finance settings and on corporations for illustration purposes, but we should bear in mind that questions related to claimant identity can arise in other settings. Subrogation in the insurance context is another example.[7] With that noted, I will begin with the litigation finance context, and then turn to corporate redress.

When we consider litigation finance, the exact form of the arrangement may be new, but there is a long common law history that bears on the general subject. Maintenance and champerty loom large here, and not every jurisdiction adopts the same approach to the permissibility of litigation finance arrangements.[8] That said, increasingly, investors are permitted to finance a lawsuit and receive some portion of the proceeds if a legal claim succeeds. The advent of this practice means that, in certain cases, a legal claim results in substantial payments to someone other than the wronged party—and, perhaps, that some control over how a claim is pursued is shifted to a third-party investor. As with tort reform, I will largely bracket the overall policy merits of litigation finance in general and specific variations in particular. Our concern here will be with the implications of a redress-centred picture for this development, in at least some circumstances (while noting that not all litigation finance arrangements share the same structure).

For discussion purposes, let's assume a case in which a litigation finance arrangement effectively means that a very substantial portion of a plaintiff's rights have been transferred. Assume a hypothetical case that either amounts to alienation of a legal claim, or a case that at least approaches that result in substance. One might think that civil recourse theory is inconsistent with the transfer (or effective transfer) of legal claims. Civil recourse empowers plaintiffs to bring suit, but arguably in a way that is personal to the specific parties who were

[7] See ibid. 17 (noting in subrogation contexts that '[t]he insurer essentially takes an ownership or equity interest in the claim to recoup its policy obligations'). Arguably, there are other important examples of this phenomenon. Donahue and Witt suggest that contingent fee arrangements place attorneys in an ownership stake position. See ibid. 16. And, interestingly, they group settlement agreements in the same category, describing them as the alienation of a tort claim. See ibid.

[8] For helpful discussion of approaches, see Michael Abramowicz, 'On the Alienability of Legal Claims' (2005) 114 Yale LJ 697; Anthony Sebok, 'The Inauthentic Claim' (2011) 64 Vand L Rev 61.

wronged. With very limited exceptions, substantive standing limitations generally restrict the class of potential plaintiffs to those individuals whose rights were violated by the defendant. It is natural to think that a redress-centred account is likewise in tension with a legal structure that substantially shifts control over litigation and, ultimately, changes the beneficiary of a legal remedy.

Anthony Sebok has rejected such concerns from a civil recourse perspective. He contends that civil recourse theory is consistent with claim alienation. According to Sebok,

> Zipursky may be correct that private law—especially with its unique feature of substantive standing—changes the character of the normative relationship between victim and defendant, such that the significant normative fact is the power the victim gains over the defendant to pursue redress. However, it is not clear why this means that the right created by the wrongdoing must be satisfied by the wrongdoer providing redress only to the person she wronged.[9]

In other words, there may be a disconnect between the criteria for a plaintiff's standing to bring a private right of action and a third party's standing to pursue or benefit from that private right of action.

Furthermore, as Sebok adds:

> The right to seek redress was a product of the wrongdoing, and it is not clear why the rightholder cannot do what she wants with that right—destroy it, ignore it, or give it to someone else. The normative fact that gave rise to the right will not be undermined, and it is not clear why the courts should not respect the sovereignty of the rightholder to exercise unlimited control over that right.[10]

In many contexts, a legal power is transferable and, as a conceptual matter, a right to civil recourse seems open to transfer. At the very least, this interpretation of recourse norms is plausible.

And yet there is a still a potential challenge if we turn to remedies, for their significance may be altered profoundly. Before considering damages remedies, consider an arguably more personal remedy: the apology. Imagine a hypothetical legal regime in which courts regularly order apologies. Apologies fit comfortably within a civil recourse approach, or at least some versions of it. This is

[9] See ibid. 132–3.
[10] See ibid. 133.

particularly so for those accounts that emphasize the expressive component of a private right of action. As an example, consider Jason Solomon's understanding. Solomon sees tort law as a system of equal accountability, with civil recourse as a way of expressing the equality of individual citizens and their accountability to each other. As Solomon argues,

> [A] civil recourse view . . . might see a genuine apology as precisely the kind of interpersonal expression of equality and accountability that ought to be promoted. The apology has the unusual and quite powerful qualities of personally acknowledging and affirming the right of the person harmed to demand an explanation and the obligation of the wrongdoer to provide one.[11]

On this view, a court-ordered apology is one way a tortfeasor can be held to account. Note also that, for Solomon, the expressive effects brought about by civil recourse are strengthened by having the remedy directed to the victim.[12] What would happen if an apology were instead directed to a third-party transferee? If a particular tort is a tort for which an apology is an apt remedy, we might think that the transferee would acquire a right to an apology. Yet this sounds strange. It is not hard to conceive of a transferee acquiring a right to insist on the defendant's apology to the tort victim, but a transferee's right to insist on the defendant's apology to the transferee does not really make sense. The problem here is not a commodification problem; it is a problem of conceptual fit.

Admittedly, we might think that apologies are a special case.[13] They can play a role in tort law settings, but, in all likelihood, claim transferees will not be interested in seeking apologies directed to the transferee. That said, apologies illustrate what can happen to a remedy when a claim is transferred. Apologies indicate that it is at least possible for a remedial concept to fit badly post-transfer. The transfer of the claim may be perfectly legitimate, but at least one of the remedies that go along with it may grow doubtful. Even if this feature of apologies has little bearing on the typical case, it demonstrates the existence of an important phenomenon: some remedies may not retain their original meaning post-transfer.

[11] See Jason M Solomon, 'Civil Recourse as Social Equality' (2011) 39 Fla St U L Rev 243, 267.

[12] See ibid.

[13] We should also bear in mind that apologies are not necessarily examples of allocation back, although they can be. For helpful discussion from a corrective justice perspective, see Gardner, *From Personal Life* (n. 3) 150–1 (suggesting that the continuity thesis 'only recommends apology when apology can be used to repair'). There is also an additional nuance, for reparative measures can likewise work as apologies. *See* ibid 152–3.

What about the idea of recourse as a means of holding someone accountable? Accountability is a tougher question, and our answer may depend on what we mean by accountability. If we take Solomon's expressive view, then what is communicated by recourse may change when the right to hold someone accountable is transferred. It is not clear that this change would be significant enough to really distort the concept. Perhaps the right to hold someone accountable can be transferred without dramatic alterations in the expressive component of accountability. The expressive component might be weakened, but not substantially altered. Still, subjective reactions regarding transfers of a right to hold someone accountable may differ from one person to another.

One reason for divergent reactions may be that accountability is a somewhat vague word. The identity of the plaintiff may not matter much, depending on what we mean when we refer to accountability. This can be illustrated by language usage. It would hardly be odd to hear a third-party transferee say, 'I held him accountable for his wrongdoing to the victim'. Examples like this suggest that accountability can be relatively impersonal in some cases. On the other hand, what if accountability means 'getting satisfaction'? It might seem odd to hear a third-party transferee say, 'I got satisfaction for his wrongdoing to the victim', unless, perhaps, the third-party is a family member who has an emotional connection to the original victim, or perhaps acts as an agent of the victim. Like revenge, getting satisfaction in response to an affront may have a personal quality that cannot readily be possessed by unrelated third parties.

Enforcement rights, on the other hand, should pose no conceptual problems.[14] They can be transferred without difficulty, assuming it is legal to do so. For example, suppose some personal property is converted, and the victim has a legitimate claim to the value of the converted property. This fact pattern implicates recourse as enforcement. There is nothing that would seem odd if a third-party transferee brought a claim for the property's value on the transferee's own behalf. To the extent that many remedies can be understood in terms of enforcement rights, a large part of tort law poses no conceptual difficulty for the alienability of legal claims. This form of civil recourse is more easily transferred.[15]

[14] On the other hand, notice that if remedies go to a third party instead of the original plaintiff, we may no longer have an allocation back fact pattern. Accordingly, we may no longer be engaged in redressive justice. Private law, however, does sometimes respond to wrongs by doing something other than allocation back. A good example arises in cases of bribery in the fiduciary law setting. For discussion, see Matthew Harding, 'Constructive Trusts and Distributive Justice' in Elise Bant & Michael Bryan, (eds), *Principles of Proprietary Remedies* (Thompson Reuters 2013) 31–3.

[15] Note that similar puzzles arise in cases involving subrogation and insurance. As Donahue and Witt suggest, '[t]he insurer essentially takes an ownership or equity interest in the claim to recoup its policy obligations'. *See* Donahue & Witt, 'Tort as Private Administration' (n. 6) 17.

It is also worth recognizing that litigation finance arrangements have the potential of encouraging a plaintiff's morally wrongful insistence on his rights, much like the examples of wrongful redress discussed in Chapter 8. That result is by no means inevitable, but the ability to reconcile litigation finance with a redressive justice picture does not mean that all instantiations will be desirable. We should likewise bear in mind that some cases could advance a different set of authorship values than those typically involved for a private right of action. The wronged party may now have a diminished role or interest in the litigation, while on the other hand he may still feel that he set in motion a process that undoes the wrong he suffered.

B. Corporate plaintiffs

Corporate plaintiffs raise related questions, but for different reasons. Here, too, we may wonder if this is a party that should have standing to seek redress. Particularly if redress is thought to be a response to the feeling of insult that a wrong causes, it seems a little odd to ascribe such motivations to corporate entities. Generally speaking, corporations do not have emotions, attachments, and projects in life.

While civil recourse theory has evolved and expanded its scope over the years, recall that under a classic version, it addresses the *affront* of being wronged. As Zipursky argues, the 'entitlement to recourse does not spring from the need precipitated by injury. It springs from the affront of being wronged by another.'[16] Goldberg and Zipursky describe cases in which tort victims have been 'injured in a way that warrants thinking that someone else is responsible for mistreating them and that their wrongdoer is an appropriate person from whom to demand redress or satisfaction.'[17] Jason Solomon, in turn, discusses the idea that tort law is supporting 'the instinct to hold another accountable.'[18]

Does it really make sense to say that a corporation has suffered an affront? Even if it does make sense, should we take the further step of arguing that a corporation is in a position to demand a response in light of its suffering an affront? And do corporations ever have instincts to hold another party accountable? One could quite easily answer each of these questions in the negative.

[16] See Benjamin C Zipursky, 'Rights, Wrongs, and Recourse in the Law of Torts' (1998) Vand L Rev 1, 87.

[17] John CP Goldberg & Benjamin C Zipursky, 'Tort Law and Moral Luck' (2007) 92 Cornell L Rev 1123, 1162.

[18] Jason M Solomon, 'Equal Accountability Through Tort Law' (2009) 103 Nw U L Rev 1765, 1814.

While these problems are not altogether new to corrective justice and civil recourse theories of private law, they are more often debated in another private law theory context. Theories of contractual obligation likewise must contend with the detached, impersonal quality of corporate entities. Significantly, even if a special relationship between contractual promisors merits enforcement of agreements being human beings, it is harder to say that two corporations can have such special relationships. A variant puzzle has thus emerged in contract theory debates, and given the more developed literature in that sphere, it is helpful to see how participants in those debates have struggled with the topic.

A number of contract theorists build on the idea that contracts create an intrinsically valuable relation between the parties. Yet, as noted, it is not clear what kinds of relationships corporations are truly capable of having. With this concern in mind, Alan Schwartz and Daniel Markovits have noted several potential ways of conceptualizing contracts between corporations.[19] On their view, formalist contract theories of contract law focus on relationships involving a valuable joint activity. These theories are accordingly faced with challenges where corporations are the ones engaged in contracting. Schwartz and Markovits thus consider how such formalist theories can make sense of inter-corporate contracts, and their analysis offers more than one answer. They suggest one might think in terms of the human beings who own the corporation; one might ascribe intentions to corporate entities; or, one might focus on the agents of the corporation who enter into contracts on its behalf.

Consider how these ways of thinking could be extended to civil recourse theories (and in particular, civil recourse theories that emphasize accountability or getting satisfaction). As noted, an initial move is to shift the focus to actual human beings who own the corporation. Turning from contract theory to the problem of civil recourse, we can see how this perspective might help. If a claim is in substance brought by human beings who stand as principals behind a corporation, we can imagine how they might suffer an affront from a legal wrong. One may think that under the right circumstances it is really the shareholder 'owners' of the corporation who are aggrieved when a corporation suffers a wrong, just as in some veil piercing settings it is the shareholders who are on the hook for commission of a tort. This theory limits the settings in which one would plausibly be able to support a claim for civil recourse—veil piercing is exceptional, and by implication the contexts in which this theory works would also be rare. That said, a one-person corporation that suffers a contract

[19] See Alan Schwartz & Daniel Markovits, 'Function and Form in Contract Law' in Andrew S Gold, et al., (eds), *The Oxford Handbook of New Private Law* (OUP forthcoming) 10.

breach or a tort is a setting for that one person to feel an affront. On occasion, this approach has merit.

The second possibility is to conceive of corporations in a way that allows for them to form their own intentions. And, indeed, people do sometimes think of corporations in just this way. The premise that people perceive corporate intentions in certain contexts is not enough to demonstrate that corporations have such intentions. Still, let's assume for discussion purposes that the argument has enough plausibility to work in support of recognizing corporate contractual obligations. Even if there are corporate intentions sufficient to enter into a binding contract, it is a substantial further step to think that corporations can experience an affront or that they are capable of demonstrating reactive attitudes like resentment or indignation. Corporate-level intentionality is not sufficient to ground corporate reactive attitudes, and this makes the idea of a corporation 'getting satisfaction' seem less realistic.

A final option is to look for human agents of the corporation who hold the appropriate states of mind. At least in the right circumstances, a corporation's agents (or a near equivalent—its directors) are effectively the decision-making apparatus for the corporate entity. It cannot act on its own, and perhaps sometimes a corporation's agents are the true parties in interest. This point takes on added force when a corporation's agents are the very parties who negotiated a contract, or the ones who were most involved in a contract's drafting.[20] And there is certainly legal precedent for ascribing an agent's mental state to the corporation in liability settings, such as securities fraud cases. The difficulty is that, in the ordinary case, legal claims are ascribed to the corporation itself and not its agents. Civil recourse belongs to the corporation.

Overall, the conceptual challenges are severe. If we adopt the internal perspective of corporate law, then the first and third possibilities are usually off the table. Corporate personality is not easily reduced to the shareholders or other constituents with an interest in the corporation, nor to those who work for the corporation.[21] From the perspective of corporate law, the corporation is its own, separate entity—and it is the corporation that holds rights of civil recourse. Barring exceptional cases like those involving veil piercing, the legal

[20] Cf. Seana Valentine Shiffrin, 'The Divergence of Contract and Promise' (2007) 120 Harv L Rev 708, 746–9.

[21] For discussion, see Paul B Miller, 'Corporations' in Andrew S Gold, et al., (eds), *The Oxford Handbook of New Private Law* (OUP forthcoming); Paul B Miller & Andrew S Gold, 'The Corporation as a Category in Private Law' in Hanoch Dagan and Benjamin C Zipursky, (eds), *Research Handbook on Private Law Theories* (Elgar forthcoming).

point of view rules out a picture in which corporate claimants are identifiable with the people who stand behind the corporation or who work for the corporation.

Moreover, such problems are not cabined to corporate contexts. The state is another artificial entity, and it too enters into contracts with various parties (including both corporations and individual human beings). Such settings are realistically seen as private law settings, notwithstanding the presence of the state as a litigant.[22] They likewise pose challenges for corrective justice theorists and, for that matter, some civil recourse theorists. While the focus here is on corporations, the conceptual challenges posed by these entities are but a subset of a larger phenomenon.

These challenges again recede once we talk of enforcement rights. While a corporation is a product of the legal system, and while it does not plausibly benefit from pre-legal rights, it is nonetheless a relatively easy step from a corporation's primary and remedial rights to a corporation's legal enforcement rights. Enforcement rights are not entailed by primary or remedial rights, but they can be made available without building on unlikely corporate mental states. Corporations need not experience affronts, need not feel instincts to hold another accountable, and need not otherwise be personified in a way that involves emotions or desires. It is enough for redressive justice purposes that corporations can possess an enforcement right to allocate back, and that it makes sense (given policy and coherence concerns) to recognize one.

What differs, necessarily, is the justification for an enforcement right's existence in the corporate setting. As noted, there is no pre-legal right belonging to a corporation that carries over into the legal setting, and no such right will explain and justify the corporation's legal rights of redress. Nor, for that matter, is it obvious how the value of authorship would help to support corporate rights of redress. While we need not worry about how corporations could feel aggrieved, there are still reasons to wonder what justifies a legal system's provision of rights of redress for corporate plaintiffs.

As Chapter 3 suggested, rights of redress enable several important kinds of authorship that are otherwise difficult for citizens to obtain. This changes once the parties at issue are corporate firms. The value of authorship is now an uncertain source of justification, as corporations are not in a position to

[22] For helpful discussion, see Thomas W Merrill, 'Private and Public Law' in Andrew S Gold, et al., (eds), *The Oxford Handbook of the New Private Law* (OUP forthcoming) 3 (discussing the significance of such cases).

experience a feeling of self-reliance, nor are they the right kind of thing to have dignity. Even if the agents who represent corporations can feel self-reliance, and even if the shareholders who own corporate interests have dignity, neither of these parties have the relationship to corporate rights that plaintiffs ordinarily possess when bringing suit. It is telling that successful derivative litigation on behalf of a wronged corporation results in damages paid to the corporation itself, and that directors do not even have standing to initiate a derivative suit.

Concerns over what can justify a corporation's right to civil recourse is genuine, but they should not be overstated. What needs to be remembered is that the values associated with authorship are not the only justifications for legal rights of redress. Efficiency is an important goal, and the ability to plan is also vital in commercial settings. While investors and other corporate constituents may not be parties to corporate contracts, they may very well be better off if the corporations they form or have an interest in are treated as legal claimants in a way that mirrors the treatment received by human parties.

Indeed, the value of coherence is compelling in the corporate context, particularly in settings like contract law where the ability to map private law concepts onto corporate transactions is largely a matter of substituting the corporation for a human being. A legal system that speaks of corporations having rights in their own name has good cause to treat corporations the same way that other contracting parties are treated. To do otherwise risks communicating that a 'contract' has a different meaning in corporate settings, and the potential costs of uncertainty and perceived arbitrariness could readily justify treating corporations as close to human beings as possible. These challenges are compounded when we recall that corporate contracts often have human counterparties, so that at least one of the parties to a transaction will experience a contract obligation in the ordinary human way.

Even so, if the justification for rights of redress plays out differently, the conceptual structure still works. Rights of redress do not require us to ascribe any special import to authorship, nor do they require any close connection between the victim of a wrong and the party who initiates suit. For that matter, there is no requirement that a plaintiff should possess any particular reactive attitudes. Recognition of these facts is itself a step forward. What these cases show is important for understanding rights of redress more generally: such rights advance a number of values, but not all at once or in every context.

IV. Consent, Arbitration, and Class Actions

A. Arbitration

Arbitration is a longstanding practice, and not a new encroachment on private law structures. But it has grown substantially in importance with an increase in boilerplate consumer contracts, with the advent of internet purchases, and with a collection of United States Supreme Court decisions that largely insulate arbitration from judicial review. This chapter will discuss two of the challenges below: concerns that arbitration is not adequately grounded in consent, and concerns that arbitration renders private what ought to be public. I will consider each of these in turn.

In the arbitration setting, a consent failure could bear on redress in at least two ways: the value in authoring redress may be changed (perhaps lost), and the success of redress itself might be threatened. Each possibility is important. Failures of consent are not always fatal to the legitimacy of redress—consider cases in which a guardian seeks redress on behalf of an incompetent ward—but they generally raise serious doubts.

Some of the most basic concerns about arbitration in the modern era centre on problems of consent that are linked to technology. When making purchases online, people often electronically click an 'I agree' panel to indicate their assent to a boilerplate contract. They don't read all of the contractual provisions, even if they have clicked on something that says they did. Indeed, it is quite common that purchasers do not read any of these provisions whatsoever (and they may be rational in making this choice). This is not the traditional understanding of what contractual consent looks like, and where arbitration is a required result of such provisions this may arguably undermine the legitimacy of the resulting pathway to redress.

The consent implications should not be overstated. Not all of these cases involve genuine consent failures, even where consumers have failed to read some (or perhaps all) of the terms that allegedly bind them. To see how consent can exist in such cases, consider the following example, offered by Randy Barnett:

> Suppose I say to my dearest friend, 'Whatever it is you want me to do, write it down and put it into a sealed envelope, and I will do it for you.' Is it categorically impossible to make such a promise? Is there something incoherent about committing oneself to perform an act the nature of which one does not know and will only learn later?[23]

[23] *See* Randy E Barnett, 'Consenting to Form Contracts' (2002) 71 Fordham L Rev 627.

The answers to Barnett's questions will depend on our theory of consent, but it is reasonable to think that we can commit ourselves in this fashion.

Omri Ben-Shahar offers a similar example to the envelope scenario. As he notes:

> People can agree to buy a surprise. Sometime[s], the surprise is an attribute of the product or service. The most extreme example is a lottery ticket, in which the 'surprise' is affirmatively sought. But more commonly, various products or services are purchased knowing that they might not perform as hoped (. . . [for example] the arrival time of the flight, or the sweetness of the watermelon).[24]

Just as a contracting party may consent to these more tangible forms of surprise, that party may consent to surprises with respect to the terms of the contract itself. As long as the presence of hidden terms is unsurprising, and as long as the contract itself can be avoided, a blanket assent could be valid.

But these examples may seem fanciful, and in boilerplate settings the consent problems can be dramatically worse. As Margaret Jane Radin notes, some mass-market boilerplate involves terms that the individual never sees, and never even knows about.[25] Sometimes, people are told they have consented to a contract simply because they visited a website. Radin rightly challenges the idea that this is consent. She asks whether you can agree to something just by 'walking past a sign.'[26] The answer is no, at least under conventional understandings of what consent is. It might be different if one had read and understood the sign first, but the fact of walking past it is not enough.

These cases matter from a redress-centred perspective. At least where consent is absent or severely defective, this calls into question the authorship value in redress. Such failures may also call into question the legitimacy of arbitration as an institution, even if redress is otherwise effectively obtained; a redressive justice analysis does not obviate legitimacy concerns. Granted, these are not the only concerns about the modern practice of arbitration. Arbitration before a biased arbitrator, for example, may lead to partial redress or its failure altogether. I note the import of these issues, but I will bracket them here. Instead, I wish to focus on the public–private features of arbitration.

24 Omri Ben-Shahar, 'The Myth of the "Opportunity to Read" in Contract Law' (2009) 5 Eur Rev Cont L 1, 9.

25 Margaret Jane Radin, 'Reconsidering Boilerplate: Confronting Normative and Democratic Degradation' (2012) 40 Cap U L Rev 617, 628.

26 See ibid. 626.

An especially prominent aspect of arbitration is that it takes into the private sphere—at least to a degree—phenomena that are often considered appropriate matters for the legal system to handle directly. If we look past any doubts about the effectiveness of redress and focus instead on questions of public versus private status, the analysis of arbitration fits in with a broader pattern we have seen in other contexts. Arbitration can be situated along a continuum of redress-based options. Arbitration is a largely private source of redress, much as recaption of chattels is largely private—and this is in contrast to private rights of action, which rely more heavily on a state-supplied apparatus. Or at least this is what one might think at first glance.

There is another option. We might instead see both private rights of action and arbitration as importantly public, and recaption of chattels is then distinguishable as a more private mode of redress (assuming we reject the idea that right holders are stand-ins for public officials). Indeed, there is an understanding of both private rights of action and arbitration as institutions that draw on state power and authority. For some, the advantage of this perspective is that it helps to justify a more involved state role, and accordingly facilitates greater state oversight of the ways that arbitration can be misused.

A way to bring arbitration and private rights of action into this public realm is to see both settings as cases in which a form of state power is used by private parties. One might discern a continuity between arbitration and private rights of action rather than a distinction.[27] As Matthew Shapiro indicates, the power to initiate a lawsuit is 'not in itself coercive', yet there is more at stake when people bring suit.[28] Plaintiffs have the ability to hale the defendant into court, and this power at least is effectively a state power assigned to private parties. Civil recourse could thus be seen as a legal practice that draws on a delegation of state power.[29] In both cases, then—arbitration and private rights of action—private parties are exercising delegated state power. The implication could be that both cases are also, in an important sense, cases in which private parties get to use public powers.

Yet, the analysis is necessarily complex, and the conclusion is open to debate. From the civil recourse perspective, a private right of action is also understood to involve a delegation from the *plaintiff* to the state. Zipursky has referred to the 'power the state affords to private individual litigants', as Shapiro rightly notes.[30] And civil recourse theorists are well aware that private rights of action

[27] Cf. Matthew A Shapiro, 'Delegating Procedure' (2018) 118 Colum L Rev 983.
[28] See ibid. 999.
[29] See ibid. 100–1.
[30] See ibid. 1003 n. 76 (quoting Benjamin C Zipursky, 'Torts and the Rule of Law' in Lisa M Austin & Dennis Klimchuk, (eds), *Private Law and the Rule of Law* (OUP 2014) 139, 148).

involve and require the use of a state-provided legal apparatus. But Zipursky has also offered a broadly Lockean argument for the view that private rights of action implicate a wronged party's pre-legal right to redress.[31] If there is a direction of delegation on this view, it is for the most part from the private party to the state, and not the other way around—and this has bearing on how we should interpret the legal powers that plaintiffs get to exercise in civil recourse settings.

Seth Davis offers another picture, and it tracks what I take to be the classic civil recourse account. On this view, private rights of action implicate a type of standing that is importantly private. As he argues, '[p]rivate standing entails the power to stand for one's private preferences in court'.[32] Citizens get to 'pursue redress on their own behalf'.[33] One might add that private parties characteristically have an enormous amount of discretion in their choices to sue and pursue their claims.[34] Arbitration is a match for this picture as well, and I will proceed on the assumption that arbitration is understandable as private and not distinctive on that basis. What may differ is the degree to which arbitration is private.

Assuming arbitration is substantially a private source of recourse (notwithstanding the import of the state's enforcement role), that is not at all problematic from a redress-centred perspective. To the contrary, arbitration may offer a valuable type of authorship precisely because it is private to a larger than ordinary degree, assuming we adopt that view. Recall that recaption of chattels is an important example of private parties exercising their right of redress; it is entirely legitimate for private parties exercising self-help to be acting on their own behalf. While not nearly so private as recaption, arbitration is on solid footing even if it is a more private manner for injured parties to coerce wrongdoers, acting on their own behalf when they do so. The manner in which arbitration is arranged and operates is nonetheless unique. What remains strikingly different as between arbitration and private rights of action is the judicial role. Arbitration typically means a substantially more circumscribed place for judges. Yes, judges sometimes review arbitration proceedings and outcomes, but the limitations on such review are many and they are often effective.[35] By

[31] See generally Benjamin C Zipursky, 'Philosophy of Private Law' in Jules Coleman & Scott Shapiro, *The Oxford Handbook of Jurisprudence & Philosophy of Law* (OUP 2002) 623. For Zipursky's nuanced account of the state's role, see especially ibid. 649–50.

[32] See Seth Davis, 'Standing Doctrine's State Action Problem' (2015) 91 Notre Dame L Rev 585, 604.

[33] See ibid.

[34] See Gardner, *From Personal Life* (n. 3) 201 (describing how a plaintiff's legal powers are 'radically discretionary').

[35] For a series of examples, see Shapiro, 'Delegating Procedure' (n. 27) 1053–4.

and large, when we speak of arbitration, the neutral third party that decides a given dispute is effectively the arbitrator and not a judge. The arbitrator is private and that is a very real difference.

There is also something different as between arbitration and recaption, and it is likewise a notable distinction. While recaption does not involve a third party at all—except where it is subsequently reviewed after the fact in a court of law—arbitration by definition requires a third party. It means that there are decisions made by arbitrators who are not themselves participants in the parties' dispute. Arbitration does not involve one party unilaterally coercing another party in order to undo a wrong. Moreover, as with settlements, the redress that results will—hopefully—reflect the authorship of the parties and not just the authorship of the arbitrator: arbitration begins with an arbitration agreement.

This is not to say that arbitration is itself the best of both worlds, for a more expansive judge's role may offer a range of important benefits (including a potentially stronger claim to neutrality, the imprimatur of the state, and an expansion of the legal precedent pool). Likewise, self-help may be more effective than arbitration in some circumstances and it offers a particularly important type of authorship in its own right. There is also the more general question of how arbitration works in real-world settings. In practice, the critiques of arbitration are legion, ranging from challenges to the voluntariness of arbitration agreements, to doubts about arbitration procedures, to questions about the selection or neutrality of arbitrators, to concerns about arbitration awards.[36]

Arbitration is also not unique for having private rights of redress conjoined with a private third-party decision-maker. Legal systems have long co-existed with extra-legal, community-centred forms of adjudication. Consider the way that disputes among diamond merchants have been resolved within the Jewish community, or the way that tuna purchasers resolve disputes at the Tsukiji fish market in Japan.[37] These are private forms of dispute resolution and they operate largely independent of legal systems. Arbitration differs in the source of its authority and in the relationship it bears to private law. From a critic's perspective, it may be the latter feature that is especially significant: for some, arbitration 'allows private parties to tap the coercive power of the state without any meaningful oversight'.[38]

[36] *See* ibid. 1051 (listing various concerns about arbitration). See also David Horton, 'Arbitration as Delegation' (2011) 86 NYU L Rev 437; Judith Resnik, 'Diffusing Disputes: The Public in the Private of Arbitration, the Private in Courts, and the Erasure of Rights' (2015) 124 Yale LJ 2804.

[37] *See* Lisa Bernstein, 'Opting Out of the Legal System: Extralegal Contractual Relations in the Diamond Industry' (1992) 21 J Legal Stud 115; Eric A Feldman, 'Law and Norms in the World's Premier Fish Market' (2006) 94 Cal L Rev 313.

[38] *See* Shapiro, 'Delegating Procedure' (n. 27) 1051.

But what should we make of arbitration's relationship to private law oversight? The above analysis doesn't rule out ex post policing. Oversight, however, may not be justified on the basis that arbitration involves a delegation of state power; rather, it may be justified on the basis that redress without oversight could be compromised in various respects. And, while courts have a more limited role, the state can still be complicit in wrongful or unjust acts of redress through arbitration that the state facilitates, even if that redress is not understood to primarily involve delegated state power. Given the aim of enabling redress to be pursued fairly and effectively, policing by the state may take on significant importance even if arbitration is largely private.

B. Class actions and opt-outs

Although notice is an important component of class action litigation, people often do not realize they are members of a class, and in any event they only rarely opt out. Indeed, given the burdens involved, it may be rational for them to remain in a class even if they have no particular interest in the litigation.[39] Attorneys often call the shots to a very substantial degree, and settlements are sometimes more advantageous for the law firms involved on the plaintiffs' side than for the plaintiffs themselves.[40] These features hardly show the undesirability of class action litigation, or even the undesirability of a class action system with opt-outs and other standard features of today's class action process. But with that said, class actions do raise significant questions for civil recourse theory in general, and for a redress-based account in particular. Much like litigation between corporate firms, class action litigation raises questions about authorship. This time, however, the salient concern is with the right holder's level of control vis-à-vis her claim.

Notwithstanding a chance to opt out, the most prominent control-related worry is that members of the class will end up as plaintiffs when they do not actively wish to occupy that role. As a conceptual matter, the right to sue does not entail a right not to sue, but the two rights are closely connected. Indeed, the right not to sue is itself bound up with the value of authorship, as a decision to sue is worth a lot less if we couldn't have chosen otherwise. Such rights have

[39] See Ryan C Williams, 'Due Process, Class Action Opt Outs, and the Right Not to Sue' (2015) 115 Colum L Rev 599, 631.

[40] For discussion of some of the concerns, see Sergio J Campos, 'Mass Torts and Due Process' (2012) 65 Vand L Rev 1059, 1063. Campos, it should be noted, does not ultimately support litigant autonomy in the mass tort class action context.

unsurprisingly been linked to civil recourse theory principles, as an implication of that theory's substantive standing analysis.[41] And we might think that a power to act against someone who wronged us is not very empowering if we have no choice about whether to exercise that power, and little control over how it is exercised.

There is, perhaps, another way to link redress and control: by looking to norms of justice. On reflection, we might conclude that redressive justice in its ideal case calls for not only a full allocation back, but also for an allocation back under the control of the right holder. Just as failures to fully allocate back are examples of redressive justice in an imperfect form, redressive justice without right holder control could be imperfect as well. Given a common understanding of the judicial role, courts should also try to avoid providing a second-best version of justice. On this view, courts should aspire to provide full right holder control over legal claims to redress, to the extent feasible. This view on the implications of redressive justice may be right, though I confess to being unsure. The answer may hinge on context.

In any event, we cannot readily answer the question of how much control a right holder should have by turning to the value of authorship. The value (or values) of authorship help to justify some legal rights of redress, but that doesn't mean that authorship failures leave these rights without a justification.[42] This was our lesson from the corporate right holder example. Again, the justifications for recognizing a legal right to redress can extend beyond authorship concerns and, accordingly, authorship-based justifications on their own may not fully answer questions of how control should be allocated.

For example, consider the guardian–ward setting. Wards will not always be in a position to choose; in the extreme case, a ward may not even be conscious. Imagine that Jane has suffered a severe injury as a result of another's negligence and that, in consequence, she is in a permanent coma. It can still make sense to say that a claim brought on Jane's behalf counts as a mechanism for achieving redressive justice. If so, however, this means that there is no requirement that redress must incorporate a right holder's choice on whether to sue. If instead Jane is conscious but is incapable of making well-reasoned choices in light of a head injury, should her guardian ever be permitted to

[41] See Williams, 'Due Process, Class Action Opt Outs' (n. 39) 624.

[42] Perhaps ironically, respecting an interest in authorship could also make redressive justice less likely as a practical matter. It may be that authorship is important enough to a right holder that she would prefer an unsuccessful attempt at redress that gives her greater control over the process, rather than a successful attempt where someone else (such as her lawyer) makes most of the key decisions. A legal system that requires substantial deference to client wishes might be a legal system in which redress comes about less frequently, or less successfully.

pursue a claim of redress on her behalf when she states that she would prefer not to sue?

These are cases in which the plaintiff has no possibility of choosing whether her suit should be brought, or else cases in which her choice is in some way compromised. Given that these cases involve an allocation back on behalf of the right holder who was wronged, it is reasonable to conclude that they are genuine examples of redressive justice. The guardian–ward cases described above involve redress, and no doubt there are other settings with similar features. In theory, then, class actions without effective opt-outs—or with opt-outs that are unlikely to be exercised given the cost—may still provide redressive justice. Arguably, we can go a step further: the redress they provide may not be a defective or subpar version.

Suppose, however, that the ideal case of redress incorporates right holder control. The implication then is not only that effective class action opt-outs are important; there is also an implication for legal representation. Attorneys often play an outsized role in class action contexts. In the extreme case, they pick their client, and not the other way around. Cases where attorneys have an unusual degree of power—and potentially conflicting incentives as repeat players, or as parties with a stake in assuring a certain fee level—suggest that the authorship values that support rights of redress also bear on questions of professional responsibility.

As Howard Erichson and Benjamin Zipursky emphasize:

> When a client has chosen to sue, the fact that she has employed a lawyer to do so on her behalf does not mean that the claim is no longer hers. To lose the right to decide whether to settle one's claim, and on what terms, is to lose control of the claim in a very real sense.[43]

The expectations of class action attorneys are thus important not only for general professional responsibility reasons, but also because they may increase the chances for a particular kind of redress: redress that falls under a right holder's effective control.

Several recent theories of the attorney's role emphasize the importance of an attorney's deference not only to a client's instructions, but also to the client's values, goals, and objectives. Whether it is the negative capability account espoused by Daniel Markovits or the fidelity-based account described by Brad

[43] Howard M Erichson & Benjamin C Zipursky, 'Consent Versus Closure' (2011) 96 Cornell L Rev 265, 313.

Wendel, these theories foreground the client's perspective.[44] If part of the value of redress stems from a right holder's control over her acts of redress, it will also be valuable for attorneys to defer to a client's subjective preferences and goals. Courts may be an effective means for a plaintiff to seek redress, but this is often contingent upon the plaintiff's lawyer showing the right kind of fidelity to her client's wishes.

V. The Dimensions of Redress

We are now in a position to see that redress occupies several overlapping continuums—a continuum from more private to more public, from more unilateral to more multilateral, from more right holder controlled to more third party controlled, from more personal to more detached. Up to a point, none of the established positions along these dimensions is inconsistent with redressive justice. But the reasons for selecting one position over another are complex, and the overall merits of each option depend not only on context, but also on the weighing of incommensurables.

Largely private, unilateral cases are easier to justify if authorship of a certain type is especially valued or if necessity is common (as when recaption is the only viable path because without it a thief will escape). Cases of redress in which a right holder's control is limited may be easier to justify if the right holder is poorly situated for exercising that control, as in a guardian–ward case. Incomplete redress may be reasonable if it is a product of consent, or if it is the best we can hope for. Some cases, moreover, are distinctive because of the nature of the plaintiff, as with corporate lawsuits, subrogation, or claim alienation. More or less private versions offer their own pros and cons.

In trying to bring order to these structures of private law, there is no need to reason outward from a central case of redress. Recaption of chattels may be even more fundamental than the private right of action; it is surely the most simple case. Yet it is legitimate to wonder if recaption is a desirable template for the private right of action. The variations are also many and, as a consequence, there may not be one salient case of redress from which all of the other instances can branch out. It happens that private law concepts are oriented largely around private rights of action, but the frequency and judicial encouragement of settlement agreements should give us pause before describing the

[44] Daniel Markovits, *A Modern Legal Ethics: Adversary Democracy in a Democratic Age* (Princeton 2008); W Bradley Wendel, *Lawyers and Fidelity to Law* (Princeton 2010).

private right of action as the centrepiece of private law redress. We should also bear in mind that legal institutions show the effects of path dependency.

Note that more subtle differentiations emerge when private rights of action are assessed across private law fields. Thus, for example, redress often takes a form that includes gain-based remedies in the fiduciary law setting, while it rarely takes that form in the contract law setting. Particular subsets of a private law field also come with unique limitations, as where certain torts include damages caps, while other torts do not. In other words, even if we adopt the private right of action as a model for redress, its contours and effects can diverge in significant respects. Indeed, redress for contract breaches is not the same in its meaning as redress for torts, or for fiduciary disloyalty. The kinds of ex ante authorship opportunities that these different settings for redress can restore will vary as well.

As repeat player settlements, insurance coverage, class actions, and arbitration grow in both importance and frequency, the typical case of legal redress may also evolve. The list of pathways to redress is not closed—there is no *numerus clausus* for redress—and private law could invent other valuable types, with their own distinctive benefits. Such changes are not enough to unseat rights of redress as a core private law feature, as would be the case if New Zealand-style systems were the norm. They instead suggest that redress can successfully be pursued through an indefinite number of avenues and that the merits of each avenue will depend on a complex set of considerations. These include the likelihood that a wrongful transaction will be undone (i.e. whether redressive justice will be obtained), but they also include the importance of authorship, attribution, deterrence, administrative efficiency, and expressive effects.

Settlement allows private parties to experience equitable authorship—they can undo a wrong in a virtuous way, and perhaps also experience the value of joint authorship with the defendant.[45] Arbitration allows for private authorship, for joint authorship, and also for third-party decision-making. Private rights of action allow for private authorship and the imprimatur of the state—what Jason Solomon refers to as the 'best of both worlds'.[46] Class actions allow for a kind of shared authorship and, perhaps, also an increased likelihood of a plaintiff's obtaining redress (although the latter benefit may be limited). Class actions can also help to solve the problem of desirable suits that for whatever

[45] Note again that settlement is a borderline case of redress, as it involves co-authorship with the wrongdoer.

[46] *See* Solomon, 'Equal Accountability Through Tort Law' (n. 18) 1795.

reason aren't being brought. Recaption offers effectively unilateral authorship and this aspect has its own distinctive value. Recaption may also mean an increased likelihood of obtaining redress, albeit for very different reasons from the class action. A similar set of features can be elaborated for each form that enforcement takes.

Some variants only implicate a specific subset of the benefits usually associated with redress. Thus, it is not the case that a corporation obtains a valuable type of authorship when it obtains redress against a party that wronged the corporation. Indeed, some variants do very well along one dimension while quite poorly along another. Thus, class actions may offer an etiolated authorship for aggrieved right holders, while proving effective in giving defendants incentives not to commit wrongs against others in the future. Yet we also need not think that some versions are inevitably 'better' versions, while others are second-best. On this point, we might fruitfully compare trials with a judge and trials with a jury—both could bring about the same form of justice (whether corrective, redressive, or some other type), yet the mix of values advanced in each case will be different. Jury trials may not be inherently better, any more than bench trials are inherently better, even though each will have contexts in which it is the superior choice. So, too, with redress; different forms offer different benefits.

***

My aim is not to show that redress is kaleidoscopic, although in some respects it is. To the contrary, the basic idea of redressive justice is straightforward. There is a special kind of justice when a right holder or someone acting on his behalf undoes a wrong he has suffered. But simple legal structures can produce highly complex results, and something as basic as the private right of action can lead to variants like the class action or the sophisticated settlement agreement.[47] The value in redress is varied—even for a single type of redress—and our choices of when to permit, facilitate, or impede acts of redress raise a multitude of questions. This book is intended to address a number of these questions, while encouraging a vastly greater number to be pursued further.

A common theme is that redressive justice is enabling. We can live our lives in a different way if we have the opportunity to undo a wrong we suffered.

[47] Cf. Henry E Smith, 'Systems Theory: Emergent Private Law' in Andrew S Gold, et al., (eds), *The Oxford Handbook of the New Private Law* (OUP forthcoming) 12 (noting that '[b]ecause property forms are flexible like building blocks, new purposes can be served (up to a point) using existing rules').

Private enforcement can restore things that are meaningful to us, and enforcement can be meaningful in itself. On the other hand, all of the above avenues for undoing wrongs have something in common, and it is likewise fundamental: they are each ways of doing justice. That matters irrespective of other goals or policy concerns. Private law offers many ways of doing a valuable form of justice—the justice in redress.

Index

Note: *For the benefit of digital users, indexed terms that span two pages (e.g., 52–53) may, on occasion, appear on only one of those pages.*

Printed and bound by CPI Group (UK) Ltd, Croydon, CR0 4YY